ESSENTIAL
WINETASTING

ESSENTIAL
WINETASTING

MICHAEL SCHUSTER

MITCHELL BEAZLEY

For Monika, whose support made it possible

Essential Winetasting by Michael Schuster

First published in Great Britain in 2000 by Mitchell Beazley,
an imprint of Octopus Publishing Group Ltd,
2–4 Heron Quays, London E14 4JP.

Copyright © Octopus Publishing Group Ltd 2000
Text Copyright © Michael Schuster 2000
Maps Copyright © Octopus Publishing Group Ltd
Map reference/design, Michael Schuster/Lovell Johns

Reprinted 2001, 2002
Paperback edition 2005; reprinted 2006

A CIP catalogue record for this book is available from
the British Library.

ISBN-13: 978 1 84533 020 0; ISBN-10: 1 84533 020 X

Commissioning editor: Rebecca Spry
Executive art editors: Tracy Killick, Philip Ormerod
Special photography: Russell Sadur, Reuben Paris
Managing editor: Hilary Lumsden
Design: Miranda Harvey
Editor: Stephanie Horner
Picture research: Clairé Gouldstone
Map reference/Design: Michael Schuster/Lovell Johns
Map assistance: Adrian Tempany
Production: Catherine Lay
Index: Mary Kirkness

Typeset in Vectora and Meridien
Printed and bound by Toppan Printing Co., (H.K.) Ltd

contents

before the bottle

introduction

This is a 'how to?' and 'why?', rather than a 'what?' book. It is not a factual volume, there are plenty of those, but an exploration of how to taste, observe, describe, evaluate and enjoy wine. It aims to help you make up your own mind confidently, by giving you the means to do so.

The book is made up of four parts:

1 Before the bottle: is about how to taste and assess wine, about how grapes are grown and how wines are made.

2 In the bottle: describes the wines of the world, largely by grape variety.

3 In the glass: is a 'Do It Yourself' winetasting course, based on the courses I run myself.

4 Reference: consists of maps, some vintage assessments, further reading and a glossary.

How to use the book

The book is written in a logical sequence, but it is organised into sections, panels and captioned illustrations to allow you to dip in and make sense of any section on its own. There is, however, plenty of matter, and to help you navigate and make connections there is a cross-referencing system throughout.

There is a grey 'See also' box in the bottom right hand corner of most double pages. It takes key words or subjects, marked with an asterisk in the text, and leads you elsewhere for further explanation (*italic* numbers refer to captions).

In the bottle: the world's most expensive wines are not discussed in this book, and there is a notional bottle-price ceiling of £30/$50, *see* p57. The '£' symbols in this and the tasting section are a price guide, *see* p118.

In the glass: read How to Use the Tastings p117 carefully to get the most out of this section.

The course and my method of tasting are one approach. This is what works for me. It will give you ideas which you will adapt as you discover what you are comfortable with, and what works for you. The questions the course asks, the wines you try, and discussions with friends, will help crystallise your ideas and give you a permanent means to discovering your palate and preferences. Enjoy the discovery!

Acknowledgements

This has been a complex book to put together and I owe a big thank you to many. Above all to the designer, Miranda Harvey, who put in enormous overtime with me to ensure that the layouts made the ideas look clear, and easy on the eye. To the whole team at Mitchell Beazley, in particular to Rebecca, Hilary, Tracy (who chose two great studio photographers, Russell and Reuben), to Phil, and to my editor Stephanie. Also to Jane Aspden, Margaret Little and my tenacious agent Andrew Lownie.

For their time, expertise and tasting samples, I am grateful to all the winemakers whom I have visited, to those who helped organise the visits, and to the UK wine trade who provide those like myself with an unparalleled opportunity to taste, and without whose generosity a book like this would be impossible. There are too many to name, but you know who you are. Thank you!

Michael Schuster

1. you and your senses

sight

The appearance of a wine is an essential part of its overall harmony, and very much part of the pleasure of drinking it. Beauty and brilliance of colour immediately offer us a mouthwatering prospect.

Aspects of appearance

Brightness, hue and depth are the three attributes of colour.

✓**Hue:** is colour proper: red as distinct from purple, yellow as opposed to green.

✓**Brightness:** describes the light energy a surface emits, ranging from dull to radiant, the difference between a 20 watt and a 150 watt bulb, for example.

✓**Depth:** qualifies hue: for example, 'deep' purple or 'mid'-yellow.

✓**Clarity**

✓**Sediment or CO₂**

✓**bubbles:** if present.

✓**Viscosity**

Without being able to see what we are drinking we feel much less certain about judging what we see and smell. But although visual impressions can be strongly prejudicial, the information they convey is limited.

Colour reveals little about quality or flavour, though it may offer clues as to grape variety, origin and age in a blind tasting*. Brightness, on the other hand, gives you an immediately reassuring indication of health and freshness.

Overall clarity is important too, for we expect wine to be clear, and it appears much less appetising if it is not. In all cases, what matters is to develop a sense of what is appropriate for a given type and age of wine, to judge accordingly, and to be suspicious of extremes.

Clarity: looking through the wine will show how clear it is. A clear wine, with no suspended matter, is a healthy one. If a wine looks murky for reasons other than stirred-up sediment, you have reason to worry, but that is extremely rare in bottled wines today. Vocabulary for appearance can be found in the boxes on p11. (Pink margin boxes are used for vocabulary throughout.)

What appearance tells you — from above

With your glass standing on a white surface and your hands away from its base, look at the wine from directly above, as though you were looking straight down the stem.

FAR RIGHT All wines are examined from above, as though looking straight down the stem, for clarity, brightness and depth of colour.

RIGHT We want milk to be opaque, but we like our wine to be brilliantly clear. The wine on the left, hazy from a fine deposit, is much less appetising to behold.

Brightness: is a general impression, more easily perceived if you adjust your focus to the surface of the wine. Brightness is related to acidity*, and a dull or lacklustre appearance usually indicates a lack of acidity and, in consequence, a possible dullness of taste. Wines can be clear without being particularly bright, but brilliance is both a pleasure to behold and a quality feature in its own right.

Brightness is especially important for white wines, but a lustrous appearance in reds often precedes a particular fineness of flavour too.

Depth: the degree or intensity of colour, as opposed to a wine's hue, is easier to see from above, and the visibility of the stem is a useful reference point here. Bear in mind that the more wine you have in your glass the darker the wine will look and, if you are comparing wines, ensure you have a similar volume in each glass.

Carbon dioxide (CO₂) bubbles: are, of course, abundant in sparkling wines, but still wines also contain some residual CO_2 from the fermentation process, which contributes to their vitality – young wines more than old, whites more than reds. In most still wines CO_2 is at a level which is invisible to the eye and imperceptible on the palate.

Where residual CO_2 is visible, the tiny bubbles can be seen clinging to the inside of the glass – mainly in young wines – and usually, but by no means exclusively, those from warmer climates. The higher level of CO_2 gives zip, and sometimes a touch of spritz, to flavours which are felt to be lacking a little freshness. It may contribute to, but is not solely responsible for, the emulsion of bubbles which sometimes results simply from pouring wine.

Sediment: is uncommon in most wines. Where it does exist, it may muddy the wine's appearance in the glass and possibly its flavour too. Old wines, reds more than whites, often throw a deposit made up of colouring matter, tannin* and tartrate crystals*. If sediment mars your glass, you have the dregs of the bottle! Refer to the section on decanting on pp138–39, and blame the pourer, not the wine!

Influences on appearance

Glasses: should be clear, plain (*ie* undecorated), without coloured stems, and tulip shaped so that the wine does not spill when they are tilted.

The background: against which you examine the wine should be plain white so that there is no distortion of colour.

Light source: northern daylight allows the truest colour comparison. After dark, daylight simulation bulbs are ideal, where possible – these are bulbs fitted with a blue envelope that sheds a 'cold' light close to natural daylight. Standard household bulbs tend to filter out the purple and blue hues in red wine, making it look redder, browner and hence older than it really is. Fluorescent lighting distorts and flattens the colour of all wines.

What appearance tells you – <u>from the side</u>

CO₂ bubbles: viewed from eye level you can sometimes see CO_2 bubbles just sitting under the surface of the wine.

Viscosity: ah, those tears! Tears or 'legs' form on the sides of the glass as a result of alcohol evaporation, and they are related to alcoholic strength and sugar content, both of which increase viscosity. While they may be beautiful and intriguing, they tell you little about a wine's quality that your palate won't reveal a lot more clearly. In 20 years of winetasting I have never paid them much attention.

BELOW *A view from the side to check for clarity, possible CO_2 bubbles and, after a swirl, to look at the wine's viscosity.*

Influence of grape and climate on red wine colour

Cochineal
This culinary dye has but one pigment, as its uniform, monochrome appearance reveals; much plainer to the eye than multi-pigmented red wine.

2-year-old Pinot Noir, Burgundy
Pinot's cooler-climate preference and relatively thin skin usually produce a wine that is only moderately coloured, here barely showing signs of maturity at the rim at only two years old. This colour is typical for Burgundian Pinot but would be weak for Australian Shiraz.

4-year-old Shiraz, South Australia
Typically inky-purple hues of hot-climate Australian Shiraz, a grape variety with a high anthocyanin content. Such a colour would be abnormal for Pinot Noir. Little maturity showing here, even at four years.

8-year-old Cabernet, California
A deeply pigmented, warm-climate Cabernet, which, at eight years, shows the mahogany hues at its core and brick tints at the rim which indicate age and/or maturity.

Looking at wine with the glass tilted

BELOW *Depth of colour is easier to see from above. But the actual hue and graduations from 'core' to 'rim' are best examined with the glass well tilted against a white backdrop.*

With your glass no more than one-third full, and holding it by the base (or foot) of the stem, tilt it away from you until the wine comes almost to the edge of the bowl. Because most of us describe colour relatively rarely, it is easier to compare two wines side by side which will thus provide colour reference points for each other.

Origins of colour in red wines

The flesh of most winemaking grapes is colourless. Colour in red wines comes from a group of pigmented chemical compounds, called polyphenols, in the grape's skin. The two principal groups are anthocyanins and tannins, both extracted during winemaking. Colour is extracted* first, by contact with water in the juice; tannins* later, by increasing alcohol.

Their quantity, hue and intensity vary according to the grape variety, its state of ripeness when picked and the extent of maceration*. Anthocyanins are purple and dominate the colour of young wines, but their colour is relatively unstable and disappears before that of tannins.

Tannins are orange, amber and yellow in colour. Both groups polymerise slowly with age, *ie* their molecules combine and become larger until they are eventually insoluble, at which point they precipitate and form part of the sediment.

Anthocyanins do this more readily than tannins so their purple is the first colour to go, leaving the orange and brick red hues of the tannins in more mature red wines. Tannins eventually precipitate in the same way, but more slowly. The pace of this change varies according to the grape, origin and vintage.

Depth of colour: on the whole we tend to prefer to see darkly coloured red wines because of their promise of abundant taste sensations; and a notable lack of colour for a given type of wine may indeed indicate deficiencies: excessive yield*, grapes that are less than fully ripe, a rainy harvest, inadequate maceration for example. However, whilst intensity of colour is frequently associated with *strength* of flavour, it is not an indication of *quality* of flavour. At the other extreme, inappropriately deep colours can be just as undesirable, suggesting excessive extraction* or the addition of too much press wine*, both of which can make for very coarse characteristics.

Origins of colour in white wines

This is much less well understood than colour in red wines. Some of the colour appears to come from polyphenols, but of a different type from those which colour reds, and their quantity is small as there is comparatively little contact between juice and skins.

Tan colour of white wines increases as they age, as a result of both polymerisation and oxidation. Sweet wines made from nobly rotten* grapes are often a deep gold to begin with, and the caramelisation of their sugars over time contributes to their darkening with age. In all cases low-acid wines (very ripe grapes, hot climates) will become both dull in appearance and deeper in colour more rapidly.

Evidence of the effect of fermentation and ageing in barrel* is conflicting. The combination of contact with the wood and greater exposure to oxygen will tend to darken a wine, whilst contact with yeast lees tends to protect against this oxidative darkening effect.

Brilliance and subtleties of hue in whites: our eyes – and our initial judgements – are very sensitive to absolute clarity, lustre and subtlety of tone in white wines. Any hint of dullness, haze, or excess colour for age and type will tend to prejudice us against a white wine at first sight.

Colour: aspects to note with the glass tilted; and colour vocabulary

The core   The rim

Examining red wines: look for the principal colour at the 'core' of the wine as well as the different tint at the 'rim', purple in young wines, increasingly brick-hued with age. Red wines lighten in colour as they age: inky, purple, violet, red, ruby, garnet, mahogany, brick, orange, amber, brown.

Examining white wines: intensity of colour in whites is less important than for red wines, what matter here are absolute clarity, brightness, and degree of colour for type and age. Whites become darker in colour as they age: water-white, greeny-yellow, pale-yellow, lemon, straw, gold, old-gold, amber, brown.

Rosé wine colours: pale red, rose, salmon, pink, onion-skin, orange. Here colour is not necessarily an indication of age, since rosés are generally drunk young; rather, these different hues reflect the variety of red grapes used and the relatively short period of skin contact when the grapes are in the vat. For all wines, excessive browning, considering type and age, will usually indicate storage conditions that have been too warm, and therefore premature oxidation.

Influence of grape and climate on white wine colour

2-year-old Riesling Spätlese, Mosel, Germany
Lively and limpid, yet almost colourless, appearance of a young, cool-climate Riesling which will gain colour very slowly. The residual CO_2 bubbles result from slow, cool fermentation and early bottling (*see* pp9,22).

2-year-old Chardonnay, California
Bright, clear, pale gold of a young barrel-fermented and barrel-aged Chardonnay. Riper, warm-climate grapes and lower natural acidity typically produce a warmer, deeper colour which will darken more rapidly than the Riesling (*see* pp11,40–1).

Appearance

Clarity: clear, limpid; muddy, murky, cloudy, hazy.
Brightness: radiant, lustrous, luminous, vivid, lively, bright; lacklustre, dull, flat.
Depth: opaque, deep, dark, dense; pale, light, weak, watery.

---

*See also

smell

The finest wines are those richest in aroma, the plainest are aromatically impoverished, and it is our sense of smell which makes the distinctions. The nose of a wine reveals much about its identity, origin and quality even before you taste.

Aromas: a selection

Floral: rose, violet, acacia, jasmine, lime-tree.
Vegetal: grassy, green or bell pepper, pine, resin, bruised leaf, tea, mint, undergrowth, truffle, hay, green or black olive.
Continued on p14.

Smell is a cerebral prelude to the palate's carnal gratification, conjuring up intensely vivid memories of people, places, occasions and emotions. It is, by a long way, the most important of our senses for both winetasting and wine drinking. Most of what we describe as 'taste' is in reality 'smell'; a fact we appreciate better, as adults, when we realise we cannot taste our food or drink when we have a cold.

How smell works

Children told to hold their nose to avoid the unpleasantness of cough mixture will indeed escape it until they let go of their nostrils. At this point, as they breathe out, the medicine's taste will penetrate their being as intensely as if they hadn't grasped their nose at all.

Smell consists of odour molecules which react with numerous tiny hairs bathed in the mucus that covers our smelling mechanism, the olfactory bulb, situated at the top of our nostrils. The molecules need to be in a vaporous state to be perceived by these hairs, which then convey the message of smell to our brain.

A ribbon of odour-laden air crosses the olfactory bulb, drawn from the base of the nostrils as we breathe in (the wine's 'nose'), and a different current crosses it, expelled from the throat after being warmed in the mouth, as we breathe out (most of the wine's taste and aftertaste.) *See* illustrations.

Influences on smell

Four important factors affect what we are able to smell. Being aware of them helps us to maximise our perception and may also help us to interpret what we smell.
Adaptation: describes the way our sense of smell gets used to, 'adapts' to, what it is smelling and as a result becomes less sensitive to it, less able to perceive it. For this reason, first impressions are usually the most telling.

Nose

Olfactory bulb (enlarged for the purposes of illustration)

Odour-laden air perceived as *smell*

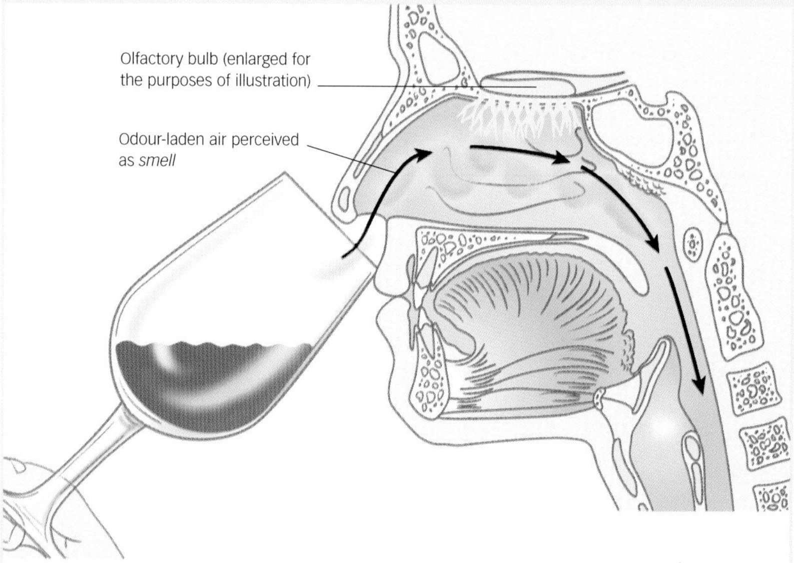

Nose: odour-laden air from the glass crosses your olfactory bulb, the smell mechanism, as you breathe *in* through your nostrils. This is perceived as smell, the wine's 'nose'.

Taste

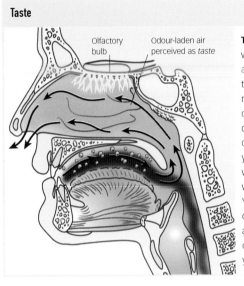

Olfactory bulb

Odour-laden air perceived as *taste*

Taste: the mouth's warmth along with air drawn through the wine help release the wine's odours. These are driven *out* over the olfactory bulb from your throat as you work the wine gently with jaw and tongue. You perceive these odours as 'taste' by association with the other sensations in your mouth.

Aftertaste

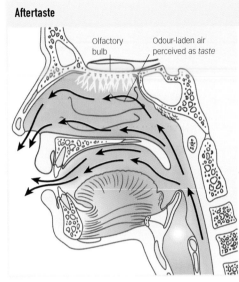

Olfactory bulb

Odour-laden air perceived as *taste*

Aftertaste: as you breathe *out* through nose and mouth after swallowing, the surfaces of, and the air in, your nose, mouth and throat remain saturated with residual odour/taste sensations. This is called the 'aftertaste', which lingers more or less, according to the quality of the wine (*see* also p27).

If you find you can no longer 'get at' smells you think are there, stop trying, leave the wine alone for a while and then go back. Our sense of smell tires in this way rapidly, but it recovers its acuity rapidly too.

Temperature: affects how odour molecules vaporise; the warmer the wine the more easily vaporisation occurs, the colder the wine the more reluctant it is to yield its scents. The perfect temperature is a will-o'-the-wisp, it is almost always a compromise (*see* p125).

What you have just smelled: will make any smell you move on to seem particularly clear, at least to begin with. This is the dual effect of contrast (with the previous odour) and sensitivity (to the new smell) prior to adaptation. The immediate comparison may put either odour in a better or worse light, but it will usually help to define them both.

Glasses: the size and shape of their bowl, in particular, have a marked effect on how the bouquet of a wine comes across, but, given certain minimal criteria, any standard glass will do. Those basic requirements are that the glass should be plain, not too thick, large enough to allow for a vigorous 'swirl' without spilling, and with a tapering bowl to 'gather' and concentrate the wine's aromas. When comparing wines you should endeavour to have identical glasses. The same wine smelled

in different glasses will smell different, even if it doesn't taste different; though one's perception of the nose is likely to influence one's impression of the palate too.

The exceptionally wide range of glassware made by the Austrian manufacturer Georg Riedel results from the theory that there is an ideal shape to bring out the best on the nose and palate for each wine type and grape variety. There is no question that the shape of the bowl makes a big difference to the way in which a wine's bouquet emerges. But, apart from the very first impression upon sipping, I don't believe it affects the way we perceive a wine's most important attributes after the initial attack, *ie* texture, aromatic interest, length across the palate and the qualities and

BELOW *A tasting sample in a horizontal International Standards Organisation (ISO) tasting glass. The tulip shape enables you to tilt it thus, without spillage, meaning you can examine the hue closely and easily.*

Aromas (continued)

Fruity: orange, lemon, lime, grapefruit, tangerine; pear, peach, apricot, melon, apple, quince, gooseberry; red cherry, redcurrant, strawberry, raspberry, blueberry, blackberry, mulberry, black cherry, blackcurrant, cassis; lychee, pineapple, mango, passion-fruit.
Mineral: earthy, chalky, volcanic, slate, stony, gravelly; petrol, wax.
Animal: venison, game, gamey, damp fur, wet wool, leather, musk, cat's pee.
Spicy: black/white pepper, clove, cedar, liquorice, aniseed, cinnamon, vanilla.
Dried fruit: nutty, hazelnut, walnut, bitter almond, fig, prune, raisin, fruitcake, jam.
Burnt: tar, coffee, toast, butter, caramel, chocolate, honey, 'roasted', singed, smoky, tobacco.
Chemical: see p151.

BELOW My wife and I drink out of glasses we enjoy the look of, like the range here, broadly grouped into white, on the left, red in the middle, and Champagne on the right. But this has more to do with conventions of size than anything else. Second from left is our favourite, the Riedel Rheingau. Sixth from left is a family glass, enjoyed for sentimental reasons. The antique Champagne pair are lovely, full stop.

persistence of the finish. My wife Monika and I use Riedel stemware because it is the most beautiful range available to the wine-lover, but the limited selection we have is chosen on the basis of shapes and sizes we like, rather than on what we are likely to drink.

Where smells come from

(These topics are covered in more detail in the section Viticulture and Vinification pp34–51.)

Grape variety: the best winemaking grape varieties vary considerably in their aromatic characteristics, and it is these characteristics that are the prime source of the individuality of flavour in their wines.

Location and viticulture: the grape's aromatics* are themselves affected by where they grow, and how and to what extent they ripen. Sauvignon Blanc from New Zealand smells clearly of its grape variety, but though recognisably Sauvignon Blanc, it is a very different version of the aroma from that encountered in Sancerre from France.

Aromas are also affected by yield (high yields dilute them), how vigorously the vines grow (excess leaf cover* often leads to herbaceous characters), whether the overall climate is warm (softer, riper but often less well-defined smells) or cool (crisper, more intense characteristics), see pp130–31.

Vinification: the most obvious vinification-related odours are the mildly dairy-like smells deriving from malolactic fermentation*, and the vanillary aromas (amongst many others) which come from contact with new-oak*.

Bottle age: some of the most subtle and seductively desirable smells in wine are to be found in quality wines that have been given time to mature in bottle, anything from a couple of years to a couple of decades and more.

How to smell wines in the glass

It is worth gently rinsing wine all round the interior of a fresh glass, just to mask any traces of washing-up residue, musty storage odours or the like.

Before agitation (glass resting on the table, or hand-held but still): odour molecules of smell differ in their volatility, *ie* in their ability to escape from the liquid and vaporise. The lightest emerge naturally from the wine's surface when it is at rest, unagitated. You need to smell the wine in this state, before swirling, or you may well disperse what are often some of the most delicate and transitory smells. Sniff gently, but deeply, noting the different smells as you identify them.

After agitation: weightier molecules need encouragement. Give the glass a good 'swirl': a small, circular motion (anticlockwise for right-handers, clockwise for left-handers), sufficient to drive the wine up the walls of the glass. This creates a broad expanse of thin liquid from which the heavier smells

ABOVE *Giving the glass a good swirl drives the wine up its walls, creating a broad expanse of thin liquid from which the molecules of aroma can vaporise more easily. There is often a succession of scents as the wine subsides.*

can evaporate more easily. Smell immediately, letting your nostrils drink deep at what is now a well of aroma-rich mist in the glass, and again note down the scents you now detect.

You need to concentrate to identify the smells, and you will probably find they are at their most clear-cut and intense between three and eight seconds after you begin. Experiment with how profoundly you need to breathe in to suit yourself and the individual wine. After swirling, particularly with older wines, you may well note a succession of elusive, fleeting scents before the wine becomes still again. There is not invariably a marked difference between 'before' and 'after', but you should always give yourself the opportunity to see if there is.

Occasionally after a shake: if a wine seems very 'dumb', or stinky, try covering the glass with your hand and giving it a really good shake to rouse it from its torpor or to disperse the pong.

After emptying the glass: some of the heaviest molecules and richest odours only emerge after considerable contact with oxygen, which happens when there is little wine and lots of air. You will understand this if you have ever savoured the residual bouquet in an empty glass of fine Cognac or malt whisky – the morning after! This is what the French call the *fond de verre*, bottom of the glass.

Aroma versus bouquet: as general terms these are pretty much interchangeable. Used more specifically, aroma describes the primary, varietal, fruit-based smells in young wines. The phrase 'highly aromatic' is reserved for wines with an impressive array of aromas/flavours on the nose, in the mouth and on the finish. Bouquet is used, by analogy with the variety of scents in a bouquet of flowers, to denote the softer, sweeter, more subtle smells that evolve with bottle age.

Honing your sense of smell

Just as our eyes can 'see' a wide palette of colours, so our nose can 'sense' a wide range of smells. But in both cases we are not good at putting names to what we perceive. Developing our sensitivity to smells and an ability to identify them is simply a question of application and practice. Concentrating on identifying everyday smells in the home is a start; a more efficient way is to use a specific list such as the ones in the margins on pp12,14, as a trigger and memory aid whilst tasting, matching names to smells as you go. A more expensive, but much more precisely efficacious tool is the *Nez du Vin* series of reference aromas which you can use to train your olfactory memory (*see* margin illustration). Mine is nearly 20 years old and still in use.

Smell: aspects to note

Health: clean; grubby, dirty; faulty (specify if possible, *see* p151).
Intensity: closed, dumb; weak, light; open, medium-intensity; intense, strong, concentrated.
Characteristics: grape variety smells; those associated with vinification and barrel-ageing; state of maturity, bouquet smells associated with bottle age. *See* the margin listings pp12,14.
Quality: indistinct, neutral, vague; plain, common, ordinary; simple straightforward; clear-cut, frank; delicate, subtle, complex; penetrating, long, refined, classy.

ABOVE *The large Nez du Vin box of reference aromas. The small phials come in sets of different sizes, including one devoted to wine faults.*

*See also

grape aromatics **40**
leaf cover *38-9*
malo fermentation **41**
new oak **48**

taste and tasting

We have already considered wine's appearance and smell, and now we turn to taste: wine in the mouth. Here, in the final phase of tasting, the word 'taste' is used in two of its many senses: the physiological one first, and then the aesthetic.

The physiological meaning of taste refers to the perception of sensations that we call tastes (sweet, acid, salty, bitter); the aesthetic meaning involves questions of judgement (How good is it? What is it worth?). As far as the winetaster is concerned, neither is possible without the medium of language. The following three sections, Taste and Tasting, Words and Qualities, and Values,

look at these three aspects of tasting and how they interrelate.

What makes a good taster

In contrast to prior conviction, recent science tells us that there is an enormous variation between the number of taste-buds that each of us has and that, in consequence, those of us blessed with a very large number must be 'supertasters'. But don't bother to rush to the mirror to start counting! Taste-bud incidence is likely to be an extremely poor indicator of whether you will make a good taster. Firstly, most of what we call taste is in fact smell, and most of the qualities we appreciate in wine are related to aspects other than those sensed by the taste-buds (aroma, texture,

LEFT *The problem for beginners tasting wine is how to look, and what to look at to make sense of it. In the picture of Adam and Eve embracing there are three images: Eve's profile to the left, Adam's to the right, and an imprecise composite (like a mouthful of wine). Unless you focus on Adam or Eve individually, it is impossible to see either clearly, and in practice awareness flips from one to the other. But knowing there are two faces, you can adjust your gaze and concentrate on one at a time to see each more clearly. Similarly with wine in your mouth, you can focus* on its elements separately, and consider them individually, before returning to an impression of the whole. Experience, and guidance from others, will show you which elements to look for in the first place.*

length, balance…). What the taste-buds of the mouth perceive, the so-called 'primary' tastes* of sweetness, acidity, saltiness, bitterness (and possibly umami*), are but a minor part of what wine has to offer.

Secondly, what counts in any case is not so much your potential sensitivity to these limited aspects of taste, but how your mind processes, interprets and communicates what you perceive. And that is a question of practice, of developing your vocabulary, of a set of values, and, above all, of motivation. Children – and dogs even more so for that matter – are much more sensitive to tastes and smells than most adult humans, but as they cannot pass on their perceptions we would hardly call them supertasters, not in any useful sense of the word. If you want to be a good taster, and work at it, the likelihood is that you can be.

Tasting versus drinking

Drinking wine, like listening to music, is mostly a passive, albeit very conscious, sensual pleasure; we relish the sensations without giving them too much thought. **Tasting** wine involves a deliberate and considered act of scrutiny, more or less brief according to what the wine has to offer or what you are trying to do, the ultimate aim of which is to amplify your enjoyment. In this respect it is no different from studying any subject you fancy, be it art, literature, sport, gardening, music….

In the company of someone who knows, as well as by reading and experiment, you discover what to look for, and how to look for it: brushwork, form and colour in painting; melody, textures and harmonies in music; movement, plays, strokes and strategies in sport; plants and their placement in gardening.

Increasing familiarity leads you to notice more and more easily, you begin to take pleasure in variations on themes* you recognise and in discussing them with others; and you broaden your taste by sampling the unfamiliar. And, in the case of wine, when you go back to just drinking, simply letting the sensations wash over you, you appreciate them all the more.

The importance of words

A look, if an oversimplified one, at the interdependent relationship between perception and words is a useful background to understanding how to develop your overall tasting ability. Here is what happens: a physical or chemical stimulus excites your sensory apparatus (vision, smell, taste) and creates a sensory message. This sensation is automatic, registered as a reflex. But from the brain's viewpoint, no colour, scent, taste or texture is such until it is consciously recognised. Our senses are constantly bombarded with stimuli, but our perception of them is mostly passive – and therefore, in effect, non-existent – until we direct our attention to them, at which point we become consciously aware.

Think of background music, always there, but on the periphery of perception, swimming in and out of our consciousness depending on whether or not we direct our attention to it. But even conscious perception works at two levels: we can be aware of a sensation but unable to put a name to it – or uninterested in doing so – partial perception if you like; and we can perceive it fully by identifying it with a word or a name.

Words help us to notice things. The capacity of our senses to perceive far exceeds our ability to articulate all the sensations we can experience (just consider colour and smell), and of course we don't need the words to have the experience.

But once acquired and linked to the appropriate sensations, words help us to locate and identify them subsequently. They make perception more rapid, more efficient. And when we taste with a wide vocabulary, an active search of the mind generates the words, which in turn capture and crystallise the sensations.

This is why we find the thoughtful, 'expert' commentary of others helpful, because it heightens and clarifies our awareness; and why enlarging our own stock of active words is so essential. Even professionals benefit from reviewing their vocabulary periodically.

The taste of wine

Describing the taste of wine is more complicated than assessing its appearance or smell. There are more aspects to consider and a limited time (whilst you have the wine in your mouth) to mull over them before you need to swallow or spit. Thus the principal difficulty facing you is knowing where and what to focus your attention on, and in which order to look. This is made easier by having a consistent, systematised approach. So let's dissect and consider:

- How to direct your attention.
- The order in which to consider things.
- The technique of tasting.
- Tastes and sensations to focus on.

How to direct your attention

The location of your taste-buds: knowing where your taste receptors are located and which locations are more highly sensitive to specific sensations helps your mind home in on these tastes as you explore the liquid. Becoming familiar with the 'taste-bud map'

of your palate is also a good way to discover how easily you can direct your attention to different aspects of wine, in particular sweetness, acidity, bitterness and length. For details, *see* the box below.

Other more abstract qualities – balance*, texture*, aroma and individual flavours, for example – are not perceived by the taste-buds as such and are therefore less easily pinpointed. But the principle of directed, focused attention is the same.

The order in which to consider things

It is useful to think of tasting in two broad phases: information first, interpretation second. **Information:** in this first phase you use your senses to get as much information as possible (or as much as you want) from the wine. You need to search actively to 'see what there is to see', putting words and names to what you notice as you go, tasting the wine fully by considering its component parts separately. This analysis provides you with a factual

---

Taste-buds on the tongue, with their traditional taste-sensitive locations

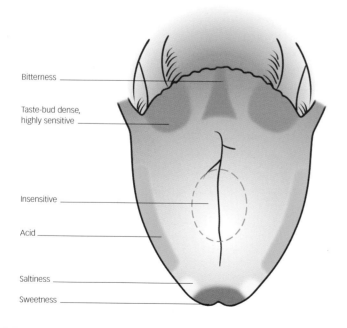

Bitterness

Taste-bud dense, highly sensitive

Insensitive

Acid

Saltiness

Sweetness

This traditional 'map' of the tongue is rightly discredited because its oversimplification – sweet-sensitive taste-buds at the tip, bitter-sensitive taste-buds at the rear and so on – is scientifically inaccurate. It seems that most taste-buds can respond to each of the primary tastes, though perhaps not with equal sensitivity. But if its shortcomings are clear from a scientific point of view, the map of the tongue is still a useful reference for winetasters. For almost everyone's experience shows that different parts of our tongue are indeed more sensitive to one taste than to another, the traditional locations are broadly correct for most people, and they continue to be practical focal points when winetasting. For practice in locating these areas, and to find out about your own particular sensitivities, consult the exercise on pp120–21.

summary. Indeed a definition of this first phase of tasting might be: **an attempt to maximise the number of sensations you can perceive and identify in the wine.**

At this point you can stop and simply enjoy your drinking; the very act of tasting attentively will have revealed to you much that might otherwise have gone unnoticed. Or you can proceed to the second phase:

II **Interpretation:** armed with the individual perceptions from phase 1, you can now:
a) put the parts together again in order to see the wine as a whole.
b) go on to evaluate it, asking a wide range of questions relating to quality, value for money, typicity and so on, which are dealt with under Values*.

You might think of these two phases in a number of ways: in essence they are What? and So What? respectively, or information followed by interpretation. Either can be simplified or refined to whatever extent you like or, more importantly, according to what seems appropriate for the wine concerned.

The technique of tasting

As with considering a wine's appearance and then its smell, the actual 'mechanics' of tasting are easy to learn (steps 1 and 2 below). It's what you *make* of your perceptions that counts.

Below is a detailed outline of the tasting* process and sequence. This is an ideal, if you like, because common sense tells us that not all wines require or reward such close examination, in which case you just curtail the procedure. Other wines, however, take more time to get to know, but repay the effort. Your tastes, time, interest and the occasion will decide what is suitable.

1 **Technique, step 1:** take the equivalent of a good teaspoonful of wine into your mouth – 6–7ml is what I find comfortable. Beginners often take too little – and then taste mainly the harsher aspects of the wine. Too much is wasteful, especially if sample size is limited, but more to the point it is cumbersome to explore in the mouth and then messy to spit.

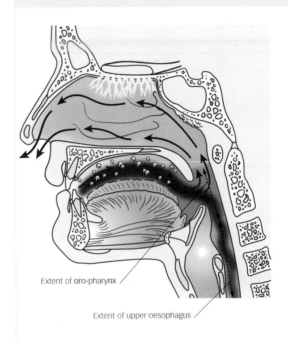

Taste-buds other than on the tongue

Extent of oro-pharynx

Extent of upper oesophagus

The location of taste-buds is not limited to your tongue. They are also located in the oro-pharynx, the area directly behind your mouth, and in the upper part of the oesophagus (the tube that leads down to your stomach). In addition to being further focal points, these are important from the taster's point of view because they account, in part, for the physical sensations of 'length' of flavour – one of the principal measures of quality in a wine. (See also illustrations p27.)

2 **Technique, step 2:** alternate between **working** the wine gently round your mouth, **aerating** it and **swallowing** a little. You work it round to make sure it reaches all your taste-buds, and to feel its texture; you aerate it in order to release the molecules of aroma, in effect a large part of the taste; you swallow a little to get the tastes and scents to those important receptors in your throat, and also to drive them up to your olfactory bulb before spitting. With a little practice this should become a physical rhythm which is second nature.

Information, during your first taste: concentrate on making a **quantitative summary** of the wine, noting its basic 'dimensions': body (alcohol), acidity, tannin (in reds), and concentration, focusing your attention as necessary on different areas of your palate, different aspects of the wine, always searching for the appropriate words. You may find you have time to note the most obvious flavours during this first taste too. Then spit. This will have given you a broad outline of the wine, a good idea of its overall quality, and, crucially,

*See also

balance **31**

tasting tech, summary **133**

texture **28**

values **29-33**

Dryness/sweetness

Bone-dry, dry, off-dry, medium-dry, medium-sweet, sweet, intensely sweet, cloying.

Acidity

Rising levels, from insufficient to excessive: flat, flabby (inadequate acidity); soft, fresh, lively, crisp, mouthwatering, firm, vigorous; and for excess: tart, sharp, green, biting, acid.

Comparative tasting

The contrast effect, or adaptation: if you taste a high-acid wine and then a low-acid one, the latter, even if well balanced, will likely taste rather flat. Taste them the other way round and the acid wine will taste disagreeably sharp.

Your palate having become 'adapted' to one sensation will experience its 'contrast' even more keenly. This may be a distorting influence on your perception of many aspects of tasting: sweetness, body, intensity of flavour, quality and so on. On the other hand, it may also be usefully revealing, depending on the context. What matters is to be aware of it.

whether it deserves further exploration and to what extent – one more taste, two... etc. You will find that the simplest wines probably need only this one look.

Information, during subsequent tastes (as required): as you continue to work, aerate and swallow a little wine, note individual flavours/aromas; their intensity, variety, subtlety; the balance of 'fruit' as opposed to 'aroma'; the character and qualities of the wine's texture; its middle-palate length and interest; the quality and persistence of its aftertaste.

This requires considerable concentration as you make sure you cover each aspect, and as you search your mind for vocabulary. A regular pattern of scrutiny will ensure you don't miss anything. Clearly, only the finest wines will merit or repay such detailed examination; experience (and pleasure!) will rapidly tell you which they are.

Details of the more quality-oriented aspects mentioned here are dealt with in the section Words and Qualities*.

Interpretation: you have the information, now you decide which questions, to do with various values, you want to address. They may be none at all: 'I just want to sit back and enjoy this without thinking too hard any more', or at the other extreme you may want to consider numerous questions relating to quality, style, typicity, value for money, readiness to drink, and so on. See the section Values*.

Tastes and sensations to focus on

The primary tastes: are sweet, acid, bitter and salty (and possibly umami, see box p21). Outlined here are their origins, how (and where) you perceive them, how they interact in a wine's overall balance, and some of the vocabulary you can use to describe them. (See margin boxes.)

Dryness/sweetness

The term 'dry' in winespeak is the opposite of 'sweet'; it simply means an absence of any sugary impressions. 'Cloying' is a term used to indicate insufficient acidity to balance the sugars.

Origins: the principal sources of sweetness in dry wines (those with all the sugar from the grapes fermented into alcohol) are alcohol itself, and the flavours of naturally ripe fruit.

Alcohol, at the level it is in most table wines (8–14%), contributes a sweetness which is easily demonstrated (see p121) if not always perceptible as such. Modest quantities of glycerol, a by-product of fermentation, may also add sweetness. In sweet wines the main sweet taste comes from the **fructose** and **sucrose** sugars in the grape's juice which have not been fermented into alcohol. This is called residual sugar*.

Perception: sweetness is perceived primarily, but by no means exclusively, on the tip of the tongue. The two sites at the rear sides of the tongue are also sensitive to it. If you have a sweet tooth (as I do), you will probably be less aware of low levels of sweetness precisely because you indulge in it frequently. Perhaps for this reason I perceive sweetness very much as a general impression. If you dislike sweet things, you are likely to be much more sensitive to it.

Role and balance function: for most people, sweetness is the only flavour which has any appeal on its own. It moderates and counterbalances acidity, astringency and bitterness; and in turn its own intensity is moderated by them.

Acidity

Origins: the most important acids in wine, tartaric (the principal one) and malic, come from the grape. But acid can be 'adjusted' up* during fermentation in warmer climates when there is insufficient acid in the ripe grapes. Small amounts of other acids are produced during fermentation: notably lactic acid, during malolactic fermentation, and acetic acid, a natural and normally imperceptible component, but a fault when present in excess (see p151).

Perception: the sharpness of acidity is clearly perceived on the upper sides of the tongue, so it is easy to focus one's attention on it.

An unpleasantly high level of acidity also tends to thin one's saliva and thus create a slight feeling of astringency as well. An agreeably high level is appetising, mouthwatering in the literal sense that it makes you salivate, it 'makes the juices run'.

ii **Role and balance function:** acidity shapes and puts into relief the flavours in wine just as it does in fresh fruit. Its level varies enormously according to the type and/or origins of the wine, and just what constitutes an appropriate amount varies as much as it does with different types of fruit.

Acid is especially important for white wines as, in the absence of tannin, it constitutes their principal element of 'structure'. Familiarity will enable you to describe it relatively objectively, as well as helping you decide whether it is adequate or not, both for the type of wine, and for your personal taste.

To what extent you actually taste acid depends very much on the levels of the wine's other main constituents: alcohol, sugar and tannin. The sweet aspect of alcohol takes the edge off acidity, but in white table wines with high alcohol (say 13.5% and above) *and* high acidity it can make the acid taste even harder. Sugar itself moderates and diminishes acidity as we know, delaying and to some extent masking our perception of it. High levels of tannin and acid accentuate each other.

Bitterness

i **Origins:** bitterness can come from a number of sources: unripe tannins in barely ripe red grapes, bruising of grape skins and pips during both red and white winemaking*, excessive 'extraction' during maceration in red winemaking, excess oak contact for white wines. It frequently has a simpler origin, namely high alcohol, especially in white wines with only a modest amount of flavour.

ii **Perception:** mainly, and clearly, tasted at the rear (base) of the tongue, sometimes seeming to reach back into the throat. The taste is like that of quinine in tonic water, or of strong black coffee. It is sometimes confused with tannin; but though they may be associated, bitterness is a taste, tannin is a tactile sensation. Its taste location at the back of the tongue explains why bitterness, when it is found, is usually perceived as part of the 'finish' or 'aftertaste' of a wine.

iii **Role:** bitterness plays no crucial role in wine's structure (unlike acidity and alcohol), it is simply a taste. Individuals' perception of bitterness varies a great deal, as does their liking and/or tolerance for it. It is sometimes present in young, tannic red wines which require ageing, and it is a light, agreeable attribute of many Italian red wines for example.

Saltiness and umami (*See* margin box.)

Touch or tactile sensations

Although they are not, strictly speaking, tastes, tactile sensations are a significant part of what we perceive when tasting. They play an important role in the balance of wine, and they can strongly affect our impressons, positively and negatively.

Alcohol and 'body'

i **Origins:** ethyl alcohol or ethanol is the main product of fermentation, where grape sugars are fermented by yeasts. In cooler climates, if the grapes are considered to have inadequate natural sugar (for the wine's required level of alcohol), this can be boosted by the addition of sugar* to the must during fermentation. Most standard table wines contain between 8% and 14% alcohol by volume. (This can also be expressed as 8° or 14°; it means the same thing.)

ii **Perception:** alcohol is a complex liquid whose properties are such that it has both tastes and textures. We have already seen that it has sweet and bitter tastes (*see* above). It has a perceptible warmth in the mouth, especially at levels above 13%, which, in excess, can make table wines taste 'hot', sometimes even 'fierce'. It also has a perceptible 'thickness', a palpable viscosity of texture, especially by comparison with water.

iii **Role and balance function:** alcohol's sweetness has been discussed above. Its

Bitterness

Indications of intensity are usually sufficient: quinine bitterness; slightly bitter, bitter, very bitter.

Saltiness and umami

Although wine contains salts, the taste of saltiness as such is rare. Some people claim to find it in Manzanilla sherries. **Umami:** this Japanese word meaning 'savoury' refers to the flavour of monosodium glutamate. Most European palates, mine included, have insufficient experience in identifying umami for it to be usefully considered a fifth primary taste, as it is, apparently, in the Far East.

*See also

acid adjustment **41,50**
addition of sugar/
    chaptalisation **44,49**
bitterness/winemaking
    40,44-6
residual sugar **42–3**
values **29–33**
words & qualities **24–28**

Alcohol

Relating to alcoholic weight or 'body'. What is perceived as too little alcohol for a given type is described as weak, thin, watery; in between they are light-, medium- or full-bodied, ample, generous, potent. Too much makes for wines that are heavy, hot, alcoholic, fierce, spirity.

Astringency

Quantity: lightly, moderately, very or abundantly tannic.
Quality: fine-grained, soft, silky, velvety, matt, dry, firm, chewy; ripe, rich, savoury; green, vegetal, herbaceous, tough, coarse, aggressive, astringent. See also pp28,47–8.

CO₂

Pearly, prickle, a touch of spritz, spritzy, pétillant.

'presence' in the mouth is something we 'feel', the very essence of 'wineyness'. This is part of the impression that we call 'body' or weight in a wine, and is the aspect of alcohol that has most words associated with it. Like all the principal aspects of a wine's make-up, what is an appropriate level is very much a question of the type of wine. Alcohol also carries and spreads the flavours of wine around the mouth, and helps prolong them on the finish.

Astringency

Origins: most astringency in wine is produced by tannin, and most of that is in red wine. There are two sources: the skin and pips of red grapes, and new wooden barrels. Tannin from grapes is extracted during both fermentation and maceration* (the period when grape skins and pips remain in contact with the wine after fermentation). Tannin from wood is extracted during the ageing of wine in new-oak* barrels.

Perception: astringency is the drying, furring, puckering sensation you get in your mouth when your tongue and gums no longer 'slip' against each other smoothly. Tannin creates this effect by combining with and coagulating the proteins in your saliva so that it no longer has its normal lubricant properties. Its effect is more or less intense according to both the quantity and the quality of the tannins.

Role and balance function: at the start of the 21st century tannins continue to defy scientific analysis. We know what they do, but we still don't really understand why. More than anything else tannins affect the texture of a wine, how it feels in the mouth, and the vocabulary of tannin reflects this. But they appear to contribute to its overall sapidity as well, to its savoury richness, particularly when they come a) from really ripe grapes, and b) from careful vinification.

Insufficiently ripe grapes and/or brutal handling of the grapes during vinification can produce herbaceous, bitter and excessively astringent* characters. As a preservative, tannins allow fine red wines to age; and if they are good quality, not overly astringent, then they will soften over the course of time, making the wine's texture softer, smoother, glossier.

The astringency of tannin is accentuated by acidity and for this reason red wines with abundant tannin generally don't have as much acidity as those without. Nor do they need it, for the presence of tannin gives some of the 'shape' and definition to red wine that acidity does to whites, or to reds with very little tannin. Without tannins the feel of red wines in the mouth would be just like that of white wines. Tannic astringency is softened by sweetness in the form of sugar or alcohol, and sugars also delay its perception in the mouth.

As with acidity, what is judged an appropriate level of tannin is closely related to the grape variety and type of wine.

Carbon dioxide (CO_2) in still wines

Origins: along with alcohol, CO_2 gas* is the principal by-product of fermentation and newly fermented wines are saturated with it, but the bulk of this disappears naturally, or via racking, prior to bottling. However, a few white wines are deliberately made to retain enough CO_2 for it to be both tasteable and sometimes visible too: Vinho Verde, Muscadet Sur Lie, many Swiss, German and warm-climate New World white wines, for example.

Perception: occasionally you can see CO_2 bubbles clinging to the interior of the glass, and if you can see them you can almost certainly taste them, usually as a first impression, and just as a light prickle on the tip of the tongue. Even when the bubbles are invisible, you may sometimes notice them. CO_2 and water produce the mild carbonic acid with which we are familiar from carbonated water and fizzy drinks. The warmer the wine is, the more obvious CO_2 will be.

Role and balance function: all wines, and young ones especially, contain a little CO_2, usually imperceptible to both eye and palate, but contributing nonetheless to brilliance of appearance and to freshness of both nose and flavour. The more tannin red wines contain, the less CO_2 they will have because, as a mild acid, it would tend to accentuate any astringency.

Identifying focal points and getting your bearings

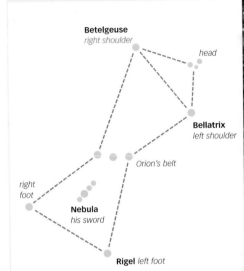

Betelgeuse
right shoulder

head

Bellatrix
left shoulder

Orion's belt

right foot

Nebula
his sword

Rigel *left foot*

Finding your way round wine is like navigating the sky at night, you need to recognise the reference points to get your bearings. Until you are 'shown' the particular bright stars, you don't 'see' the pattern called Orion the Hunter. But once identified, Betelgeuse, Rigel and Orion's Belt become easily recognisable focal points because they stand out so (his raised right arm is missing, his 'shield' is in the right hand corner). Wine too has 'focal points' to help you get your bearings. Its 'bright stars' are the structural elements of alcohol, acidity, and tannin, and individual aroma/flavour/texture traits. Once you recognise them, you can home in on them, consider them, and thus establish the 'patterns' which identify the various grapes and wine styles.

Flavour

The categories above describe the basic structural elements of a wine's make-up, and they account for a large part of our experience of the wine. However, their vocabulary doesn't say much about more commonly identifiable 'tastes' or their concentration.

i **Concentration:** the degree of concentration of flavour, and how you judge it, is to some extent relative; necessarily dependent on the type of wine you are tasting, but a lack of flavour might be described as: **empty, weak, dilute; stretched;** then to convey increasing concentration: **lightly, moderately, fairly concentrated; concentrated, dense, strong, extracty.**

ii **Specific tastes:** these are, inevitably, closely bound up with smell. Every conceivable fruit can and has been called to service, along with all available vegetables, herbs, spices, mineral impressions, and as many everyday flavours as your dining table, kitchen, larder, indeed household, can offer.

Perhaps in an attempt to be complete – or to avoid looking at other aspects – such listings* often owe as much to imagination as to reality. And whilst it is useful to try to identify the predominant tastes, naming these in isolation reveals very little about what our experience of a wine is like. There are no flavour vocabulary boxes because the possibilities are infinite!

ABOVE *Until you establish reference points in the night sky, you simply drown in wonder. Wine is similar, but its reference points are easy to get to know.*

*See also

CO_2 **9,11**
excess astringency **44-6,50**
'listing' flavours **25**
maceration **44-6**
new oak **48**

words and qualities

Imagine relishing a delicious meal with a friend, seeing a remarkable match point at the end of a tense tennis duel, being overwhelmed by the music at a concert: and having no reaction, making no comment. Inconceivable, don't you think?

It is human nature to want to share enjoyment, applaud achievement, or record disappointment at poor performance. And once you get beyond grunts of satisfaction or shouts of excitement you have to use words to communicate passion. This applies equally to wine as to any other activity that generates pleasure. We have seen how words can help 'reveal' individual sensations – literally 'drawing back the veil' from them – and of course we also need language if we want to convey the physical realities of what we experience. This matters as much for winemakers discussing wine production as it does for consumers appreciating their efforts.

RIGHT *Jean-Marie and Mainke Guffens-Heynen; an extraordinary husband and wife team. She looks after the vineyards and he does the winemaking. They make Mâcon and Pouilly-Fuissé of exceptional purity and character. Again technical ability is just the servant to a quality ideal which lies in their palates – taste is the constant and final arbiter.*

Wine language

Simple wines need few words. If they are good, the pleasure they give is real enough, but what they contain that merits description is very limited. At the other extreme, the finest wines are so full of nuance that they challenge our ability to perceive and describe in much the same way as fine art and music.

How is this possible? After all, wine is just a drink is it not? Drink, yes. Just a drink, no. Beyond its beverage function, three factors account for our fascination with it: one, wine is demonstrably a complex mixture with multiple, often individually discernible, sensations, and a seemingly infinite number of possibilities of combination; two, our nose and mouth can perceive an extraordinary range of tastes and textures; and three, the transparent, liquid nature of wine allows the palate and olfactory system to scrutinise it easily over a period of time, enabling us to perceive, separate and consider its individual elements. These prerequisites don't occur to the same degree in anything else that we eat or drink.

Is there, then, a language of wine? Yes. Albeit a 'specialist' one (like that of art, music, sport) in that it combines words rarely used outside its own area: **Chardonnay**, **tannin**, **volatile**, **alcoholic**; along with some that we use unambiguously every day: **sweet**, **bitter**, **acidic**; and many that we understand easily in other contexts: **crisp**, **cloying**, **elegant**, **creamy**, **dumb**, **fine**, and so on. The initial problem in winetasting is knowing which words to attach to which characteristic, to which sensation.

The associations are not instinctive, but if we want to learn them we do so in the company of someone who knows, and the relevant vocabulary quickly becomes a reflex. For the most part we simply reassign one of the well-known meanings of a word to another area, in this case wine, and if we choose with care, the word soon makes sense in its new context. We do this with language all the time.

Consider a few meanings of the word **flat**, depending on context: accommodation, lack of business, a musical note below pitch, a deflated car tyre, a horizontal perspective without relief; or a sparkling wine that has lost its fizz!

Context is important; in this respect wine is no different from any other use of language, and the vocabulary boxes in this book list groups of generally accepted words, across a spectrum for particular features and contexts. **Ambiguous, inaccurate, nonsensical, excessive:** some of the criticisms regularly aimed at the language of wine are that it is full of ambiguity, a tower of Babel, or wildly exaggerated. Where these are justified, and they often are, I think it reflects more a lack of will to use words with care than that words cannot be used meaningfully to describe wine.

True, wine language is imprecise, but no more so than that of music or art – both subjects dealing with taste and perception – and the context usually avoids ambiguity. Beyond the vocabulary of basic tastes, words for sensations are very much a question of imagination, and they are, necessarily, impressionistic; but this does not mean they have to be either nonsensical, or extravagant.

You need only read thoughtful wordsmiths such as Hugh Johnson, Gerald Asher or Andrew Jefford to see that wine can be described in a manner that is clear, evocative, illuminating, and without excess. But this is not achieved without effort! **Appropriate words and meaningful relations:** some wine language communicates very little and is rightly mocked. When basic wines are subjected to inflated writing, they simply cannot stand the burden of all the verbiage. The meaningless gulf between the torrent of adjectives that bears little relation to the wine in question, and the reality of a plain, if pleasant beverage is then rightly held up to ridicule; it isn't appropriate.

Just as lacking in enlightenment are the long lists of fruits and vegetables detected in a wine, along, it seems, with anything that has ever been tasted or smelled, with no indication as to how they interrelate. If they do give *some* idea of the wine, the overall result is more akin to enumerating all the colours you can identify in a painting, or all the instruments that are used in a musical composition, without saying anything about the way they are used or how they blend. In other words, you might just as well be reading descriptions of individual pieces of a jigsaw, for you remain completely ignorant of the actual picture, or the piece of music.

What matters is how the constituent elements *relate* to each other, not just the elements by themselves. It does require a bit of active thought though.

Making tasting notes

In the section Taste and Tasting pp16–23 we looked at identifying individual elements of taste, because it is easier to start by looking at

ABOVE *Quality starts in the vineyard. Mainke's pruning is short so yields are low, and the violets reflect a healthy soil. No chemicals are used, only cow dung for manure. Organic viticulture is increasing, and is laudable practice. But regulations vary by country. And though it provides better fruit, alone it doesn't guarantee a better wine – a good winemaker is essential too. When the two go hand in hand, however, you are likely to get wines which taste purer and more characterful.*

one thing at a time. Describing how they fit together, what sort of a whole they make, is more demanding because you have to consider several aspects at once, and you will begin to make value judgements, or ask questions if things are not what you expect. Here is a simple example of how you can practise shaping your impressions.

After looking at its appearance and smell, let's say you have tasted a New Zealand Marlborough Sauvignon Blanc*, and you have noted the following dimensions 'individually', during your first taste*:

Alcohol*: medium-full

Acidity*: crisp

Flavour: abundant

You could write these more fluently thus: **'A medium-full wine with a crisp acidity and abundant flavour.'** This gives a clear impression of the wine's 'size' and style, without, yet, mentioning the type of flavour or its quality.

If you had qualified crisp with 'typically', you would be going a stage further, indicating your appreciation that this is the norm for Marlborough Sauvignon Blanc. If, on the other hand, you had initially noted the acidity as 'soft', this would call for some comment, because it would be unusual for this type of wine – you might ask the question in brackets: (hot year or harvest?) or if you knew that was the case, as in 1998, for example, you could simply mention the fact.

Your second taste might note:

Sweet/dry*: dry

Flavours: mouthfilling aromas of ripe gooseberry and tropical fruit ·

Aftertaste: long, very aromatic (gooseberries), plenty of fruit persistence too – lychees.

Which you could polish to:

'Dry to taste, with mouthfilling aromas of ripe gooseberries and tropical fruit, followed by a long finish, full of fruit persistence and lingering, lychee, Sauvignon scents.'

You now have a complete, well-observed 'palate' note, without any explicit 'evaluation', but with plenty of 'information' which will have helped imprint the wine on your memory, and which will recall it accurately if you refer to the note subsequently, both important reasons for making careful notes. Full note: **'A medium-full wine with a crisp acidity and abundant flavour; dry to taste, with mouth-filling aromas of ripe gooseberries and tropical fruit, followed by a long finish, full of lychee-like persistence and lingering Sauvignon scents.'**

Practising this sort of exercise at home with plenty of time and a variety of wines will quickly reward your efforts. Clarity of thought will produce clear notation, and as you establish a rhythm of perception and build up your vocabulary, fluent, informative notes* like this will come increasingly easily as you taste.

Quality: length

We have already looked at the basic structural elements of a wine, its framework of alcohol, acidity, tannin, and concentration of flavour. We considered them first because they are the easiest attributes to identify and record by tasting, as indeed they are to measure scientifically. But wines of similar dimensions can of course differ enormously in character of flavour and in quality.

Quality is subjective if only because it involves, along with personal preference, a host of abstract concepts, difficult to measure, and therefore easy to disagree over. These are discussed in the next section: Values. But there is one quality feature in wine which is sufficiently concrete to be easily measurable by our senses, if not by scientific instruments. And because it can be applied, relatively objectively, to all wines, it comes close to being a universal measure of excellence. This is length. There are always two crucial lengths to examine when tasting: palate and finish.

Palate length in the mouth: you sense this in two ways, physical and temporal.

Physical length: with a 'long' wine, having swallowed a little, you can feel the presence and tastes of the wine extending and remaining beyond the back of your tongue and down into your throat, a literal perception of physical 'reach' (*see* illustration 1, opposite). The flavours

---

Palate length

Empty, hollow, short; moderate-, long-middle-palate, long across the palate, sustained, prolonged, tenacious.

Finish, aftertaste

Length: brief, short; moderate, medium; long, lingering, persistent, endless.
Principal characteristics: fruity, core flavour of…, aromatic, scented, light, strong, resonant, powerful.
Excess: possible defect: acid, acidic; astringency dominant; alcohol burn, alcohol bitterness.

1 Physical length: a long wine

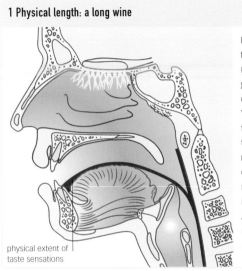

physical extent of
taste sensations

In addition to temporal length (*see* text), long wines give a clear sensation of physical length. You sense their flavours all along the length of your mouth, at the rear of your tongue, and reaching way back into your throat. An almost literal measure of linear span.

2 Physical length: a short wine

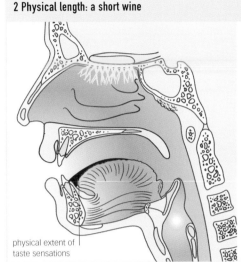

physical extent of
taste sensations

Short wines are not only brief in terms of the length of time their flavours last. A short, 'hollow' wine will seem barely to cross your tongue before its sensations fade. A better wine will actually reach the back of your mouth before its tastes die (*see* tasting 1 p124).

of 'short' wines seem barely to cross your tongue before they die (*see* illustration 2, above).

Temporal length: the second way you perceive palate length is chronological so to speak, and is one of the most important means of judging quality. Here you consider the length of time over which the wine continues to hold your attention as you explore it in your mouth, for how long it carries on stimulating your taste-buds, teasing your palate.

You will find the finest wines seem to have an inner energy and range of sensations which keep you savouring so that you finish the liquid in your mouth before you have exhausted its possibilities. This is often referred to as the middle-palate, or length across the palate. As an absolutely key feature of quality, this is a measure well worth mastering.

How long to keep wine in your mouth: palate length has an important implication for how long you keep the wine in your mouth when tasting. It is pointless, indeed self-defeating from a quality assessment point of view, to try to taste each of the wines you are comparing for the same length of time.

Wines that are brief, even if enjoyable, warrant only brief exploration, long wines are almost endless in what they have to offer. The quality of the wine, as your palate perceives it, will dictate how long you want or need to explore it.

Taste two wines of a similar type, but of clearly different quality levels, going to and fro and comparing how long you want to 'savour' each one, how long it speaks to you.... You will quickly see the difference and grasp the principle (*see* p146).

Length of finish, length of aftertaste: finish and aftertaste refer to the same thing – the tastes and aromas which persist after you have finished tasting the wine (having swallowed it or spat it out, that is), and for how long these last: the longer the better.

The taste of a short wine will disappear almost as soon as you have swallowed it. A premium wine will last at the back of your mouth primarily as a continuation of its fruit tastes. The finish of really fine wines combines sensations of the wine's core flavours reaching back into your throat, with lingering aromas which seem to perfume not only your palate, but your psyche as well – a resonance of all the preceding tastes and scents. Naturally, length in the mouth and length of finish tend to go hand in hand.

Length as a defect: quality length assumes that the wine is otherwise well balanced, and attractive to taste. But any of the three strongest constituents of wine – acid, tannin, alcohol – can be present in excess, and where this is so they may give rise to a false impression of quality simply because their taste sensations

ABOVE *Experts can't seem to agree on taste-bud location. But if there is a question over their precise extent, there is no question about the physical reality of the taste sensations which reach way back into your throat in the finest wines. And no question that you need to get a little wine there to sense this length.*

can be very 'long'. Where one of these becomes the primary character on the finish, to the exclusion of the wine's fruit and aromas, then, whatever its 'length', it is unbalanced, poor rather than good quality. It is an important distinction to make.

Acid length: sufficient acidity supports and defines a wine's length, indeed a lack of acidity often leads to a limp finish. However, acid as the principal impression is no more pleasant than the 'length' of pure lemon juice or vinegar. The most common causes are unripe grapes, excessive yields or over-enthusiastic acidification during winemaking.

Tannic length: the presence of tannin is an essential ingredient of quality red wine. But where a strong astringency dominates the finish of the wine, masking rather than enriching its flavours and aromas, then the prolonged tannic grip reflects poor winemaking; usually excessive extraction or over-oaking. When the tannin is of good quality, and in balanced proportions, it also remains present, but allows the wine's scent and savour free passage as well.

Alcohol burn and bitterness: a wine's alcohol, at whatever level, is unobtrusive so long as it is balanced by the other flavour components. Where this is not the case, it gives rise to a lingering bitterness on the finish, often accompanied by a marked warmth or burn, neither of which is pleasant and both of which are tiring aspects when drinking. As a flaw, excess alcohol tends to be more noticeable in dry whites than in red wines, and in both at alcohol levels above 13%, where there is

inadequate flavour. High yields in hot climates (high sugar and low flavour in the grapes) or excessive chaptalisation (*see* pp44–5,49) in cooler climes are regular culprits.

Quality: texture/mouthfeel

Touch is a significant source of pleasure, whether it be giving or receiving a caress, running fine silk through our fingers, sinking our teeth into a crisp apple. And one of the aspects of wine that we value most is its tactile quality, for it is remarkable how sensitive our mouths are to the 'consistency' of wines in general, and to the 'feel' of red wines in particular.

Tactile impressions often involve a visual element: rough surfaces are granular in appearance as well as feel, glossy ones are smooth. Although we cannot 'see' the surface of a wine as we taste it, its feel will often conjure up visual analogies alongside the tactile ones.

'Mouthfeel' is a new combination word which is accurate but which I simply dislike, preferring the more descriptive 'texture'.

'Texture' has its origins in the Latin words for fabric and weaving, and quality textures in wine have long been evoked by comparisons with expensive, high-quality fabrics; those that we have valued down the centuries for their combination of tactile and visual appeal: lace, taffeta, satin, silk, velvet. Ordinary fabrics have little to offer by way of analogy, but the visual difference between types of fabric 'weave', close-knit in contrast to loose-knit, for example, can be a helpful reference for making texture distinctions between wines.

Texture/mouthfeel

Smooth, pliant, supple, soft, mellow, fleshy, yielding, rich, opulent, unctuous, muscular, chewy, hard.
Textured, close-knit, close-woven, highly wrought, filmy, lacy, satiny, velvety, glossy, polished.
Thin, stringy, lean, loose, taut, sinewy, granular, grainy, rough, coarse.
See also Oak pp47–8 and Astringency p22.

RIGHT *Tactile impressions often involve a visual element, and textures in wine have long been evoked by language related to fabrics. 'Matt' or 'loose-knit' (left) in contrast to the 'fine-spun', 'glossy' sheen and 'silky' feel of the satin and silk on the right.*

values

Read, listen to opinions, but above all taste. Taste, compare, identify what you like and what you don't like and, if possible, try to say why. Ignore fashions if you don't agree with them, for the conviction needs to come from inside you, otherwise it will never make sense.

Not all criteria apply to all wines, and they need to be applied appropriately. It is important to remember that good quality exists at all levels. It is not a monopoly of expensive wines; but simple wines have modest ambitions and we should judge them by relatively modest standards. Where wines are expensive and make claims to higher quality, though, we are rightly more demanding as consumers. Equally, wine is not just a continuum ranging from the very ordinary to exceptional examples of a single product.

At anything beyond the most basic beverage, wine is made in a very wide range of different styles, with different purposes in mind, and often with considerable effort involved in achieving those aims. It would be ridiculous not to take these intentions into account when judging. Make up your own mind and be prepared to support your opinions with reference to some of the categories outlined here.

Value for money

This is an important practical consideration, if not an easy one to decide. Line up any number of different bottles of the same type of wine at the same price, and after comparing them it is not difficult to say which is 'the best value for amount x'. The comparison is simple and relatively precise because it has few variables. At a given price, for a product we know and purchase regularly, we make implicit comparisons like this all the time.

Trickier to resolve are more general questions of value for money, especially for more expensive wines. Today, above a notional £15/$25 or so, there seems to be an increasingly erratic price/quality correlation, indeed scarcity and fashion rather than quality often appear to be the guides. So much so, that many wines are now sold at prices which seem, to me, to be out of all proportion to the pleasure they give.

BELOW *Value for money? It depends on your disposable income and, especially, on what gives you pleasure. Here are three expensive tickets for different leisure activities – luxuries like expensive wine. £55/$80 may seem money well spent on a cup final ticket to the football fan, whereas to the opera buff it may appear incomprehensible, and vice versa. To the person who has no interest whatsoever in any of these, all three might be regarded as criminal extravagance! What you pay for what you fancy has always defied logic.*

Hierarchies of wines

It is human nature to want to impose some sort of order on the chaos of experience. The world of wine is full of attempts to grade its quality fog via an assortment of more or less useful hierarchies.

The most famous of these is Bordeaux's 1855 classification of the wines of the Médoc (*see* below). Burgundy's Côte d'Or vineyards were graded into three quality levels in the 1860s: Village, Premier Cru and Grand Cru, a ranking which was largely incorporated into the official appellation system in the 1930s. These provide a rough quality calibration* across a notional spectrum, where the borders are inevitably blurred, and to some extent arbitrary.

1855 Classification: The wines of the Médoc

Premiers Crus		Château Ferrière	Margaux
Château Lafite	Pauillac	Château Marq. d'Alesme Becker	Margaux
Château Latour	Pauillac	Château Boyd-Cantenac	Cantenac
Château Margaux	Margaux	Quatrièmes Crus	
Château Haut-Brion,Graves	Pessac	Château St.Pierre-Sevaistre	St.Julien
Château Mouton-Rothschild	Pauillac	Château St.Pierre-Bontemps	St.Julien
Deuxièmes Crus (1973)		Château Branaire-Ducru	St.Julien
Château Rausan-Ségla	Margaux	Château Talbot	St.Julien
Château Rauzan-Gassies	Margaux	Château Duhart-Milon	Pauillac
Château Léoville-Las-Cases	St.Julien	Château Pouget	Cantenac
Château Léoville-Poyferré	St.Julien	Château La Tour-Carnet	St.Laurent
Château Léoville-Barton	St.Julien	Château Lafon Rochet	St.Estèphe
Château Durfort-Vivens	Margaux	Château Beychevelle	St.Julien
Château Lascombes	Margaux	Château Le Prieuré-Lichine	Cantenac
Château Gruaud-Larose	St.Julien	Château Marquis-de-Terme	Margaux
Château Brane-Cantenac	Cantenac	Cinquièmes Crus	
Château Pichon-Longueville-Baron	Pauillac	Château Pontet-Canet	Pauillac
Château Pichon-Longueville-Lalande	Pauillac	Château Batailley	Pauillac
Château Ducru-Beaucaillou	St.Julien	Château Grand-Puy-Lacoste	Pauillac
Château Cos-d'Estournel	St.Estèphe	Château Grand-Puy-Ducasse	Pauillac
Château Montrose	St.Estèphe	Château Lynch-Bages	Pauillac
Troisièmes Crus		Château Lynch-Moussas	Pauillac
Château Kirwan	Cantenac	Château Dauzac	Labarde
Château d'Issan	Cantenac	Château Mouton-Baron Philippe	Pauillac
Château Lagrange	St.Julien	Château du Tertre	Arsac
Château Langoa-Barton	St.Julien	Château Haut-Bages-Liberal	Pauillac
Château Giscours	Labarde	Château Pédesclaux	Pauillac
Château Malescot-St-Exupéry	Margaux	Château Belgrave	St.Laurent
Château Cantenac-Brown	Cantenac	Château Camensac	St.Laurent
Château Palmer	Cantenac	Château Cos-Labory	St.Estèphe
Château La Lagune	Ludon	Château Clerc-Milon-Mondon	Pauillac
Château Desmirail	Margaux	Château Croizet-Bages	Pauillac
Château Calon-Ségur	St.Estèphe	Château Cantemerle	Macau
		Château Haut-Batailley	Pauillac

This famous hierarchy reflected prices achieved over many years, long before the advent of multi-media influence. It has stood the test of time surprisingly well. Such a league table would be impossible today, given the instantaneous influences, on both winemaker and consumer, of competitive tastings, fashion, rarity, wine scores and guru pronouncements.

That said, tasting and comparing good examples of the different levels shows that they can provide useful, albeit imprecise, benchmarks which reflect clearly perceptible quality distinctions on the palate.

The pleasure principle

I like it: an empty bottle, especially one that has emptied faster than you can credit; this has to be one of the best measures, and one of the most important values. After all, enjoyment is the point and the pleasure principle has to be the first, and possibly the final, arbiter. But we don't all like the same wines, and as soon as we begin to discuss any disagreement, and to go beyond a simple matter of personal opinion, all sorts of other value questions arise.

'I like it' is not the same as 'it's good': where wine is concerned, it is fashionable to say that you are always 'right' about what you like. And it clearly doesn't make sense for anyone else to tell you that you are 'wrong' about your own reactions, or that you don't really feel what you say you do. But on its own that doesn't get us very far in assessing a wine.

It says more about you than about the wine; and it certainly doesn't tell us that the wine is good or bad. Here is a teasing illustration. It must be the case (because there are so many bottles of it) that many people enjoy wine that is corked – technically faulty to a greater or lesser degree (*see* p151) – because they simply don't recognise that there is anything 'wrong' with it. Are they wrong to like it? Presumably not. Is it 'good' wine? They might say it's good because they enjoy it, a professional would have to say it was defective, bad wine.

Personal taste is one thing, standards of quality which refer to more or less accepted criteria, another. Both matter, and it matters to be clear about the difference. The values by which we judge wine are a complex amalgam of subjective taste and more objective standards. The categories and criteria I outline here are not a series of prescriptions, but suggestions as to how you might think about wine, a means to interpreting and assessing what you taste.

Personal taste: not everybody likes the same things. Intelligent comment can happily combine tolerance of other people's likes and dislikes with argument for a different point of view. Nor are we born with a sense of good taste, but we can cultivate it if we are interested.

We learn about different styles, standards and measures, we develop preferences as we taste widely, and we change and extend them as our interest and exploration progress. But however convinced we are of our good taste, we also need to remain aware that we tend to forgive or overlook flaws in wines we love or with which we are familiar (providing they are not too gross), and to exaggerate those in wines we are predisposed to dislike, where the minutest point of distaste simply serves to confirm a prejudice. We are only human after all!

Balance

Balance describes the way in which the principal constituents of a wine – alcohol, acid, tannin and flavour – relate to each other, and ensuring that there is neither excess nor deficit of each or any of these is obviously a prime measure of quality. But there is no such thing as one perfect set of proportions.

There are numerous different ideals* which relate above all to individual grape varieties and to the geographical origins of the wine. Ripe grapes contain differing levels of sugar, acid and tannin according to the grape variety and the limitations on ripening of the climate in which they are grown. Wines from cooler climates will tend to have more acidity and less alcohol than those from warmer areas, where the reverse will be the case.

The balance in a given wine will reflect that of its grapes when picked*; and what is appropriate and 'well-balanced' in one region or grape variety will not be so in another – and you need to judge them accordingly. To do so you have to become acquainted with the various styles, to develop a sense of what is 'typical' for different combinations of grape and origin. The next two sections, In the Bottle and In the Glass, will help you here.

Typicality or 'typicity'

Wine is not just 'wine'. The essence of its appeal lies in its huge diversity and, as I just mentioned, the bulk of this diversity derives from different grape varieties and different geographical origins.

Where wines have been made in a certain area for a considerable time, empirically successful combinations of grape varieties and local conditions will have given rise to certain styles and conventions over the years. This is usually a perfecting of what experiment and experience have shown that they combine to do both naturally and well.

This style, with its attendant flavours and proportions, eventually becomes an established archetype, the wine becomes a 'typical' expression of the grape in the locality and begins to be made deliberately to these criteria. And it also starts to be assessed according to how well it achieves these ideals.

Drinkers come to appreciate the unique features of such wines, to value them both in their own right and as qualities which distinguish 'this' from 'other' wines. They then look for, indeed expect, these when purchasing the wine, and measure it according to the extent to which it meets the established norms, also taking pleasure in recognising anticipated characteristics and in subtle variations on the theme. Many of the world's most delicious and distinctive wines are deliberately made to traditions* that have arisen like this. And whether you like them or

LEFT *The fine wine market is a strange place! Le Pin is a tiny Pomerol property making a very fine, succulently flavoured and seductively textured Merlot based wine; a style which also happens to be particularly fashionable at the moment. Recently, once on the open market, it has been fetching prices way above what the château owners themselves sell it for, and which would seem quite ludicrous to most rational people. It poses the interesting, and complex, question of to what extent a free market price today is an accurate reflection of quality? (The 1855 hierarchy was based on long term free market prices.) Le Pin only makes 500 to 600 cases of wine a year. What if it were to make 5,000 or 6,000 cases of the same wine? Or 20,000, like some of the Médoc First Growths? It clearly couldn't sustain the same price. But would that mean it was any less good than it is now? Or that it is any better for fetching silly auction prices?*

*See also

not personally, it is perverse not to judge them, at least partly, on their own terms, for what they set out to be, on their 'typicality'. After all, we don't blame a pear for not being a peach, just because we prefer peaches.

Expectation and performance

Expectation plays an enormous part in our appreciation of what we taste. Whatever we buy, be it food, clothing, pencil sharpeners or motor cars, we don't do it at random, but with specific functions in mind. The extent to which the purchase then fulfils or falls short of our expectations will understandably colour our judgement of it.

In the case of wine, our expectations are set up by a number of things: brand, price, grape variety, origin, style, type, reputation and so on; and when we open a bottle, we are set up, so to speak, for a certain type of experience. If the bottle then doesn't perform, we have every right to feel dissatisfied.

If the wine was inexpensive, we may not worry too much because our hopes would not have been high. But the more expensive and illustrious the wine, the more demanding we are entitled to be, the more important it is that it lives up to expectations, and the greater our disillusion if it doesn't. These are essentially functional criteria, *ie* does this wine do the job it was designed to do? Does it work well for its type? How good is it for what it says it is?

Aesthetic ideals

Many of the attributes that we use to describe our impressions and appreciation of proportion, form, beauty and performance in other spheres of life may also apply to our appreciation of wine. If the words* to describe them fit, and are used thoughtfully, there is no need for them to seem absurd. How desirable any of these criteria are depends, of course, on the wine in question. Here are a few that can be useful in relation to wine.

Complexity: suggests a multiplicity of individually perceptible flavours and scents. This is the audiophile's 'information rich'. Given the choice, we tend to prefer this to simplicity, especially in more expensive wines.

Clarity: we value clear impressions in contrast to blurred ones. Useful analogies are with focus and definition in photography for example, or with separation in good Hi-Fi speakers, where the better they are, the more clearly you can discern the individual strands of the music.

Effortlessness: the best wines, at whatever level, be they simple and inexpensive, or profound and costly; and in whatever style, be they delicate or forceful, taste good from the word go. They immediately impress with their natural harmony, and they have an overall feeling of 'rightness', of performance achieved with absolute ease, with an apparent absence of effort, like that of a great athlete or musician. This is preferable to the opposite impressions of stress, effort, distortion*, rigidity, overworking.

Concentration, power: particularly fashionable virtues at the beginning of the 3rd millennium. We all enjoy our senses being overwhelmed by dramatic, assertive characteristics, particularly when starting to explore wine. But this is easily overdone, and we don't want it all the time.

Finesse, delicacy, subtlety: often undervalued, in contrast to the above, and frequently mistaken for dilution or weakness, which are not the same thing at all. As virtues they are less immediate to the senses, but nevertheless pleasurable. And if they require a bit of getting to know, they will usually more than repay your time and effort. As our tastes evolve, many of us find some of our most intense experiences come from pleasures that are delicate, be they a caress, a perfume, music or wine.

Fruit versus aroma: a wealth of ripe fruit is easily perceived, just as it is in black cherry jam, and most of us relish its presence in wine, red wines especially. Some wines stress aroma and scent, rather than an abundance of fruit, and their virtues will be revealed as you aerate them in the mouth, and on the aftertaste. They are neither better nor worse, just different. Many of the best wines are generous with both. And don't we just love those!

Context: can make a huge difference to our experience of a wine. Take a bottle of heady Tavel rosé. Sampled in the clinical context of the taster's bench it may seem bland and alcoholic. But let's put it in its proper place: alfresco, on a baking-hot, azure-skied summer's day; a table heaped with Provençal fare: black olives, ratatouille, ripe tomatoes in olive oil and basil; tuna, sardines, salads, abundant herbs and crisp baguettes. Chilled, in good company, there will seem to be no better wine in the world. A fig for objectivity and scores *then*!

*See also

competitive **155**

distortion **50**

words which fit **24-5**

In the vineyard

The principle is simple enough: fully ripe, quality grapes plus intelligent winemaking equal good wine. Of course it's more complicated than that, but as a basic equation this is a useful generalisation.

ABOVE AND BELOW
Deinhard in Germany and Sileni in New Zealand; 350 years apart. Considering the time span, surprisingly little has changed in vineyard work. But science means we can better explain practices that were only understood empirically before.

It is impossible to make good wine without good ingredients in the first place. And then, however good your ingredients and your equipment, without common sense and a good palate* as guides, it is easy to make a mess of the winemaking recipe. The parallels with cookery, and gardening, are numerous. The grape variety and the climate in which it is grown are the two seminal influences on the final style and quality potential of the wine.

Grape variety

The choice of grape variety will depend on what type of wine you have in mind and, more importantly, how it will flourish in the vineyard at your disposal. Of the two, the latter is the more important initial consideration because if your grapes won't ripen in the first place, you can forget about the niceties of style. Different varieties, like any plant, have different requirements and some are choosier than others.

Climate

Where your vineyard is situated matters more than the specific site or the type of soil, for this will govern the three crucial variables of temperature, water and light. All three are essential, in moderation.

Sunshine is the primary requisite for the photosynthesis which produces the grape's sugar. It works most efficiently, as does the general ripening of the grape, when the temperature is warm but not excessive, somewhere between 15 and 30°C (60–85°F).

The vine can no more survive without water than you or I, and inadequate water inhibits photosynthesis and the whole ripening process. Too much water, on the other hand, tends to produce oversized grapes and/or excess vegetation, both of which result in unripe or dilute flavours.

Site

A wide range of vineyard sites produce good wine all round the world. Pronounced gradients or the direction in which the vineyard faces (aspect) are of special significance only where they are needed to moderate extremes of weather

and climate. Slopes make for good drainage after heavy rainfall and provide a slipway to lower ground for frosty air. A slope, along with a sun-grabbing aspect, concentrates the limited sunshine in marginal climates, whereas in hot climates, high altitude and/or a slope facing away from the sun can temper the heat.

Soil

Even if our palates appear to taste mineral or earthy impressions* in many wines (and they do), there is no scientifically proven correlation between particular soils and specific tastes.

What science has shown is that the most important role of soil is in ensuring a constant, but not excessive, supply of water to the vine, as well as adequate air circulation for the root system. Both of these depend much more on soil structure than on its chemical constituents.

Ideal soils for wine are also low in fertility, so that the vine doesn't grow too vigorously*. Where specific soil types* seem important, they are discussed in connection with the relevant grape varieties.

Viticulture

Good winemakers will know their grapes and vineyard intimately. They will literally have their footprint in the soil. And they will tell you, as will any gardener, that every year is different in the vineyard. If there are general principles, there are no precise formulas. The goal, though, is always the same: ripe, healthy grapes at harvest time. In addition to keeping

the vine and its fruit disease-free, the main challenge is in 'managing' the leaf canopy, ensuring a balanced vine that will ripen the fruit as required.

A balanced vine

This refers to an ideal area of leaves exposed to the sun to provide sufficient sugar for the weight of fruit on the vine. In poor, low-fertility soils – those with an abundance of stone, gravel, rock, slate – the vine's natural vigour is controlled so that not too much effort need be expended on its training or management, and its leaf to fruit balance is relatively easily achieved.

This is the case with most European vineyards. But given half a chance, in so-called 'vigorous', fertile soils (much of the New World), the vine will put all its energy into producing abundant greenery. This results in too much shade within the canopy. Many leaves then don't photosynthesise efficiently. The new shoot tips, especially, compete for the vine's sugars, and the grapes don't ripen properly, leading to thin, green, herbaceous and peppery characteristics in the wine.

Trimming the vegetation often simply encourages it, so the solution lies in numerous different forms of training the vine to achieve the right balance. Too much fruit (from insufficient spring pruning) can have the same unripe consequences: there simply isn't enough sugar to go round! (*See* photographs and captions p38–9.)

ABOVE *Morning fog above the Sonoma and Napa valleys in California; created by the cold Pacific Ocean, and drawn through the coastal valleys by the rising heat of inland Californa. These fogs help cool the valley floor vineyards during the hot Californian summer, making for better balanced grapes. Vineyards the world over have local climatic features which make their grapes and wines what they are, subtly different from others.*

the grape

When is a grape ripe? From a biological or physiological point of view, it might be considered ripe when its pips can reproduce the plant, or when its sugar content is at a maximum. The winemaker's viewpoint, however, is not quite the same.

Ripeness

BOTTOM FAR RIGHT A winemaker with his footprint in the vineyard, who knows his soil and fruit intimately, will make better harvest decisions and better wine. Like Hubert Laferrère here, starting a new vineyard from scratch in the Mâconnais, France.

BELOW Spring pruning aims to keep the vine healthy and to limit the number of grape bunches, avoiding excess yield.

From a winemaking point of view, ripeness (*ie* when you want to pick) is when sugar, acid, skin colour, flavour and tannin are all at the ideal level for the type of wine you want to make. This is difficult to define in theory, even more so in practice.

Theoretically the 'ideal' occurs when these important parameters all coincide at their optimum level. But if sugar and acid levels are relatively easy to measure scientifically, flavour and tannin ripeness are not; indeed, sampling the grape is probably the best way of deciding whether these are 'ready'. In practice the grape's ripening pattern differs according to the climate, location, annual weather pattern, and even varies within bunches of the same grape.

More mundane realities may also be at least as pressing in deciding when to pick: Are the heavens threatening to open? Have you got all the pickers you need? Or if you own part share in an expensive mechanical harvester, is it your week to use it? The timing will be a compromise, more often than not.

Yield

Yield expresses the volume of wine which results from a given weight of grapes, or from the grapes harvested on a given area of land. This depends on numerous factors such as grape variety, pruning, vine age, weather conditions, irrigation, and economics.

The oversimplified wisdom is that the lower the yield, the better the quality of the wine. And as yields can be 'managed' to a large extent, especially by pruning methods and irrigation, how much wine to make is usually a calculated compromise between demands of the bottom line (more wine, blander taste, greater income) and quality considerations (less wine, more intense flavours, but fewer bottles).

The correlation between quantity and quality is a definite but by no means a direct one. White wines are less affected than reds because the grape's skin is not used during vinification, whereas the proportion of skin to juice clearly matters in red winemaking.

Very high yields retard ripening and certainly dilute flavours in all grapes, but very low yields, especially for red wines, probably end up offering diminishing quality returns.

Sugar

Sugar, in the form of glucose and fructose in roughly equal proportions, accumulates continually as the grape ripens. Its rate of increase is accelerated above all by high temperatures, and retarded by a heavy crop of fruit, excess vegetation competing for sugar, poor photosynthesis as a consequence of cloud cover, and either very low or excessively high temperatures. As the principal source of alcohol, or of sweetness in sweet wines, it is the most important measure of ripeness, but certainly not the only one. Sugar ripeness is not necessarily overall ripeness. Take two extreme, but not unusual, examples:

Hot New World climate, red grapes:
the grapes can be sugar ripe, already past the optimum acid level, yet with their ideal flavour and tannin ripeness still lagging behind. Waiting for the tannins to mature (a longer 'hang time') will improve the flavour, but entail the disadvantages of yet lower acid, which can be corrected later, and higher alcohol, which cannot. Result: potent, flavoursome wine after some acid bolstering.

Cool New World climate, white grapes:
with plenty of sunshine, white grapes can be sugar ripe and flavour ripe, but still with too much acidity (cool temperatures, cold nights). Waiting for the acidity to fall will also mean allowing the sugar to go on rising. Result: wine with both high alcohol and, still, a relatively high acidity (even after malolactic fermentation), both hot *and* hard on the mouth.

These ripening problems can be evened out to a large extent by experimentation with grape varieties, training methods and canopy management, but you only get one attempt a year so the solutions don't appear overnight. In much of northern Europe, insufficient sugar (often as a result of greedy yields and therefore barely ripe grapes at harvest time) can be corrected by chaptalisation (*see* pp44–5).

One of the advantages of these variations is, of course, the diversity of styles on offer, but good balance remains good balance whatever the style. As a consequence of perceived critical and public taste (and possibly global warming?) there has been a definite tendency in the recent past to aim for later picking, so as to get riper fruit, and, willy-nilly, higher alcohol. This has been facilitated by vineyards that are healthier on the whole, and by many of the new vine clones which ripen rapidly and early. But whilst some wines wear their high alcohol well, I feel that a greater proportion are uncomfortable with it.

For most table wines, a well-balanced 12.5–13% alcohol is an easier drink (if not a more impressive taste) than 13.5–14%. Indeed one of the major challenges for hot-climate viticulture now appears to be how to get grape *flavours* ripe at somewhat lower sugar levels (*see* also cultured yeast caption p49).

ABOVE *Drip irrigation on the vineyards of Cloudy Bay in New Zealand. Vines need regular water to keep them alive and healthy (just as we do) where there is not enough rainfall. Quality vineyards avoid excess watering as it dilutes flavour.*

ABOVE AND BELOW
Differently trained, adjacent Cabernet Sauvignon vines at Dominus in California. The vine above is barely trained, a traditional method known as 'California sprawl'. You can see the excess greenery, and that much of the fruit is 'shaded'. The vine below is trained on a wishbone shaped trellis to allow more sunshine to reach the grape bunches, whilst allowing sufficient leaf area to photosynthesise* adequately. Here, at harvest time, I compared the taste of the grapes from the two methods: the traditional vine's fruit was herbaceous, and with a hard, green tannin; that from the new form was riper, softer, sweeter. An impressive demonstration of the effects of thoughtful vineyard management.

Acid

The grape starts to ripen, properly speaking, at *veraison*, when the small, hard, green berries begin to soften and colour to yellowy-green or blackish red. At this stage it has the least sugar and most acid*.

During the months following *veraison*, one month in the case of the hottest climates, two in the case of the coolest, the grape will ripen fully. And, from a maximum of around 20 grams per litre, tartaric and malic in equal proportions, the total acidity will diminish during ripening by two-thirds or more, depending on the climate. The 'greener' tasting malic acid decreases much more rapidly than tartaric, especially in hot, dry, sunny conditions, as it is this acid which is used in the plant's breathing cycle.

Grapes in hot climates will have very little malic acid left when ripe, often resulting in inadequate acidity and necessitating an addition of acid to the fermenting juice or wine. Conversely, cooler climates may have too much at harvest time, and this can be diminished via the malolactic fermentation.

Another important influence which reduces acidity in the grapes is the potassium level in the juice. Whilst potassium in small amounts is a normal component of grape juice, too much severely reduces acidity, resulting in flabby wines which may require excessive acid adjustment. High levels are caused primarily by the excessive use of soil fertiliser in which potassium is a significant element.

The acid content of the juice poses similar picking date problems as does sugar (*see* previous page), their relative proportions and absolute level both being important measures of ripeness.

Acidity and ageing: in terms of measurement, a wine's fixed acidity remains the same as it ages; but other reactions in the wine over time mean the acid impression may become less to taste.

Tannin

Tannins* are numerous, difficult to isolate and measure, and forever changing in their chemical nature and taste impressions. Most of our knowledge about them and their function in wine is simply based on experience. Scientifically speaking, they remain pretty much a mystery.

Tannins belong to the group of chemical compounds in the grape called polyphenols, which include the anthocyanins responsible

for colour in red wines. They occur mainly in the pips and skins of the grape, and as these are not involved in the making of white wine to any extent, white wines have very little tannin by comparison with red wines, which *are* fermented* in contact with the skins and pips.

As the grape ripens, polyphenols increase in quantity and, as far as tannins are concerned, in quality too. For this reason, makers of quality red wines often want to wait to pick their grapes until they are fully 'phenolically ripe'. As the grape continues to ripen late in the season, the tannins appear to become increasingly soft in texture, more savoury to taste, and easier to extract during winemaking. But this improvement frequently occurs after what might hitherto have been considered the optimum levels of sugar and acidity.

The danger of being enticed too far down this fashionable road is that you end up with a 'jammy' overripe character in the wines, along with noticeably high alcohol and/or a serious acid deficiency* to correct. However seductive the texture!

Measuring tannin: there are enormous differences in the texture of tannin in red wines according to the grape variety, yield, ripeness, geographical origin and winemaking techniques. And trying to measure tannin scientifically, in wine or grapes, doesn't reveal much. For whilst it is possible to measure the *quantity* of tannin, this gives you little indication of its textural *quality* from a tasting point of view. Two wines similar in almost every other respect, and with the same measured amount of tannin, will often have a completely different astringency on the palate. Knowing your grapes and tasting them is usually a more accurate indicator.

Pigmented tannins: refer to the chemical combination of tannins and anthocyanins in wine made from red grapes. These combinations are thought to be less astringent than the non-pigmented tannins from white grapes, which have no anthocyanins. This is the main reason for avoiding excess skin and pip contact during white vinification*.

Tannins and ageing: tannin molecules found in red wines made specifically for ageing grow larger with time, they 'polymerise'. As they grow, their ability to combine with (to 'tan') proteins changes.

Initially this ability becomes stronger, the tannins are more reactive with proteins in our saliva and the wine 'hardens'. As the size of the molecules increases, tannin reactivity begins to diminish; they become less astringent or become too large to remain soluble and precipitate to form sediment, and the wine softens. Eventually, as the fruit retreats, the remaining active tannins are laid bare, so to speak, and the wine becomes more dryly astringent: this is known as 'drying out'.

ABOVE LEFT AND RIGHT *Training (see illustration opposite) and canopy management aim at an ideal balance of leaf to fruit on the vine (the canopy is the canopy of leaves). The main aim is to avoid excess greenery which will compete with the fruit for sugar, and also 'shade' the grapes so that they ripen less well. Above you can clearly see where the leaf (which has been removed in the second picture) has cast its shadow. There the grapes are greener and less ripe. A crude, but clear illustration of the principle.*

*See also

acid deficiency **41,45,50**
acidity **20-1**
fermentation **44-6**
photosynthesis **34**
tannin **22**
white vinification **40-1**

dry white winemaking

When to pick is the most important decision in the winemaking calendar. In addition to the sugar/acid parameters mentioned in the previous pages, the potential aromatic character of your wine will also play a part in harvesting decisions.

RIGHT Ripe, healthy fruit makes good wine. If you start with poor quality ingredients you haven't a hope. These Chardonnay bunches are disease-free, fully and evenly ripe. Perfect!

Whereas for red grapes the tendency is to want to allow them to get super-ripe, most unoaked white wines rely more on their primary aromas for their appeal. Aromas develop and change as the grape ripens, and the freshest often appear earlier rather than later in the maturity cycle. Cooler areas or vintages tend to emphasise the earlier part of the spectrum, hotter ones the latter (*see* margin).

Dry white winemaking sequence

Steps marked with **( )** are optional practices for the winemaker.

1 Crushing/pressing: white wines are fermented without their skins and the destemmed grapes are therefore pressed to obtain the juice before fermentation. 'Crushing' is a misleading term for splitting the grape skins

Aroma progression of a maturing white grape

Two examples of white grape aroma development from early (barely ripe) to late (super-/overripe) maturity:

Sauvignon Blanc:
cat's pee, asparagus, nettle, grass, raw blackcurrant, gooseberry, passion-fruit, tropical fruit (guava, mango, pineapple).

Chardonnay:
green apple, melon, tangerine, citrus, peach, ripe fig, fruit salad, tropical fruit.

RIGHT A bladder press. The rubber bag inflates, pressing the grapes against the sieved sides to express their juice prior to fermentation.

to allow the juice to run more easily when pressed. Any brutality shows up as a coarse astringency in the wine. Chilled bunches can also be pressed 'whole', without destemming, minimising 'phenolics' (*see* margin opposite).

(2) Skin contact: between crushing and pressing, limited contact between skins and juice can draw additional flavour elements from just under the grape skin of aromatic varieties.

3 Settling and racking: to prevent coarse flavours, the juice may be chilled after pressing and given time for any excess solids to settle before it is 'racked' off, separated from the solid matter, that is.

(4) Cultured yeast: a selected strain* is often added before fermentation. It is safe, predictable, efficient and avoids 'characterful' smells! For the finest wines, makers tend to allow a diversity of natural, ambient yeast to do the work.

(5) Acidification: adding acid* is normal practice in hot countries to make up for what the grape has lost during ripening. Tartaric acid is used mostly, a few grams per litre, before or early on during fermentation.

(6) Chaptalisation: *see* pp44–5.

7 Alcoholic fermentation: most light or aromatic dry white wines will ferment in an inert container, such as a stainless steel tank. Temperatures are kept low (10–15°C/50–59°F) to preserve CO_2 freshness and primary fruit aromas. Finer, more expensive – or more ambitious – wines, Chardonnnay especially, might be fermented in new-oak barrels, often at slightly higher temperatures.

(8) Malolactic fermentation (MLF or 'malo'): if there is excess malic acid, bacteria (as opposed to yeast) can be used to transform the sharp malic into softer lactic acid – wholly or partly, according to taste. In addition to reducing acidity, this can add aromatic interest and roundness of texture to the wine.

The purest strains of bacteria leave little aromatic trace, less well-cultured versions can leave unpleasantly strong dairy and confectionery smells in their wake: yoghurt, melted butter, butterscotch.

(9) Lees* contact/lees stirring (*bâtonnage*): mostly for fine wines in barrel. The main aim is extra complexity. The lees act as an antioxidant, keeping the wine pale and fresh; and if stirred they add richness of flavour and texture. Stirred-up yeasts also protect the wine from wood tannin and wood colour to some extent.

(10) Barrel maturation: unsuitably light, or overoaked wines will develop bitter, resinous, astringent, 'phenolic' characters (*see* margin and pp47–8). In contrast to this, concentrated, flavoursome white wines are protected from astringency by their abundant proteins: the oak barrel tannins combine with these and thus lose their astringent potential for your palate, they are neutralised in effect.

In barrel-fermented wines the presence of yeast during the fermentation also acts as a buffer against excess absorption of colour, oak

ABOVE *Stainless steel vats outside at Allan Scott winery in New Zealand.*

tannin and oak aromas. Wines that ferment in stainless steel first and which are *then* put into barrel (more economical) lack this yeast protection and 'show' the oak effect much more (colour, aroma and tannic texture).

11 Racking: after fermentation wines will again be allowed to settle for a few days, and then 'racked' off their lees into a clean container. Barrel-aged wines may require periodic racking*. (*See* illustration, p43.)

(12) Blending of different lots; final acid adjustment: if necessary; according to taste.

(13) Cold stabilisation: chilling to below 0°C (32°F) precipitates unstable tartrate crystals to avoid a white crystal deposit*.

14 Fining: barrel-matured wines will stabilise and 'fall bright' naturally over an extended period. Others will have suspended matter, which might cloud the wine, removed by the use of a fining agent, typically fine bentonite clay, isinglass or casein for white wines. This is a physio-chemical process where the fining agent coagulates the unwanted elements and renders them insoluble so that they precipitate, or are filtered, out of the wine.

15 Filtration: a sieving process to remove unwanted matter (yeast, bacteria, fining deposits...) which might affect the appearance or stability of the wine after bottling.

16 Bottling: most unoaked dry white wines are bottled within a few months.

Main hazards to avoid during white vinification

Most white grape juice/wine is more fragile than red, not having the protection of tannins, and it is therefore especially sensitive to oxidation, which can produce colour, smell and taste defects.

Phenolics: Excess grape or wood tannin, owing to hard pressing or over-oaking. This soon shows up as astringency or bitterness of taste.

---

*See also

adding acid **50**

crystal deposit **50**

racking **42–3**

selected yeast **49**

lees **186**

sweet white winemaking

Residual sugar is sugar in wine which has not been fermented into alcohol. This is the difference between 'dry' wine, which contains no (or very little) residual sugar, and sweet wine, which contains sufficient to make the wine taste anything from moderately to intensely sweet.

The alcohol/residual sugar balance in 'sweet' wines varies enormously: it takes about 17.5 grams of sugar per litre (g/l) to produce 1% alcohol, so that most grapes for dry wine are picked with somewhere between 190 and 230g/l sugar, 11–13% potential alcohol.

Nobly rotten grapes for a good Sauternes will be picked with an average of 330g/l to produce a wine with 19% potential alcohol, 14% actual alcohol and 5% (85–90g/l) as residual sugar – a truly 'sweet' wine. On the other hand, the balance in a Spätlese* from the much cooler Mosel in Germany might be:

RIGHT *One way to keep unfermented grape juice (Süssreserve in German, see text), is in steel tanks under pressure, after sterile filtration which gets rid of any yeasts.*

FAR RIGHT *Periodic racking (decanting wine from one container to another) takes place to remove a wine from sediment which has settled to the bottom of its container. For expensive fine wines, aged in barrel over a long period, this is a more natural, gentle way of clarifying than fining and/or filtration.*

grapes without noble rot picked at 170g/l, less than 10% potential alcohol, to produce a final balance of 8% actual alcohol plus barely 2% (30g/l) residual sugar – a medium-dry to medium-sweet wine. Their very different acidities also play a significant role in how they taste.

Different routes to sugar in the bottle

Backblending: this is the simplest, cheapest, most widespread method of making sweet wines and, not surprisingly, it is mainly used for the blandest types. Here you make a dry wine first, and then sweeten it. Just before bottling you blend in (hence 'backblend') unfermented grape juice (known as sweet reserve from the German *Süssreserve*) to the required level. *Süssreserve* juice is sterile-filtered and then kept very cold in stainless-steel tanks to prevent any fermentation.

Special grape conditions: because of special treatment, or the conditions under which they are harvested, the following types of ripe grapes have a very high level of sugar to begin with, and the sugar remaining after the fermentation process is truly residual:

Noble rot/*Botrytis cinerea:* literally meaning an ash-coloured bunch of grapes, is the plant-marring mould (familiar to gardeners) on leaves and flowers during periods that combine warmth with humidity. In certain vineyards, alternating conditions of moisture and sunshine encourage this mould to develop on fully ripe grapes, so producing the blighted bunches that give birth to some of the world's greatest sweet wines: Sauternes, Tokaji, fine German Auslese and so on (*see* box, right).

Eiswein: originated in Germany, where healthy bunches of ripe grapes, *without* noble rot, are left on the vine in the hope that frosty conditions of −5 to −10°C (20.5–23.3°F) will literally freeze them. The grapes are picked in the most bone-chilling hours of the night, and immediately pressed, yielding a juice that is super-concentrated in sugar and acid, because the water content is left behind in the press as ice crystals. 'Ice wine' made like this has become a notable specialty of Canada but it can also be produced by 'cryoextraction', artificial concentration achieved by freezing picked bunches.

Partially dried grapes: the sugar content is raised by drying the ripe grapes until they are more or less raisin like. This can be done either by leaving them to desiccate on the vine, or by picking the bunches and hanging them up, or laying them out on racks to dry, usually in well-ventilated lofts. This method of winemaking, although relatively rare, remains strongest in Italy for *vin santo**, *amarone** and *recioto** styles.

Stopping fermentation: *see* below and margin.

Sweet white winemaking sequence

Essentially as for dry white wine, except for:

Pressing nobly rotten grapes: in contrast to standard grapes, where the final fraction of pressed juice is the coarsest, the final pressing of fully nobly rotten grapes produces the richest, darkest and sweetest juice.

Noble Rot *Botrytis cinerea*

Nobly rotten grapes, still moist from the morning mist, photographed as the sun breaks through. Botrytis spores are wind borne. The ideal conditions for them are foggy mornings that will promote the growth of the fungus on the grape, and sunny afternoons which will slowly evaporate the grape's juice and concentrate its constituents. The fungus develops initially as coppery stains, gradually colouring the skin sepia-pink to chocolate. Grey-brown fungus tufts begin to cover the surface, the skin starts to wrinkle and shrink as the juice evaporates, and the final stage is a mould covered, desiccated raisin, with a concentration of all its flavour elements except tartaric acid.

Fermentation: musts that are very rich in sugar are slow to ferment – even sugar-loving yeasts find them hard work. The very sweetest Tokaji or German Trockenbeerenauslese may take many months, even years, and then end up less than 6% alcohol. Given sufficient sugar, most sweet-wine fermentations will stop naturally at about 14% alcohol, but for reasons of balance and taste you may want to call a halt earlier and this is no place for uncertainty!

Stopping fermentation: this is normally effected by a combination of cooling to a temperature where the yeasts are inactive, adjusting the SO_2, racking, and then sterile filtering the wine before bottling to ensure there can be no yeasts to restart fermentation.

Stopping fermentation

Fermentation can also be stopped (to retain sugar) at any point by the addition of alcohol in the form of grape brandy; this is called fortification and is discussed under Fortified Wines (*see* pp110–15).

*See also

amarone **100**

vin santo, recioto **80,100**

spätlese **62**

red winemaking

Most ripe grapes have pale green flesh. The difference between red and white grapes lies in the skin's colour and constituents. If you ferment the juice of red grapes without their skins you get white wine, as in the case of Champagne, for example.

Where red winemaking is concerned, the skin, and what is extracted from it (colour, flavour, texture), is paramount; and the juice of the grapes is fermented in contact with the skins and pips. As fermentation proceeds, and possibly after it has finished, there is a progressive extraction of the skin's polyphenols*.

The art of red winemaking lies in knowing how best to effect this procedure and, above all, when to stop.

Picking dates

As with white grapes, the sugar/acid ratio in red grapes will be the primary measure of ripeness, but the quality* of the tannins in the skins and pips is just as important. Their aromas also change and develop as ripening continues (an early indicator of wine style) and again, as with white grapes, cooler regions or vintages tend to emphasise the earlier parts of the spectrum, hotter ones the latter (*see* margin).

Aroma progression of a maturing red grape

Two examples of red grape aroma development from early (barely ripe) maturity to late (super-/overripe) maturity:
Pinot Noir: redcurrant, strawberry, red cherry, raspberry, violets, black cherry.
Syrah/Shiraz: green coffee bean, green olive, raspberry, black pepper, blackberry, blackcurrant, cassis, jammy.

RIGHT *Pumping over. A regular operation early on during fermentation which draws the must from the bottom of a vat and pumps it back over the top, a bit like stirring the pot in cooking. It promotes extraction from the skins, makes fermentation more even, prevents hot spots and aerates the must.*

Fermentation

A complex reaction, but in essence:
sugar + yeast = alcohol + carbon dioxide (CO_2)
The yeasts gorge on the sugar in a frenzy, passing alcohol as waste at one end and burping CO_2 satisfaction at the other, until either the sugar is exhausted or they are overcome by their own alcohol.

Red winemaking sequence

Steps marked with **( )** are optional practices for the winemaker.

1 Destem/crush: destemming is usually, if not always, total. 'Crushing' is between counter-rotating rollers, sufficiently spaced so as just to split the skins, but without bruising them or breaking the pips which contain a very bitter astringency, as we all know from biting into them ourselves.

(2) Cold maceration: prior to fermentation, the skins and juice may be macerated 'cold' to enhance the wine's aromas. As there is no alcohol, only water-soluble aromatic compounds and colour are extracted from the skins, not tannins.

(3a) Enrichment/chaptalisation: this is the other side of the 'acidification' coin, and routine practice in moderate to cool climates. Sugar is added to the must early on during fermentation to boost the final level of alcohol. The aim is not to sweeten as such, as all the added sugar is fermented, but to use the characteristics of alcohol

(of which sweetness is one) to improve the overall balance* of the wine (*see* pp49–50). There are strict legal limits for both enrichment and acidification.

(3b) Enrichment/concentration: here the must is concentrated by removing water, either under a vacuum, or by using a reverse osmosis machine. This differs from chaptalisation in that everything is concentrated: sugar, acid, tannin, flavour, the good and the not so good! Where the need is felt for more alcohol, enrichment is increasingly used as an alternative to chaptalisation because it has the perceived bonus of concentrating the colour and flavour as well. This exercise is for expensive wines only, because, unlike sugar, it is not cheap.

(4) Acidification: if required, *see* p50.

(5) Cultured yeast: *see* p40.

6 Alcoholic fermentation: will take place in vats, as getting skins and pips into and out of barrels is impractical. Temperatures are higher than for white wines, commonly 25–30°C (77–86°F), but dependent on type: cooler for lighter wines (limiting extraction), warmer for richer, more extractive styles. Temperature control and managing the cap are the two main preoccupations. Temperature control is primarily aimed at preventing the fermentation overheating (so killing the yeast) and 'sticking'. The 'cap' refers to the mass of skins and pips which, if unmanaged, simply sits on top of the wine. It needs constant redistribution (like stirring the stock pot) to encourage complete and even extraction of colour, flavour and tannins from the skins and to prevent hot spots in the wine. This is mainly done by 'plunging' the cap back down in open-topped vats, and/or by pumping over (*see* illustration p44).

Vatting time in contact with the skins varies according to wine style. Guiding principles are that colour, being more water soluble, is extracted before tannin, and that as the tannins start to be dissolved by rising alcohol and temperature, the best-quality tannins are extracted first. Rosé wines will be 'run off' the skins after

ABOVE *M O G: 'matter other than grapes', but including mouldy bunches! Removed prior to crush to prevent taints in the wine.*

BELOW LEFT *Stainless steel, the most commonly used material for fermentation and storage, here at Léoville Poyferré in St-Julien.*

Main hazards to avoid during red vinification

Excess phenolics: coarse, bitter, astringent tannins will result from a) brutal treatment of the grape's skins or pips before fermentation, and b) over-extraction from too long a maceration after fermentation.

*See also

balance of wine **49-50**
quality of tannins **39**
skin's polyphenols **10**

24 hours or less, with practically no tannin. Light red wines may be taken off after three or four days with plenty of colour and moderate extraction. Fine wines made with noble grapes (*see* p124) will spend anywhere between a week and a month macerating depending on the type of wine. The alcoholic fermentation of most red wine will be complete within a week.

(7) Barrel fermentation: imaginatively Australian in origin, this stage avoids excess tannin extraction in red wines which do not need it. The not quite fully fermented wine is run off the skins and the fermentation finished in barrel.

(8) Post-fermentation maceration: the winemaker can choose to steep the wine on its skins after fermentation is over to extract more tannin and flavour. The process needs careful and constant monitoring so that it is not overdone. The quality of the grapes, tradition, the winemaker's experience and, above all, his or her taste, will be the arbiters (*see* pp49–51).

9 Run off and pressing: the free-run wine (so called because it drains freely off the skins and pips in the vat) is often kept separate from the press wine. The latter is carefully pressed from the saturated mass of skins and pips after they have been taken out of the vat. If press wine is kept separately, its best fractions may be blended judiciously with the free-run wine. Great care is needed though, for press wine, though usually richer, is also often much coarser.

10 Malolactic fermentation: (*see* p41) standard practice for red wines because malic acid (*see* p38) clashes with tannin, but, in contrast to white wines, the process leaves no aromatic imprint.

(11) Barrel maturation: oaked red wines often have a 'drier' astringency to taste than their white counterparts, especially early on. Oak-barrel tannin is not neutralised in red wines in the same way that it is in whites, which have little natural tannin of their own to combine with their proteins (*see* p41).

Before red wine goes into barrel its own abundant tannins have already combined with its proteins; these are not therefore available to 'deactivate' the oak tannins as happens with rich white wines. Thus the oak tannin is superimposed on the wine's grape tannin, and often tastes like a finely dry, almost a chalky, additional astringency, more apparent than it would be in a comparable dry white (*see* pp48,98 margin).

12 Periodic racking: decanting the wine off the settled lees and into clean containers, whether tanks or barrels, is part of the continuous natural clearing process for quality red wines.

(13) Blending of different lots; a final acid adjustment: if necessary; according to taste.

14 Fining: *see* pp41 for the principles. Freshly beaten egg whites are still the best red wine fining agent. The quantity is two to six egg whites per 225-litre barrel, depending on how much tannin you want to remove; well-stirred in and allowed to 'settle' for a month or two before racking (*see* illustration above).

(15) Filtration: *see* p41.

16 Bottling: according to taste/readiness.

oak

Barrels have been used to house wine for centuries, and experience has shown oak to be the only wood to improve both taste and texture of wine, and then only as 'new' wood, during the first two or three years of a barrel's life.

Our current obsession with oak (for such it is) is relatively new. It was the mid-1980s when the Australians introduced the world, the UK market in particular, to inexpensive wines with the seductive aromas and flavours of new wood. This was something that had hitherto been strictly limited to fine wines, if only for reasons of cost. The ripe fruit with a vanilla-cream topping was irresistible, and an instant success with consumers, critics and wine show judges alike. It has now become such a preoccupation that it is difficult to believe wood simply wasn't an issue previously.

Oak species

Of the 200 or so species of oak, the winemaker uses two for barrel-making: *Quercus petraea*, the 'brown' oak, from northern Europe, and *Quercus alba*, the pale-barked 'white' oak, known as 'American' because of its eastern United States origin. American oak produces cheaper barrels because its anatomy (*see* below) means that its staves can be sawn from the tree trunk with only 50 per cent wastage, whereas the European oak must be split,

LEFT *Carefully chosen, flawless sections of these stately 150-year-old oak trunks will yield the wood for just two 225-litre barrels, known in French as 'barriques'.*

Oak structure

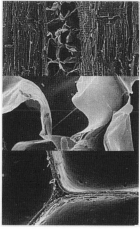

European oak: a vertical section of European oak, *Q petraea* (magnified x100), showing the 'tylose' plugging structure which makes the wood's sap-carrying vessels watertight.

European oak: the tyloses in *Q petraea* (x1000), are soft, fragile and easily torn because its walls are so thin, meaning it must be 'split' to preserve the watertight tylose structure.

American oak: the tylose walls in American oak, *Q alba* (x1000), are four to five times as thick as those of European oak, and therefore more rigid, watertight and resistant to the saw.

ABOVE *Chêne in French means oak. The 'Haute Futaie' stamp (literally 'high trunks') guarantees that the wood used for the barrel comes from fully mature forests of between 150 and 250 years of age; a quality designation.*

BELOW RIGHT *The controlled 'toasting' of the inside of a barrel after it has been made (see text for the effects of oak). Barrel toast effects: a light toast (10–15 minutes) gives a dry-edged, piquant spiciness. A medium toast (15–30 minutes) brings out the typical 'sweeter' odours of coconut and vanilla (from the wood's vanillin), along with melted butter and caramel from the toasting of the wood's sugars. High toast (30–45 minutes) impressions are more torrefied: roasted coffee, smoked bacon, cloves, ginger, woodsmoke and, at the extreme end, the 'char' of resin, creosote and tar.*

resulting in 80 per cent wastage and more than double the material cost. As a result, American oak tends to be used more, though by no means exclusively, for cheaper wines. Indeed, experiments in the 1990s showed that if American wood is treated exactly like French – its staves seasoned in the open air as opposed to being kiln dried, and subsequently bent over an open fire instead of using steam – then it can be just as 'fine' in its effects. As this is not usually the case, however, American oak's vanilla, coconut and clove characteristics do indeed tend to be more pronounced, whereas European oak, which has a tighter grain, contributes less obvious flavours to the wine.

The effects of oak: taste

Given good quality wood selection and adequate seasoning, the single most influential factor in what a barrel contributes to wine is the controlled 'toast' given by an open flame to the barrel's inside. Heat transforms the wood components to give the characteristic 'oak' aromas and flavours, *see* margin (left, below), as well as creating a barrier between the wood's 'raw' elements and the wine.

But oak not only affects the smell and taste of wine, it leaves its mark on the texture. In

both red and white wines it has a bracing, defining effect: flavours are brought into sharper focus and a 'plain' texture will develop more 'key'. It *may* soften the tannins in red wine, but this is by no means always the case, and it can also make the wines forbiddingly dry and astringent (*see* p46 for some reasons why, and p98 margin for some of the results).

Judging the influence of oak

Oak is best thought of as a condiment; and just as with food, it is easily overdone. Forceful, tasty dishes can take considerable seasoning, are improved by it, and yet don't taste of the condiments, whereas blander or more delicate dishes are rapidly overwhelmed by them. And when seasoning becomes a major ingredient, masking what it is designed to enhance, the cook has lost his or her sense of taste! So it is with wine and oak.

There is no question that oak flavours, with their reminders of the pastries trolley, candy store and spice rack, are intrinsically appealing, nor that oak improves more than just the aromas of wine. But oak flavours became such a commercial success during the 1980s and 1990s that 'oak' came to be valued for its own sake. It then began to be used on labels as a powerful selling point in its own right, and to be regarded by winemakers almost as a failsafe ingredient, the requisite super condiment, a vinous version of monosodium glutamate – and just as addictive. Something was clearly amiss!

Luckily not all grape varieties have an affinity for oak (Cabernet Sauvignon, Merlot, Shiraz and Chardonnay are some that *do*). And, weary of a decade of enforced oak addiction, the wine bibber is calling for more individuality, nuance and, indeed, the taste of grape varieties again. Some producers are listening. Paradoxically, just as Australia, New Zealand and California are weaning themselves off excess oak, in white wines especially, the reverse is the case in much of Europe and the more recently emerging 'New World': South Africa, Chile and Argentina.

winemakers

Even allowing for the compromises demanded by commerce and practicality, a winemaker's every decision should be based, ultimately, on drinkability in the glass. If this sounds obvious, the evidence in many glasses suggests it isn't. Here we look at some of winemaking's more controversial areas.

The winemaker is like a cook; indeed the parallels between winemaking and cooking are numerous. As anyone who has ever held a saucepan knows, the recipe is but a guide. You cannot cook well without tasting as you go, or without having a fairly clear idea of what you want to end up with. Give half a dozen cooks the same, proven recipe and the same good-quality ingredients and equipment, and you will likely end up with six different versions of a single concept. The odds are that one will be exquisite, one will be gross, the others will range between.

Minimal intervention winemaking

Ask good winemakers about how they achieve their results and the answer will often be something like: 'I practise minimal intervention, the wine makes itself.' This is either over modest, or disingenuous. Wine no more makes itself than an egg boils itself.

From one year to the next in the vineyard, from picking the grapes to the bottling line, the winemaker is constantly faced with options, large and small, as to what to do and when. The choices will necessarily be based on taste considerations; which is why the winemaker's palate and general wine culture are at least as important as his or her knowledge of chemistry and recipes. A talented winemaker will try to ensure balanced fruit to start with, so that the guiding hand need only be minimal, but guide it will.

Perfect fruit, or a bit of 'fiddling': in an ideal world there are always perfect ingredients. Perfect fruit that is, whose juice needs no adjustment for the type of wine you want. This is what vineyard management aims at, and why it is so important; like starting with first-rate ingredients for cooking. But in the real world, whichever hemisphere you live in, a bit of fine-tuning is often necessary.

Chaptalisation: the cool-climate remedy. The addition of sugar to the fermenting must utilises the properties of alcohol to make up for deficiencies in the juice: a lack of sugar on the one hand, excess acidity on the other. Both are the result of inadequately ripe grapes, possibly as a result of cold weather; but just as often a consequence of viticultural greed (*ie* excess yields) leaving too much fruit for the vine to ripen fully. Done with discretion, chaptalisation

BELOW *From left to right, freeze dried yeast, bentonite (fine clay) and casein (milk protein); part of the winemaker's equipment. Bentonite and casein may be used to clarify and/or fine wine, in the same way as egg white is used to 'clarify' consommé soup. Selected yeasts ferment so efficiently that they are a significant source of high alcohol (they need less sugar to produce a given level than natural yeast). But today excess alcohol can sometimes be removed by the use of spinning cone technology!*

BELOW RIGHT *The grapes in a vineyard don't all ripen at exactly the same time, and many wineries will try and keep their various pickings (or 'passes') separate, and vinify them separately, prior to deciding how to use them to best effect in final blends, based on tasting. This is a vat with wine from the Jensen vineyard at the Calera winery in California.*

BELOW FAR RIGHT *Oak chips of various sizes, shapes and 'toasts'. These can be added directly to fermenting wine, or suspended in it in a sort of tea bag. They impart the much prized flavours and aromas of oak, without affecting the wine's texture as barrel ageing does. Mainly used for cheaper wines, because they are a much less expensive source of 'oakiness'. Using them intelligently is a craft just as using oak barrels is.*

can improve the taste of a wine by making it somewhat fuller and softer. But it cannot make up for weak and inadequately flavoured fruit, and it is easily overdone. In which case, softer and fuller probably; but also hot, and *still* devoid of flavour. In other words: unbalanced.

Acidification: the hot-climate remedy. The addition of acid to the must compensates for deficiencies in the ripe grapes. In hot climates the problem is the reverse of that in cool climates: the grape's sugar and acid levels are often at the ideal level long before its flavour is fully developed. And by the time the flavour is where you want it, the acidity is too low. A discreet addition of acidity can correct what would otherwise be a want of freshness and definition in the finished wine, and it need be no more 'noticeable' than judicious chaptalisation*. But it too is easily overdone. As a corrective principle it is fair enough to compare it with chaptalisation, but it is also true that the taste of acid, being inherently aggressive, is much more obtrusive than the taste of alcohol and excess acid shows up more easily. It simply means the hot-climate winemaker's sticking plaster is less easy to camouflage than the cool-climate winemaker's, and therefore more of a challenge.

Neither correction is desirable, especially to a noticeable degree, and in both cases prevention in the vineyard is better than cure in the winery. If bacterial stability rather than taste is often the reason behind acidification*, then habit rather

than taste is just as frequently behind chaptalisation. When 'fine tuning' begins to taste like 'fiddled with' they are as bad as each other!

Evisceration and distortion: it is easy to denude a wine at the end of the winemaking process by a combination of excess fining* and/or filtration* in the name of stability and brilliance, almost literally to eviscerate it. It is just as easy, though a more recent fad, to overload a wine in the other direction in the name of greatness, profundity, intensity and so on. For red wines in particular this is done by various combinations of very low yields, super-ripe fruit, concentrating machines, high extract, extended maceration, considerable oak and so on. If most of these are laudable aims and methods individually and in moderation, they are increasingly put to immoderate use. In this case the result is distortion. Pascal Delbeck of Château Belair in St-Emilion has a nice phrase to describe such wines: the product of *cerveaux de muscle*, brains made of muscle tissue! Impressive

LEFT *Rocky O'Callaghan of Rockford, Barossa Valley (far left), and Paul Draper of Ridge, California: first-rate winemakers, who prove that good winemaking is not just about hygiene, technology and new oak, it is about taste. The ability to taste well, and a sense of good taste. Both are fundamental to good winemaking decisions. Just as no amount of technical ability will make good music if the player has no musicality, so no amount of good equipment will make good wine if the winemaker has poor taste.*

to 'taste', maybe, all but impossible to 'drink'. Evisceration and distortion are identical examples of mindless winemaking, just at opposite extremes of the same spectrum.

The influence of fashion

So rapid is the dissemination of information today that it is impossible to be unaware of fashions. Winemakers are now at least as much influenced by it as wine buyers. Red wines are especially fashionable at the beginning of the 21st century. And currently perceived attributes of value tend towards the 'super'* levels, whether of ripeness, alcohol, softness of texture, extraction (along with its tannins in this case), colour, or strength of flavour. But if there are a few wines that can manage some or all of these comfortably, there are many more that cannot.

At the moment Europe seems to feel the need to ape the New World (which can more naturally produce this style successfully) more than the other way round. Not least as a result of trendsetters belittling styles and qualities that have been around for a long time and that many consumers have learned to enjoy. It is tragic to see the rapidity with which some

winemakers discard long-held values on the assumption that particular components, valued in other contexts, must necessarily give added value to their own product, even if it is at the expense of its true identity*.

Understanding the nature of your grapes

The fruit of each vineyard has a 'voice', like the playing qualities of a musical instrument. A musician's technique can enhance or distort these qualities, depending on how he or she plays and listens to the sound. Similarly winemakers can exalt or obliterate the voice of their grapes depending on how they treat their fruit. The trick in either case is not to apply rigid formulas or preconceptions, but to explore how instrument or fruit respond when treated in different ways. In both cases, pushed beyond their natural limits they lose their identity by being 'forced'.

A tribute

This is not a bleak view, merely a caveat. Most of what follows is a celebration of the best in winemaking; a tribute to winemakers who drink and taste widely beyond their immediate horizons, who have a sense of proportion, a sense of tradition and minds of their own.

in the bottle

3. naming wines

names and labels

As we cannot sample every bottle before purchase, it is important that the information provided by the bottle shape and label should give a clear indication of what the wine tastes like.

If only it were that easy! There is little pattern or consistency in the way in which wines are named across the globe. Considering the huge variety of wines available, this is perhaps unsurprising; but as the label is the primary basis on which we choose, it can certainly be frustrating. Here, then, is a brief guide to bottle shapes, to label information, and to what they do, or don't, tell you.

Bottle shapes

There are three basic bottle shapes, known by the European wine regions with which they are associated: Bordeaux, Burgundy and Germany. The Bordeaux or 'claret' bottle (illustration 2 p54) has parallel sides and a pronounced shoulder, the burgundy bottle (illustration 3 p54) is broader and has long, sloping shoulders; the German bottle is a tall, slender shape (illustration 4 p55). The use of these bottles in any region implies that the wines have a broad similarity to the prototypes.

Bordeaux bottles: are normally used for red wines made from the Bordeaux grape varieties Cabernet Sauvignon or Merlot, or for red wines considered to be similar in weight and style – 'dry', medium-bodied and somewhat tannic. Clear Bordeaux bottles are typically used for sweet wines based on Semillon and Sauvignon Blanc, made in the image of Sauternes.

Burgundy bottles: are used for the grape varieties associated with burgundy wines – Pinot Noir in particular in the case of red wines, or generally for wines that are thought to be fuller, softer and less tannic than the average Bordeaux. Chardonnay, the white burgundy grape, is universally sold in these bottles. But so, indeed, is almost any full-bodied, oak-aged dry white!

Germanic flute: is a legal requirement for all wines from Alsace (red and white) and it is normally used for both dry and sweet wines based on Riesling, or aromatic grape varieties such as Gewurztraminer. Because its associations have sometimes been less than positive (*see* caption below), it is used less faithfully for Riesling than are the Bordeaux and burgundy bottles for Cabernet and Merlot or Pinot Noir respectively. So strong is the association

1

Marketing and the importance of image

From a distance this bottle, with its dark glass and tapering shape, suggests a classy, dry white Bordeaux, made from Sauvignon and Semillon. And this way you might give the bottle a second glance. Which you well might not, if this New Zealand Riesling were being sold in the traditional German bottle with its unfortunate, if sometimes well-deserved, image of cheap Germanic-style brands.

TOP RIGHT *The claret, on
the left, has a unique and
well known brand name,
Pape Clément, and it is clear
precisely where it comes
from – so long as you know
where Péssac-Léognan and
Graves are. But unless you
have specialist knowledge,
you will not know the grape
variety(s), 60/40 per cent
Cabernet Sauvignon/Merlot.
The Trefethen bottle suggests
it is a 'claret style'. Its well
known brand name is clear,
as is its specific origin,
Napa, and, crucially to the
consumer, so is the grape
variety. The 'Hillside
Selection' oval is, implicitly, a
superior quality designation.*

between Cabernet Sauvignon, Merlot and the Bordeaux bottle, and between Pinot Noir or Chardonnay and the burgundy bottle, it would be perverse, commercially at least, to bottle wine from these grapes in anything other than the bottle shapes so positively associated with them. Though it is precisely commercial considerations that have prompted many New World producers to forsake Riesling's traditional shape (illustration 1 p53).

Beyond these few powerful associations, bottles are but a very rough indication. Australia's potent Shiraz wines, for example, are sold in claret bottles rather than the burgundy bottle used for Syrahs from the Northern Rhône. And there is an increasing number of bottle designs and colours aimed primarily at attracting the consumer's attention rather than indicating the style of the contents.

2

Names

Essentially, wines are named in two ways: either after the geographical region from which they come, or after the grape variety or varieties from which they are made.

Geographical names: most European wines are named geographically – Bordeaux, Chianti, Rioja – because historically their style was associated with their provenance. This is, potentially, a much more subtle and detailed system than varietal naming, as wine styles and quality are so often closely tied up with their origin (*see* pp126,129,144), and that is its advantage. It is also its biggest drawback, for there are so many place names to get to grips with. And in many cases it is by no means obvious whether the name is that of a grape or a location: Nebbiolo is a grape variety, Barolo is a place name, Montepulciano is both!

Varietal names: most so-called 'New World' wines are named 'varietally', *ie* after their grape variety. This is much more user-friendly, for two reasons. First, there are only a handful of grape varieties that are used with any regularity so there are far fewer names to remember. And, second, once you are acquainted with the wine from these varieties, the name (of the grape) on the label immediately gives you a good general

RIGHT *Burgundy bottles.
On the left, not only a
Chassagne-Montrachet, but
a superior Premier Cru
vineyard and, most
important of all, the name
of a top producer: J N
Gagnard; important because
there are many who make
wine from this site. An
outstanding vintage too. But
you need special knowledge
to interpret most of this. And
what you cannot tell is that
this is a Chardonnay!
You can't miss that on
the Meerlust! Which also
has the details of vintage
(less crucial in South Africa)
and specific origin. As to
quality, the heavyweight
bottle is certainly trying to
tell you something!*

3

idea of that wine's style. But this simplicity is also limiting, because by itself it allows for practically no useful distinctions of quality and style. For that, producers of varietal wines must turn to a host of special quality indications such as 'Reserve', 'Special Selection', separate in-house brand names, or, you've guessed it, increasingly detailed place names.

Brands, and 'whose version is it?': in the most accepted sense of the word, a branded wine is one with a heavily promoted name whose supply is almost limitless. The supply is related mainly to the level of demand and degree of promotion: Blue Nun, Mateus Rosé, Mouton Cadet, for example. But most wines are 'brands', albeit in a looser sense, in that their producers' names are associated with recognised and consistent particularities of style and quality. The names of individual Bordeaux châteaux are 'brands' of claret, and many New World wine-producer names are in effect brands: Penfolds, Mondavi, Montana. And their reputation is a key clue to quality. Indeed, however one wants to define a brand, the individual producer's name is probably the most important piece

4

of information on a wine label. Amongst the host of Chardonnays, Cabernets, Merlots and so on, what really counts is whose version it is. Mini brands if you like. And the same goes for geographically named wines too.

Label information

Specific labelling laws differ from one country to another. But in most countries the following, self-explanatory, pieces of information are mandatory:

TOP LEFT *German flutes. On the right is an Australian winery which is (justifiably) proud to put its Riesling in a traditional Riesling flute, and to associate it not only with a specific region within South Australia, but with a specific vineyard as well. 'Heggies' is in effect a mini brand.*

No mistaking the importance of the producer on the German bottle; and grape, very specific origin and vintage are also clear. But considerable 'further reading' is required to understand the significance of Dr Loosen (top notch), Wehlener Sonnenuhr (top site) and Kabinett (light, medium sweet style).

BELOW LEFT *Back labels can be usefully informative or just sales puff. There is more of the latter than the former, but mostly it is inefficiently utilised space, especially for the consumer. Along with what you can see on the label left and behind, Sainsbury's back label has information on the Bulgarian region the wine comes from, a 'drink by' date, and a customer careline number. Good basic information, and no space wasted. The Italian label has some detail about how it is made, but no grape details, and also a certain amount of padding of the 'noted for its quality' sort. Simply less efficient.*

- **Country of origin**
- **Producer's name**
- Where and by whom bottled
- A measure of the liquid content, a standard bottle is usually 75cl/750ml
- An indication of the alcohol level, usually expressed as % by volume

Additional important details might include:
- **Grape variety** – for varietally named wines
- **Specific region of origin**
- **National or regional quality designation**
- **Vintage date** – the more moderate the climate the more crucial this is (*see* p166)

The items in **semi-bold** are the crucial ones and, depending on the individual wine, you would probably consider them in the following order of significance:

1 Country and specific region (geographically named wines), or grape variety
2 Producer
3 Quality designation
4 Vintage date

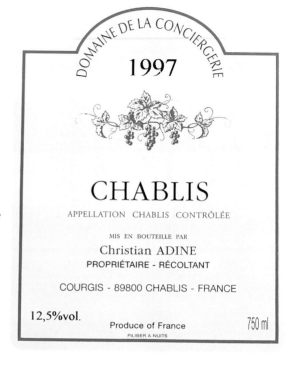

NB The three illustrations of bottle pairs (pp54–5) compare the presentation of a European 'original' alongside a New World version of a similar style of wine.

The three label illustrations here examine and compare samples of label information.

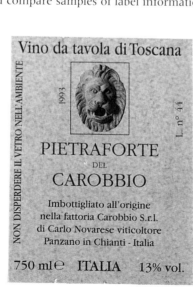

4. white grapes and their wines

Themes and variations

Comparing different wines from the same grape variety, and comparing different varieties are two of the best ways of familiarising yourself with wine's diversity. The individual grape essays here outline what to expect from where.

Within an overall kinship of taste, there are marked variations on each grape theme resulting from the influences of country of origin, climate and viticulture on the one hand, and winemaking on the other. Some indication of the possible flavour spectrum, largely dependent on ripeness (as dictated by the first three influences), is given in the margin boxes for the major grapes.

Winemaking, where it is extreme, can affect a wine's style to the point of unrecognisability. But, in a given context of country, soil and location, there is a broad middle ground for every grape, where its wines seem 'natural' and unforced. This is part of the notion of what is 'typical', and it is these wines that feature here.

This book's notional £30/$50 price ceiling applies, and the grandest wines are not generally discussed; but for possible tasting reference, a few top, price immaterial, benchmark wines for the main grapes are mentioned in the margin.

The grapes are arranged in rough order of significance. To find a particular variety, consult the index.

ABOVE *Riesling, probably the finest white grape variety of all.*

chardonnay

Chardonnay is grown all round the globe, producing amongst the very best of dry white wines, as well as much fine sparkling wine. Its wide availability and enormous quality spectrum make it a practical, interesting and pleasurable subject for comparative study.

However, its very adaptability, the fact that this grape can be grown and vinified with relative ease almost anywhere, has brought with it a certain amount of Chardonnay weariness, giving rise to the original 'ABC' slogan: 'Anything But Chardonnay', please! This was not born of a dislike of Chardonnay as such, but out of frustration with the copious amounts of indifferent, alcoholic Chardonnay produced.

Unlike Riesling or Sauvignon Blanc, for example, Chardonnay has no pronounced characteristics of its own, and this lack of

BELOW The steep Grand Cru vineyard of Bougros in Chablis showing the characteristic limestone dominated soil, and a row of oil-fired 'smudge pots' to ward off the effects of spring frosts.

identifiable personality means that it readily accommodates all manner of winemaking techniques. Its impressionability makes it an attractive challenge to the ambitious – or to the bored – winemaker. Its ease of manufacture makes it an undemanding prospect for lazy or large-scale vinification. And the brand-like recognition of its name means it is almost always a valid commercial prospect. Small wonder that it appears in so many guises, and that it is difficult to pin down!

It does, however, fall into two clearly different groups: oaked and unoaked wine, and if its individual characteristics are somewhat vague, its quality distinctions are clear to perceive, and interesting to explore.

Unoaked Chardonnay

Unoaked* Chardonnay is made increasingly widely in **France**, in the Ardèche (Louis Latour) and in the Languedoc (James Herrick) to name but two successful ventures. But the unoaked, yardstick Chardonnays still come from Chablis and the Mâconnais.

Well-made **Mâcon**, drunk young, is simple, easy to drink and a delight: medium-bodied, supple, yet fresh, with pure, straightforward, ripe-apple and tangerine flavours. Its easy-going, food-flexible, amiable nature shows just why inexpensive Chardonnay wins so many friends. Mâcon-Villages from Domaine Talmard is regularly exceptional, and the Buxy and Lugny cooperative wines are very consistent.

Chablis is 180 miles (290km) further north. And although its grapes are picked riper today, and most wines are put through malolactic fermentation*, it will have a livelier acidity (and meanness where it is overcropped), and a more minerally/stony character to its flavour. Most Chablis is still made without new wood, and pure, pristine, unoaked and beautifully clear-cut wines are made by Louis Michel, Billaud-Simon, Christian Adine, Bernard Legland, Daniel Dampt, and a reliable cooperative, La Chablisienne.

From the rest of Europe, **Bulgaria**'s best Chardonnays are peachy, Mâcon look-alikes, such as Khan Krum and Bin 63 from Vinex Preslav. Those from **Hungary** are more green-apple sharp. Northeast **Italy** makes plenty of fresh, easy-drinking, stainless-steel-fermented wine (try Lageder, Tiefenbrunner). And Alasia, part of the Araldica cooperative, makes remarkably good wine in Piedmont. In **Spain**, look for Raïmat (Costers del Segre) and Enate (Somontano).

Unoaked New World Chardonnay used to be a rarity. That is far less true now, especially in **Australia**. Amongst the most reliable are Constable & Hershon Hunter Valley, Chapel Hill and Shaw & Smith from South Australia, Browns from Padthaway and Goundry's from Mount Barker. The grapes for many of these are picked a little earlier than for the wooded versions, or come from cooler areas. The best are so refreshing and gulpably good, and apparently sell so well, one wonders why more aren't made! And an Iron Pot Bay from the Tamar Valley – juicily vivid, beautifully

balanced, gorgeously fresh – showed me Tasmania's promise. An easy to find and particularly good version from **California** is Fetzer's unoaked Mendocino Chardonnay.

Oaked Chardonnay

Of the three principal quality communes on **Burgundy**'s Côte de Beaune, it would be nice to think that, for a given quality level, the three – Puligny-Montrachet, Chassagne-Montrachet, Meursault – were always distinguishable. But if the broad distinctions are there, the influence of the producer, benign or otherwise, does rather blur them.

Meursault (Lafon, Roulot, Grivault, Jadot) tends to be somewhat fuller than Puligny, broader, more open and more buttery; Puligny is a bit tauter, purer, more peach and tangerine fruit (Carillon, Domaine Leflaive, Jadot, Champy); Chassagne is somewhere between the two (J-N Gagnard – rich, concentrated; Ramonet – delicate and fine). Variations in style abound, and quality (of actual taste, rather than what the label claims) is what matters most! St-Aubin (G Prudhon, M Colin, B Morey) is well worth exploring as an alternative to Puligny, and Auxey-Duresses (Leroy, M Prunier and J-P Diconne) as 'slighter' Meursault.

The modest appellation of Bourgogne Blanc is particularly good value from top producers such as Leflaive, Leroy and Coche-Dury. At Burgundy's southern extreme, Pouilly-Fuissé makes ripe, supple, fulsome wines (Château de Fuissé, Denogent) with fresher styles from the higher, cooler village of Vergisson (Michel Forest, D Barraud, Guffens-Heynen).

ABOVE *Burgundy: Château de Meursault, with St-Romain's compacted limestone ridge in the background.*

BELOW LEFT *The backstreets of Beaune are full of delightful details like this bell pull in the rue des Tonneliers.*

Chardonnay at a glance

Alcohol: medium to high.
Acid: mostly moderate; can be vigorous in cool climate.
Aroma characteristics: naturally low; easily marked by new oak or *terroir*.
Cool-climate/less ripe fruit: apple, melon, lime, white peach, nectarine.
Warm-climate/riper fruit: tangerine, peach, pineapple, passion-fruit, fruit salad.
Bottle age bouquet: most best drunk young, a very few top wines age splendidly.
unoaked: honeyed, vegetal, wet wool.
oaked: honey, butter, nuts, caramel, toast, *terroir*.
Styles (all dry):
• unoaked, pure, fresh.
• oaky, restrained to rich.

TOP RIGHT *Louis Carillon, source of one of Burgundy's most consistently stylish, 'village' Puligny-Montrachets.*

MID RIGHT *Gisborne, New Zealand. Numerous barrel experiments on Chardonnay: different vineyards are writ large on the casks; smaller markings refer to rootstocks, vine variety clones, yeasts and pruning methods. Chardonnay is always obliging experimental material for the curious, or the bored, winemaker.*

BELOW *Carneros, California This cooler, breezier region at the southern extremity of the Napa Valley produces particularly elegant and restrained examples of California Chardonnay.*

Spain produces a small amount of oaked Chardonnay, mainly in the northeast: crisp and lemony from Navarra (Castillo de Monjardín), and a softly, creamy, pricey Milmanda from Torres (Penedès). **Italy**'s barrel-influenced* Chardonnays come largely from that heartland of vinous ambition, Tuscany, and so far the wood tends to dry the fruit. Lageder's northern Italian Alto Adige Löwengang, however, is consistently stylish and successful.

Germany, **Austria** and **Switzerland** are also all quality-conscious producers of small amounts of wooded Chardonnay.

Easy to grow, easy to make, easy to sell – no wonder the **New World** produces so much oaked Chardonnay. Much of it is in a somewhat alcoholic, overblown Mâcon style, super-ripe, oaky, off-dry (from high alcohol and a few grams of residual sugar) and with more or less acidity according to origin. In Burgundian terms many of the best are at 'good village' or 'lesser Premier Cru' level, but generally represent much better value for money than most white burgundy of a similar quality level. Most of what are considered the 'top' wines are at 'good Premier Cru' level (*see* page 82).

In South America there is plenty of decent, oaky Chardonnay from **Chile**, as yet perhaps the best from the cooler Casablanca region (Casablanca, Errazuriz). And from **Argentina**, Catena's wines are a model of balance. So far, there is little from either country to match the best of the rest of the New World in scope. In North America, everywhere but California is a very small Chardonnay player. **Canada**'s best are light, fresh and delightfully drinkable, and **Washington State** looks like being more consistent for the grape than **Oregon**.

California's quality wines come from all along the 'coastal' vineyard regions, from Mendocino County in the north to Santa Barbara, 500 miles (800 km) further south. Particularly reliable mid-priced wines are Beringer Napa, Estancia and Château Souverain. So complex is the coastal geography, impressive from the air, it is easy to appreciate the impossibility of generalising about location and style. That

said, the best Carneros (cool and breezy) Chardonnays do seem particularly elegant and restrained: Saintsbury, Phelps, Mondavi, Acacia. Sonoma County has a high proportion of richly elegant wines: Sonoma Cutrer, Château St Jean, Matanazas Creek. From the Central Coast, heading south, Ridge, Calera, Au Bon Climat, Qupé and Edna Valley can all show 'top Premier Cru' quality. Kistler and Chalone are regularly 'Grand Cru'. A quality quartet for comparison might consist of: Fetzer unoaked (£ – *see* p118, Fetzer Private Collection (££), Saintsbury Reserve, Chalone or a top Kistler (all £££–£££+).

The best of **South Africa**'s oaked Chardonnays are increasingly consistent, generally in a lighter (13+% alcohol notwithstanding), more restrained style than those of California, Australia or New Zealand: 'peachy' regularly comes to mind. As with California, there are good wines from all the quality regions. The best at 'good village' to 'lesser Premier Cru' level, with a notably high proportion from Stellenbosch (Mulderbosch, Jordan, Simonsig, Meerlust…) and crisper wines from Constantia (Steenberg), Walker Bay (Bouchard-Finlayson, Hamilton Russell), and an excellent range from De Wetshof in Robertson, and Neil Ellis – from purchased grapes.

The majority of **Australia**'s Chardonnays are golden, generous, ripe and oaky, mostly with a more tropical-fruit accent than California. Lindeman's Bin 65 and Penfold's Koonunga Hill are two remarkably good, and consistent, 'generic' wines. And there are clear regional differences amongst the premium Chardonnays: large-scale, broad and buttery from the Hunter Valley (Rosemount's Roxburgh, Tyrrell's Vat 47); with more elegant wines from a number of somewhat cooler areas: Yarra Valley in Victoria (Mount Mary – atypically restrained for Australia, ages like good Puligny – Tarrawarra, Coldstream Hills). Plus Piccadilly Hills in South Australia (Petaluma, Grosset) and, above all, from Western Australia, where Howard Park, Sandalford and Plantagenet are deep, dry, firm and complex wines from a true Australian cool climate, Mount Barker.

Consistently, though, Australia's best is Leeuwin's Art Series: long, finely balanced, classy purity from Margaret River. A quality quartet for comparison might be: Koonunga Hill, Yalumba Family Reserve, Petaluma, Leeuwin.

By contrast with most New World Chardonnays, **New Zealand**'s stand out for their backbone of acidity. Examine the labels to see if the wine is 'regional'. Vineyards range over 600 miles (960km) from north to south, with styles broadly 'softening' the further north you are. Villa Maria's range (Private Bin, Cellar Selection and Reserve) will give you a good three-tier quality reference, and any of the wines mentioned below, an idea of differences in style. From South Island: Marlborough's Cloudy Bay and Vavasour Reserve, and Nelson's Neudorf – all, firm, elegant, close-knit wines. From North Island: Martinborough or Palliser, both from Martinborough itself – fresh and pure, with a more direct fruit. Gisborne makes rich wines, supple for New Zealand (Kim Crawford's Tietjen); Hawkes Bay's Te Mata Elston, or Kumeu River Mate's Vineyard from Auckland are full and firm, yet luscious too, both 'top Premier Cru' quality.

Most Chardonnay does not age gracefully and the vast majority are best drunk young. The warmer the climate, the sooner the better. But Burgundy's Premiers Crus and the top New World wines develop subtle, nutty, honeyed characteristics with up to a decade in bottle.

ABOVE *Boschendal Estate in Paarl, South Africa. The Franschhoek Valley is the source of some of the country's peachiest, early drinking Chardonnays.*

Top wines to taste

Burgundy, France
Chevalier-Montrachet
(Domaine Leflaive, Jadot)
Corton-Charlemagne
(B du Martray, L Latour)
California, USA
Robert Mondavi Reserve
Kistler McCrea Vineyard

*See also

barrel influences **41,48**
malo fermentation **41**
tastings **2,3,126,130**
unoaked **41,160,161**

riesling

At its best, from cool but sunny locations, Riesling makes incomparable wines which combine lightness of touch with intensity of flavour; from bone-dry to intensely sweet the wines are also triumphantly oak-free. No longer unsung but still underrated.

ABOVE *Steep, slate-strewn slopes at Bernkastel on the middle Mosel – impossible not to taste a slatey minerality in this region's delicate Rieslings.*

BELOW *Rheingau, looking south (towards the Nahe) over the river Rhein from the Rüdesheimer Berg. Riesling is at its most aristocratic here.*

Riesling is by nature a high-yielding variety and, given its head in a rich soil and warm location, it ripens rapidly and abundantly, diluting both its natural acidity and potential savour. But on poor, stony soil, in a cool climate, its yield is curbed, its acidity preserved; and, where sufficient sunshine permits a long ripening period, it develops intense yet subtle flavours. Such favoured sites are to be found primarily in Germany, Austria, Alsace and Australia, and, in tiny quantities, in New Zealand and the USA.

Riesling needs time, first on the vine, then in the bottle, unlike Chardonnay, which displays its charms early. Fine Riesling, especially if completely dry, can taste plain and hard when young, but time allows it to mellow in texture and blossom in bouquet with a most seductive combination of floral, honeyed and, surprisingly, petroleum-related aromas. Sweeter wines can be delicious at almost any age. One of its most intriguing and attractive features is a transparency of flavour which seems to allow the geology* of the vineyard to infiltrate your senses.

Germany's quality wine 'classification' (Qualitätswein mit Prädikat, or QmP) is largely based on the natural ripeness of the grape, and indicated by various Prädikat ('praiseworthy' attributes), which are, generally, in rising order of sweetness: Kabinett (off-dry to medium-dry), Spätlese (medium-dry to medium-sweet), Auslese (medium-sweet to sweet), Beerenauslese (BA), Trockenbeerenauslese (TBA) and Eiswein. BA and TBA are made from individually picked, nobly rotten* grapes – shrivelled, raisin-like for TBA; Eiswein from frozen grapes without noble rot.

Eiswein, TBA and BA are all intensely sweet, rare and expensive. There is a correlation between sweetness and quality, because the sunniest spots of the vineyard will allow the grape to ripen and concentrate best. But there are wonderful wines at every sweetness* level. Individual producers are your guide to quality.

The cream of German Rieslings comes from Mosel-Saar-Ruwer (**Mosel** for short), the Pfalz, the Rheingau, the Nahe and Rheinhessen. And though the current fashion is to make an increasing proportion of dry (*trocken*) wine, the most appealing wines, for me at least, are the

ABOVE *France, Alsace. The tiny vineyard of Clos Ste-Hune, just below the church in Hunawihr. The clay and limestone soils here make the region's top dry Riesling. By no means Alsace's strongest or most intense example, this is instead a wine of surprising delicacy, but exceptional aromatic complexity and length, especially after ten years or so in bottle. The wait is well rewarded!*

off-dry to sweet wines: Kabinett, Spätlese and Auslese. These have an alcoholic lightness (7.5–9.5%) and an unrivalled balance between fresh, ripe fruit and teasing acidity – delicious on its own! Nowhere is this better illustrated than from the best slate-strewn slopes of the tortuously winding River Mosel, which grows nearly one-third of Germany's Riesling.

The most exquisitely delineated, taut and porcelain-fine wines are produced along the River Saar (Egon Müller, Schloss Saarstein, Von Kesselstatt) but they do need a warm vintage. The 'middle-Mosel' wines, around Bernkastel, are softer, a little easier in the mouth, but so juicy (J J Prüm, Rheinhold Haart, J Wegeler, Fritz Haag, Ernst Loosen, M F Richter, and Heymann-Löwenstein on the 'lower-Mosel'). And the Ruwer wines lie somewhere between in style (Von Schubert, Karthäuserhof). Good examples have that exquisite combination of zest and succulence that so seduces in a crisp, green apple or juicily ripe peach. All are mineral-backed to some degree. The best drink well young* and age beautifully too.

Pfalz wines, from heavier soils and a warmer climate, typically have more weight and breadth, often with a marked earthiness and apparent spice. Many of Germany's top dry Rieslings, deep and strong (Koehler-Ruprecht, Bürklin-Wolf), come from the Pfalz and, indeed, from Franken (Juliusspital, Hans Wirsching).

To the north of the Pfalz, **Rheinhessen** (Gunderloch, Keller, St-Anthony) produces a gentler, more pliant style overall, with particularly fine wines from along the Rhein near Nierstein.

Rheingau, when on form (it is currently very uneven) is the most elegant, gracefully poised middleweight expression of great medium-sweet to sweet Riesling (Johannishof, J Wegeler, Leitz). Along with beautifully proportioned, sappy dry wines (Künstler, Robert Weil, Becker, Breuer).

The **Nahe** combines some of the cut of the Mosel with the elegance of the Rheingau (Diel, Dönnhof, Schönleber). Ideally, compare Kabinett, Spätlese and Auslese from the same producer and vintage, and then the same Prädikat and vintage, but from different producers or regions.

Austria's Wachau region is on the banks of the Danube between Krems and Melk, northwest of Vienna. Here cool nights, sunny days and rocky valley slopes produce Austria's raciest Rieslings (Hirtzberger, Högl, FX Pichler, Prager, S Donabaum, Knoll and Nikolaihof). These are firm, dry and minerally, and, at *Smaragd* level, between good Alsace and fine German *trocken* in style. They come in three categories: *Steinfeder* (11% alcohol maximum), *Federspiel* (12% maximum) and *Smaragd* (12.5%

RIGHT *Spitz, Austria: one of numerous pretty villages along the Danube, in the Wachau region. Here stony terraces and hot summers make for Austria's raciest dry Rieslings. In terms of style you might think of them as Alsace with a German accent.*

Top wines to taste

Alsace, France
Clos Ste-Hune (Trimbach)
Vendange Tardive (Hugel)

Mosel-Saar-Ruwer, Germany
Wehlener Sonnenuhr
Spätlese/Auslese (J J Prüm)
Scharzhofberger Auslese
(Egon Müller)

BELOW *Australia: Orlando's Barossa Hills 'Steingarten' vines make Australia's finest dry Riesling; a distinguished, long and graceful tribute to its German inspiration.*

minimum). Weighty *Smaragds* tend to grab the lion's share of the limelight, but they can be a bit potent in hot years, and then I often prefer the fresher, more delicate balance of *Federspiel* or *Steinfeder*. In general, these drink younger, and mature more rapidly than their dry German or Alsace counterparts.

The best **Alsace** Rieslings come from the southern half of the region, the Haut-Rhin. They vary from the steely, bone-dry majority at one end, to a few intensely sweet, noble-rot-affected Sélection de Grains Nobles (SGN) wines at the other. There are also a few confusingly off-dry to sweet, late-harvest Vendange Tardive (VT) wines in between. Confusing, because there is absolutely no indication as to the enormously variable sweetness level on the label; utterly unhelpful to the customer! The two large merchant-growers Trimbach (taut, restrained) and Hugel (broader, more generous) make excellent examples in contrasting styles, with price a reliable guide to quality. Other benchmark growers are Faller, Deiss, Meyer-Fonné, Blanck and Zind-Humbrecht.

Australian Rieslings are quite different in style from the European model, and none the worse for that. They are predominantly dry, and almost all have a telltale lime scent when young, with subtle, fresh-toast characters (and occasionally a touch of kerosene) as they age. Characteristically, the most successful come

from Australia's coolest locations: Clare (Grosset, Tim Knappstein, Mitchell), Eden Valley (Chapel Hill, St Hallett's) and Adelaide Hills (Yalumba's 'Heggies' – a regular, delicate favourite – and Henschke) in South Australia. And Mount Barker (Goundry, Plantagenet, Howard Park) in Western Australia. Plus two rarities from Victoria: a precise, floral, alpine beauty from Delatite, and the first Australian Riesling to show me how gracefully they can age – a 1976 Brown Bros King Valley wine, under both cork and Stelvin screw cap! This was a miracle of complex, polished, honeyed freshness at 16 years of age. There is, in fact, a good case for saying that bottle-aged, dry Riesling is Australia's finest white. For a quality range, compare Penfold's Bin 202, Penfold's Eden Valley Reserve and a Grosset, Plantagenet or Steingarten example.

New Zealand makes delicious late-harvest, botrytis* Rieslings: intensely sweet, but lemon fresh, mainly from Marlborough (Cloudy Bay, Wairau River, Jackson Estate, Merlen), but also from North Island (Villa Maria, Martinborough, Sacred Hill). And the potential is clearly there for fine, juicily vivid dry wines (Corban's Stoneleigh, Kim Crawford, Steve Smith's Craggy Range). **Canada** too, is the source of a few fine 'Icewine' Rieslings, as is **Washington State,** whilst **California** produces a handful of botrytis 'stickies' (Château St Jean).

sauvignon blanc

The essence of Sauvignon Blanc is freshness, and quintessential Sauvignon is from cool-climate vineyards. In its purest form – unoaked from France's Loire Valley or New Zealand's South Island – it combines the thirst-quenching fruit vitality of lime cordial with the most bracingly tonic aromas of any grape variety.

Sauvignon Blanc should be as rousing to the palate as peppermint, and as refreshing to the nostrils as the wilderness and greenery suggested in the origins of its French name: *sauvage* – wild. For this is, by a long way, what the grape does best. Sauvignon is a demanding grape for the winemaker, being particularly sensitive to the ideal moment for picking and also prone to excess yield*. Underripe it is tart, vegetal and lacking in aroma; overripe it loses its freshness, definition and intensity. Overcropped and its wines are simply mean, acid and empty. But seek out the best and they are unforgettably vivid.

Unoaked Sauvignon
Until very recently the Central Vineyards of the mid to lower reaches of the **Loire** in **France** could claim to be Sauvignon's most natural home, if not its most reliable source. Here,

RIGHT *Hilltop town of Sancerre in the Loire, France. Flint and limestone soils here give its Sauvignon wines their fine scent and minerality.*

in Sancerre, Pouilly-Fumé and Menetou-Salon, its aromas are the keenest, sharpest examples of its 'fresh-green', herbaceous side: gooseberry, nettles, blackcurrants, redcurrants, grass; sometimes tinned asparagus or musk. And occasionally, the sort of 'catty' pungency left by a territorial tom. These aromas are often underlain by a chalky, stony, or smoky (whence *fumé*) impression from the flint and limestone soils. This distinguishes them from their New Zealand and South African counterparts. The Loire's best Sauvignons have an excitingly crisp acidity, and demonstrate perfectly what is meant by an 'aromatic'* wine for they leave your mouth suffused with the aromas described. As such they also make deliciously

BELOW *Montana's Brancott Estate, Marlborough, New Zealand; original source of their brisk, juicy Sauvignons.*

Sauvignon Blanc at a glance

Alcohol: medium to medium-full.
Acid: high.
Aroma characteristics: strongly aromatic.
Cool-climate/less ripe fruit: grassy, herbaceous; nettles, gooseberry, blackcurrant leaf.
Warmer-climate/riper fruit: above, along with citrus and tropical fruit; fig, guava, passion-fruit.
Styles: the vast majority to drink young and fresh; a very few oaked top wines will age well.
• unoaked, dry, aromatic.
• oaked, rich/dry, complex.
• a few intensely sweet wines with botrytis.

BELOW *Mulderbosch in Stellenbosch, South Africa; where mountain slopes plus meticulous viticulture and winemaking produce world-class Sauvignons.*

appetising apéritif wines. Particularly good Sancerres are made by Vacheron, Lucien Crochet, Henri Bourgeois, Alphonse Mellot, and Paul & Francis Cottat (dense, age-worthy wines from the heavier clayey soil in Chavignol). Menetou-Salon often provides equally fine, scented examples in a more restrained, less muscular style. Two personal favourites here are Henri Pellé (Clos des Blanchais) and Jean-Max Roger. Pouilly-Fumé is often rather richer and broader than Sancerre, possibly a little more supple and polished: Château de Tracy, Jean-Claude Châtelain, Pascal Jolivet and de Ladoucette would give you a good idea of what I mean. Reuilly and Quincy are lighter and slighter in expression, and are the two other wine villages worth exploring.

Touraine, to the west of the Central Vineyards, produces the generically named Sauvignon de Touraine. These wines are lesser examples of the grape, limited in both flavour and aroma; at best they are fresh, at worst (too often?) thin and pinched from high yields.

Sauvignon's most northerly French outpost is at **St-Bris**, close to Chablis, making crisp, piquantly nettly wines.

Bordeaux's unoaked Sauvignons, mostly from the Entre-Deux-Mers and Bergerac, are much better than they used to be, though the warmer climate means they are softer and more muted in their Sauvignon character. From **Austria**, Styria is the most often mentioned source, but there are surprisingly mouthwatering wines from further north: Römerhof in Burgenland, Sonnhof from Langenlois. Light, crisp, herbal but inexpensive Sauvignons come from Sopron in **Hungary**. Pure, fresh and aromatic examples come from northeastern **Italy**: from Lageder in Alto Adige, and from numerous quality growers in the Collio region on the border with Slovenia.

Marlborough in **New Zealand**'s South Island might now justifiably lay claim to being Sauvignon's true homeland. This is all the more remarkable for the fact that Sauvignon Blanc was first planted there by Montana as recently as 1973! Yet today its wines are frequently touchstones for the grape, with the added advantage of being much more reliable than their Loire counterparts. Marlborough's cool but luminous climate and stony soils produce wines with a similar acidity to those from the Loire; but they are less dry to taste, with fatter, riper fruit, and a projection of Sauvignon aromas so forceful as to be close to caricature. To smell there is gooseberry, yes, often capsicum too, and a strong citrus and tropical-fruit accent. The two great originals, Montana (at the less expensive end) and Cloudy Bay (at the other) still provide excellent examples of Marlborough's quality span. The Villa Maria range – reserve wines especially – Jackson Estate and Lawsons

Dry Hills are also regularly amongst the best. Softer, peachier Sauvignons come from the somewhat warmer climes of Martinborough, Hawke's Bay and Gisborne in North Island. Whilst much of **South Africa's** Sauvignon Blanc is still thin and bland, its finest wines should cause some nail-biting in both France and New Zealand. Mulderbosch, from the warmer Stellenbosch region, has the rich yet vibrant juiciness of a top Marlborough, if less stridently so. Buitenvervachting and Steenberg, from the cooler Constantia area south of Cape Town, are lighter, crisper, drier; closer to the Pouilly-Fumé or Menetou-Salon model. All are world-class wines, unmistakably, emphatically Sauvignon Blanc.

Most vineyards in **Australia** are too warm to produce quality Sauvignon Blanc, but where fruit is sourced from cooler areas, it is increasingly successful. Delatite's lively, grassy medium-weight Sauvignon from the Yarra Valley; Shaw & Smith's fragrant, flavoury benchmark wine from the Adelaide Hills; Katnook's succulent, weighty Coonawarra.

Chile also struggles with this grape, mainly because the vast majority of its so-called Sauvignon Blanc is in fact the almost aromatically neutral Sauvignon Vert. For its promise, though, look to Casablanca, Santa Rita, Villard and Doña Javiera.

Oaked Sauvignon

In the cooler growing areas, new oak is rarely used for Sauvignon Blanc wines as it masks those exhilaratingly pure, fresh aromas and flavours. Nevertheless, a limited number of Sauvignon-based wines are successfully barrel-fermented* and aged. Didier Dageneau's austere, concentrated Pouilly-Fumés, their oak barely perceptible, are impressive examples from the **Loire**. Hunter and Vavasour are stylishly oaked **New Zealand** Sauvignon Blancs.

Pessac-Léognan in Bordeaux produces increasingly good oaked, Sauvignon-based wines. They are taut, yet softer than those from the Loire, fainter in their Sauvignon

aromas, with more of the Graves *terroir* 'stoniness' in their flavour. Look for Smith-Haut-Lafitte and Couhins-Lurton (both 100 per cent Sauvignon) and La Louvière. As with many oaked Sauvignons, La Louvière is blended with a small amount of Semillon, softening the Sauvignon edge, making it a bit broader and rounder, and more honeyed in maturity. In contrast to unwooded Sauvignons, oaked versions improve with bottle-age, the very finest white Graves (*see* margin box) for a decade and more.

A few expensive oaked Sauvignons are emerging from **Italy**, fine wines rather than fine Sauvignons. Terrabianca's Ortaglia from Tuscany, and Angelo Gaja's Alteni di Brassica from Piedmont – an outstandingly elegant, cedary, Pessac-Léognan lookalike.

If much of **California's** Sauvignon Blanc (often called Fumé Blanc, oaked or not) was once dreary, alcoholic and unrecognisable as Sauvignon – at least to a European palate – this is less the case today. Whilst much remains hefty and overwooded, fruit from cooler areas and a search for something more aromatically Sauvignon has resulted in some attractively individual, if still fairly weighty, expressions of the grape. Rodney Strong and St-Supéry (at the cheaper, unoaked end), Matanzas Creek, Spottswoode and Mondavi are regularly good examples.

ABOVE *Casablanca, Chile; where, like in California, the valley floor vineyards such as these are cooled by early morning mist* from the cold Pacific Ocean, making for crisper, more aromatic Chilean white wines.*

Top wines to taste

Loire, France
Pouilly-Fumé Silex (Didier Dageneau)

Bordeaux, France
Domaine de Chevalier Blanc (70/30% Sauv/Sem)

Pavillon Blanc de Château Margaux (100% Sauv)

*See also

aromatic **14**
barrel-fermented **40,48**
morning mist *35*
tastings 2,3 **126,130**
yield **14,36-7**

semillon

Semillon, like Riesling and Chenin Blanc, makes wines from completely dry to lusciously sweet. Like them, its purest dry versions can seem remarkably plain when young, and like them too, its best wines, dry or sweet, develop into great beauties given sufficient bottle-age.

Semillon has two uncontested centres of excellence on opposite sides of the globe. They make wines that are as complete a contrast in style as you could imagine: light, lean, unoaked and bone-dry at one extreme; weighty, luscious, barrel-fermented and intensely sweet at the other. The first hails from the Lower Hunter Valley, 60 miles (100km) north of Sydney, Australia; the second from Sauternes, 20 miles (32km) southeast of Bordeaux, France.

Outside France and Australia, small pockets of quality Semillon, or Semillon blends, are produced in New Zealand (Selaks is a splendid Sauvignon/Semillon blend), South Africa (Steenberg), Chile, California (Meritage – Bordeaux-style – blends), America's Pacific Northwest and even Canada. In a warm, even moderate, climate, Semillon's natural inclination is to produce fairly 'fat' wines, high in alcohol, low in acidity. For this reason, good-quality, pure Semillon wines are rare, and in many cases, for dry and sweet wines, it is blended with Sauvignon Blanc, benefiting from the latter's aromatic input as well as from its acid brace.

Australia makes three broadly different styles of Semillon-based wines: from the Hunter Valley, South Australia and Western Australia. The **Hunter Valley** wines are made from early picked grapes low in alcohol (typically 10–11.5%) and firmish in acid as a result, and without new oak or malolactic fermentation. When young, they are pale, neutral in aroma, lemony-hard and

RIGHT Château Climens in Sauternes, Bordeaux. Climens is in the commune of Barsac, where all the sweet wines may call themselves Sauternes too; consumers know that name better. It is one of the few properties here that makes its wine from 100 per cent Semillon; Doisy-Daëne is another. Climens is usually considered to be second only to Château d'Yquem in quality.

plain to taste. Ten years in bottle transforms them into waxy, smooth, direct-flavoured wines, with penetrating toast and honey bouquets, and a quite misleading suggestion of oak (Lindemans, McWilliams Mount Pleasant, Tyrrells Vat 1, Rothbury, Cassegrain).

Barossa Valley examples from South Australia are fuller (13+% alcohol), broader, richer wines, generally barrel-fermented (Rockford, Mitchell, St Hallett, Henschke). They are accessible earlier and they don't age with quite the same distinction as the best Hunters. Nonetheless, 'bottle-age will massage this into a slippery-soft yellow wine that invites itself to dinner', as Rockford's back label puts it. Just so!

Western Australia's cooler-climate wines are also usually barrel-fermented*, and tend towards Sauvignon Blanc in aroma (grass, asparagus, green peas), even when pure Semillon (Vasse Felix, Sandstone). But many are blended with Sauvignon Blanc, very sucessfully, to produce a riper Graves style, without the Graves stoniness (Amberley, Cullens, Cape Mentelle).

With the exception of a few expensive top wines, the majority of **Bordeaux**'s best dry white **Graves** have much more Sauvignon Blanc than Semillon in their blend (*see* p67). This, the cooler climate and the gravelly soil* (whence 'Graves'), give them a lighter, firmer structure, and a drier, stone-tinged flavour. Good, high-Semillon-content wines to look for are Clos Floridène and Château Chantegrive. Bordeaux's sweet wines, however, are predominantly Semillon, typically 80 per cent, the balance being Sauvignon Blanc, and occasionally a little Muscadelle. The wines are made as far as possible (or as far as economical in the case of less expensive wines) from nobly rotten* grapes. **Sauternes** are naturally luscious. Sweetness, richness and unctuosity are part of their nature, but, of course, they need enough acidity to define the flavours and prevent the wines tasting flabby. By comparison, similarly sweet Chenins from the Loire, for example, have noticeably more acid tension. And Sauternes' balance of alcohol* is at least as crucial as acidity: too much for the level of sugar (or concentration of flavour) and the wines will seem hot or hard, too little and they appear over soft or cloying.

Received perception is that Sauternes are richer than Barsacs, but quality differences of overall harmony, complexity and length are perhaps easier to perceive than stylistic ones. Compare a generic Sauternes with one from a good property (Doisy-Daëne – pure Semillon; Nairac, Guiraud, Bastor-Lamontagne, Sigalas-Rabaud). You could include a wine from Cérons, Loupiac, Ste-Croix-du-Mont, Monbazillac or Saussignac, all of which make a similar, but less intense style. All these wines are delicious when young – their fresh, primary fruit to the fore. As they age, the bouquet is more redolent of wax, musk, wet wool or lanolin (the wool oil base for polishes and ointments), and they then develop more marmalade, barley sugar and caramel tastes, and a more liqueur-like texture.

Australia's botrytised Semillons come mainly from Griffith in **New South Wales**. Incredibly sweet, unctuous, marmalade and raisin-flavoured wines (De Bortoli, Cranswick, J J McWilliam).

*See also

balance of alcohol **21,42**
barrel-fermented **40,48**
gravelly soil **84**
nobly rotten grapes *43*

chenin blanc

Top wines to taste

Loire Valley, France
Vouvray Le Mont (Huët)
Savennières Coulée de
Serrant (Joly)

Chenin Blanc makes an exceptionally wide range of wine styles, from searingly dry, through medium-sweet, to ravishingly liquorous, botrytis-affected essence. In this respect it resembles Riesling; but Chenin is also the base for a great deal of good sparkling wine.

BELOW *Loire Valley: Saumur's splendid castle and bridge in the evening light. Saumur is best known for its fine Chenin-based sparkling wines, especially its Crémant de Loire, as well as the light, succulently juicy Saumur-Champigny red.*

Chenin Blanc's home is the Loire region in France, more specifically the River Loire's broad, languid lower reaches in the sub-regions of Anjou and Touraine. And Chenin's heart is its natural acidity, a feature that endears it to the makers of both sweet and sparkling wine, as well as to warm-climate winemakers who value the acidity level it retains at full ripeness – in South Africa, California's Central Valley or in Argentina, for example. Acidity becomes a less endearing feature in a cooler climate like that of the Loire, when high yields and/or poor weather result in a meanness of flavour. And if mean acidity can be successfully masked by residual sugar (as in Germany), nothing can mask the pronounced pungency and stink from excessive sulphur, used to prevent off-dry or sweet wines from possible refermentation in

bottle. This consequence of sloppy winemaking, if less common than it once was, has turned many people away from Loire Chenin for good. More's the pity, as the grape's acidity also allows the best Chenin Blancs to improve beautifully over many years.

A rough pattern to this grape variety in the **Loire** might be exemplified by the principal wines from **Anjou**: dry Savennières, dryish to sweet Coteaux du Layon and Coteaux de l'Aubance on the one hand; and those from **Touraine** on the other: dry Jasnières, dry to sweet Vouvray and Montlouis, with the finely sparkling wines of Saumur in between. Basic Anjou Blanc is variable, but good examples are dry to off-dry, fresh, straightforward, green-appley wines. **Savennières** is rare, but strikingly individual: meagre in cold years, but otherwise

a full-bodied, powerful, vigorously bone-dry wine full of a peppery minerality from its volcanic soils. Its vitality when young can be searingly austere, but its maturity at ten years and more is a long, dry, grand, mouth-coating splendour (Joly, Château de Chamboureau, Domaine des Baumards).

South of the River Loire, **Coteaux du Layon** and **Coteaux de l'Aubance** vary from off-dry (*demi-sec*) to sweet (*moelleux*). **Quarts de Chaume** (minerality and race) and **Bonnezeaux** (luscious above all) are two Grand Cru enclaves within Coteaux du Layon, producing, potentially, the sweetest, most complex and refined of these wines. (*Moelle* in French means 'bone marrow', and the description *moelleux* suggests both its sweetness of flavour as well as its rich consistency of texture.) The best wines here are affected by noble rot, and the degree of sweetness and spicy complexity will vary according to the amount involved. Chenin Blanc's high acidity and a general lack of new oak (though its use, regrettably perhaps, is increasing) means there is a freshness and grapiness to the wines, which distinguishes them from their Sauternes counterparts. (Tasting Sauternes next to sweet Coteaux du Layon or Vouvray is always an illuminating style comparison.) The sweeter these wines are, the more raisiny and liqueur-like they taste, and the best have a concentrated, yet finely drawn, thread of sweetness which makes sense of the allusion to bone marrow (Patrick Baudouin, Château de Fèsles, Yves Soulez, Domaine des Forges, Domaine du Petit Métris).

Vouvray and **Montlouis** (generally a slighter version of Vouvray), from lighter, limestone soils, as opposed to schist in Coteaux du Layon, are more restrained, generally less rich and powerful wines for a given style, than those from Anjou. Unoaked here, they have more emphasis on the faint bitterness of quince, and on an apple, lemon and honey purity. Both dry and sweet wines age with extraordinary grace to become keen, delicate, ethereal wines, often with some of the wax, musk and lanolin characteristics of mature

ABOVE *Rural Loire, upstream from Saumur, at La Croix Blanche in Vouvray. Chenin planted in Vouvray is on lighter soils than those in Anjou, and its still wines have less power, spice, fire, and more restraint. Completely oak free here, they age beautifully and with great purity.*

Riesling and Semillon (Huët, Domaine Foreau, Château Gaudrelle, Brédif, Bourillon d'Orléans). Gently honeyed, *demi-sec* Vouvray has a combination of restraint and riverine freshness that seems to make it a natural partner for freshwater fish in a *beurre blanc* or light, lemon-cream sauce. It makes a good apéritif too, as does sparkling Vouvray, which can be particularly fine-textured and refreshing (Domaine Foreau).

In **South Africa** Chenin Blanc is also known as Steen and accounts for nearly one-third of the country's vines, making, as in the Loire, every style of wine, from bone-dry to sweet and botrytised to sparkling. The great bulk, though, is well-made dry to off-dry wine: light, clean, appley, crisp and fresh. A few LH (Late Harvest) wines are made, in a medium-sweet style; even rarer are SLH (Special Late Harvest, similar to German Auslese) and NLH (Noble Late Harvest) wines. Almost unique, and the finest by a long way, is the intensely sweet NLH Nederburg Edelkeur.

Chenin Blanc is not rare in **California**. However, most Chenin comes from the **Central Valley**, where it goes to make jug wine, whose appealing freshness and fruit are usually blunted by residual sugar. Small quantities of off-dry, Loire-style and the occasional dry Chenin are also made. Australia, too, makes a small amount of Chenin table wine, as does **New Zealand**, where three North Island Chenin sources stand out: Collards' crisply fruity dry wine, Millton's classy, classic, Loire-style dry and sweet versions, and Esk Valley's Vouvray-like dry, reserve Chenin.

BELOW *Chenin grapes in a Bonnezeaux vineyard on the banks of the River Layon. In late September they are just starting to turn nobly rotten.*

Chenin Blanc at a glance

Alcohol: medium to high.
Acid: high.
Aroma characteristics: can be wet-wool pungent. *Cool-climate/less ripe fruit:* green apple, lemon, waxy. *Warm-climate/riper fruit:* grapey, ripe apple, honey, lemon, quince, apricot.
Bottle age bouquet: better quality, dry or sweet, improve greatly with bottle age: quince, honey, wax, musk, lanolin. *and with botrytis:* raisin, marzipan, vegetal, spice.
Styles:
• unoaked, light, vivid, bone-dry to sweet.
• unoaked, powerful, dry, vigorous, spicy.
• intensely sweet, with botrytis, and now occasionally oaked.

gewurztraminer

Gewurztraminer is a particularly aromatic grape that has a special appeal to beginners in wine because, in good examples, its perfumed aromas and extrovert style are instantly recognisable. This is no shy wallflower of a wine, but a striking, unmistakably showy tropical bloom.

Gewurztraminer at a glance

Alcohol: high.
Acid: low.
Aroma characteristics: pronounced, aromatic. *Cool-climate/less ripe fruit:* lightly floral, delicate, lavender scented. *Warmer-climate/riper fruit:* perfumed, rose petals, tinned lychees, Turkish delight, spiciness; *and with botrytis:* honey, raisin, musk, vegetal character.
Styles: most are to drink young; almost never aged in new oak.
- light, dry, fresh, floral.
- full, rich, heady, off-dry, unctuous and aromatic.
- medium-sweet to sweet, sometimes with botrytis.

Gewurztraminer is grown widely round the world, if not in great quantity; for it is a tricky grape to grow, and, in spite of its obvious appeal in successful examples, well-balanced Gewurztraminer is not easy to achieve. Its naturally high alcohol and low acidity mean that 'it runs to fat' all too easily. For this reason it is unhappy in warm climates* where optimum sugar and acid levels are likely to be reached well before enough flavour and its all important fragrance have developed fully.

Alsace has the greatest concentration of Gewurztraminer, and remains the model for all its possible styles, from dry to raisiny sweet.

The grape's pinkish skin often makes for a deep-yellow wine; its aroma is a mixture of rose petals, tinned lychees, musk, Turkish delight, and its flavour is typically off-dry, perfumed, and gently spicy (*Gewürz* means 'spice' in German). Low acid and high alcohol make for a mouth-coating texture which often teeters precariously between the seductively unctuous and the sluggish. But when perfectly balanced, it is an impressively scented, all-round heady combination. Sweeter wines, called Vendange Tardive (VT) and Sélection de Grains Nobles (SGN), are made from riper grapes with higher minimum sugar levels – SGN from botrytised grapes*. But as there are no legal maximum alcohol levels or minimum residual sugar requirements, the styles are infuriatingly difficult to define (Trimbach, Hugel, Deiss, Faller, Mann, Willm).

Germany (Baden and the Pfalz especially), Austria (Styria), Switzerland, Italy (Alto Adige), Spain and Hungary make Gewurztraminer, in most cases as something of a speciality. In the New World, California (Anderson and Russian River Valleys), Washington, Oregon, Australia (Tasmania, Victoria), New Zealand and Chile (Bío-Bío) all produce good examples in cooler regions, but again in very limited quantities.

LEFT *Beblenheim, Alsace. The typical lie of Haut-Rhin vineyards: lower eastern slopes of the Vosges mountains provide ideal exposure for the vines, whilst the mountain bulk behind protects them from Atlantic weatherfronts.*

other white grapes

Constraints of space preclude a more extensive listing of all the following grapes, a number of which might fairly be considered as 'major': Muscat, Viognier, Pinot Gris, for example. A few of the pages have something of a national feel to them, but for a more precise listing, consult the index.

Viognier

Viognier is a rare grape even in its Northern Rhône home, **Condrieu**. Like Gewurztraminer, its wines are high in alcohol, low in acidity, with a rich silkiness of texture. But its fine aroma derives more from the fruit basket (peach and apricot) than the scent bottle. Again, like Gewurztraminer, it is a wine to drink young. It became fashionable in the 1990s and is increasingly, and successfully, being grown in **Languedoc-Roussillon** in France, and in **California** and **Australia**. Its naturally low yields, and the need for it to be really ripe to achieve its true perfume and viscosity, mean it can never be inexpensive. Cheap Viogniers seem to me to be pointless, just a cashing-in on the name. Look for Georges Vernay, Chapoutier, Pierre Gaillard in the Northern Rhône. And

Phelps, Alban, Fetzer's Bonterra in California. Yalumba make a speciality Viognier in Australia.

Pinot Gris

Pinot Gris is a grape with multiple names and guises, grown mainly in Europe, but also in Oregon, USA. Individual characteristics vary according to location, climate, and when it is picked. As Pinot Gris or Tokay Pinot Gris, its most impressive styles come from **Alsace**, where it ranges from dry (mostly) to Vendange Tardive sweet. Good examples have some of Gewurztraminer's alcoholic weight (but not its distinctive scent), along with considerable density of flavour (which means it can support some new oak*). Without having a noticeable acidity, it can, nonetheless, have a marked sinew to it. In **Germany**, lively, dry styles

BELOW LEFT *Terraced vineyards above Condrieu in the Northern Rhône, with the river just visible in the background. Condrieu's soft, scented, peachy but fulsome wines are the model for the Viognier grape around the globe.*

*See also

botrytised grapes **43**
new oak **40,48**
tasting 1 gewurz **122**
warm climate **34-7**

from Baden are called Grauburgunder, and from the Pfalz, richer, often sweet wines are named Ruländer, as they are in Austria. Most of **Italy's** Pinot Grigio is an early picked, crisp, if neutral, style from Friuli, whereas **Switzerland's** Malvoisie from the Valais is often a rich, classy, scented wine. **Hungary's** Szürkebarát, is generally softish, but there are broad, dry, sappy wines from Lake Balaton. And **Oregon** produces the grape's spectrum: from light and sharp, through soft and bland, to firm and sinewy.

Muscat

Muscat* is a large family of grapes with a bewildering list of names. The most important ones for wine are Muscat de Frontignan or Muscat Blanc à Petits Grains, and Muscat d'Alexandrie. Its range of wine styles varies from dry to intensely sweet, from low-alcohol sparklers, to weighty, fortified dessert wines.

The very essence of the Muscat grape is its remarkable perfume: orange blossom, or *Philadelphus*, in the garden, a scent which is enhanced by the grapey sweetness of residual sugars. For this reason, the best Muscat is sweet, and most of its wines are more or less refined, more or less scented, and more or less weighty variations on this theme. Muscat de Frontignan makes the finest wines: **Northern Italy's** gossamer-light, barely sparkling, super-fine Moscato d'Asti (5% alcohol) and the slightly fuller (7.5%) Asti Spumante; as well as the rare, rose-petal fragrant Rosen- and Golden-muskatellers from the Alto Adige. It is also the grape for **France's** pearly Clairette de Die Tradition, and for the majority of southern France's Vins Doux Naturels (sweet, fortified wines of 15.5% alcohol), such as Muscat de Beaumes-de-Venise, Muscat de Lunel, Muscat de Frontignan and Muscat de Mireval.

Similar to these are the **Greek Island** originals from Samos, Lemnos, Patras and Cephalonia. The Brown Muscat variation is behind **Australia's** great liqueur Muscats (*see* margin p75); the Black and Orange (and orange-scented) varieties behind Andrew Quady's fine **California** wines. Finally, though most **South African** Muscat is the Alexandria variety (called Hanepoot), the sweet, thick, unfortified Vin de Constance is made from Muscat de Frontignan (called Muscadel!).

The somewhat coarser tasting, more raisiny Muscat d'Alexandrie makes **France's** Muscat de Rivesaltes, and may contribute to Banyuls and Maury (*see* p103). Moscatel de Valencia and the fortified Málaga (of **Spain**), Moscatel de Setúbal (of **Portugal**), and Bukkuram (of Pantelleria, **Italy**) are also based on this grape.

RIGHT *Sometimes vineyards just catch one's eye. For reasons that have nothing in particular to do with wine or grape varieties; like the pretty purple weed here, known as Patterson's Curse, under vines back-lit by the early morning sun in Mudgee, Australia.*

Muscadelle

No relation to Muscat, Muscadelle has, as it happens, a faintly 'musky' aroma. Blended, it makes plain, dry white in **Bordeaux**'s Entre-Deux-Mers, as well as forming a very small proportion of some Sauternes. However, it is a star in **Australia**, where it makes spectacularly fine liqueur 'Tokay' in Rutherglen, Victoria. These are similar to the liqueur Muscats, but with less grapiness and more suggestions of malt, lapsang tea and burnt caramel.

Petit Manseng, Gros Manseng

Characterful **South West France** grapes, from the Pyrenees foothills. The finer Petit Manseng is used for the sweet, *moelleux*, wines. Dry wines from Pacherenc du Vic-Bilh are sappy, zesty and compact, with an aroma of wax, ripe peach and dried fruit. Many are made by Madiran producers (Laffitte-Teston, Berthoumieu). The best sweet Jurançons, from shrivelled* rather than nobly rotten grapes (no fog available!), are fresh, clear, grapily honeyed and most individual wines (Domaine Cauhapé, Charles Hours).

Pinot Blanc (Pinot Bianco, Weissburgunder)

Widely grown, making (mostly) full, round, green-apple fresh, uncomplicatedly* pleasing wines in Alsace, northeast Italy, the Pfalz and Baden in Germany; along with Canada's British Columbia amongst others, and the occasional intensely sweet, nobly rotten wines in Austria. Most attempts to oak-age* seem, to me, to be sterile in effect, merely masking the grape's appealing simplicity and direct fruit quality.

Aligoté

A naturally acid grape, grown patchily throughout **Burgundy,** from St-Bris in the north to Mâcon in the south, with Bouzeron a notable location. It is usually pretty tart, but the best old-vine, low-yield wines have an attractively bracing quality and, with a touch of oak, can occasionally taste like a good, taut village wine from the Côte de Beaune (Coche-Dury, J-H Goisot).

Muscadet (Melon de Bourgogne)

This grape has adopted the name of its only wine: Muscadet, from Nantes in the Loire. Most is very ordinary, light, dry wine. Seek out those from the heart of the region, Sèvre et Maine, and bottled *sur lie* – straight off their lees. These have a very dry, rather than sharp, gently yeasty flavour with a touch of CO_2 prickle*; and they make a great deal of vinous sense with shellfish (Métaireau, Sauvion).

Silvaner (Sylvaner in Alsace)

Medium-bodied, high-acid and plain-flavoured would sum up the bulk of Silvaner. In the Bas-Rhin of **Alsace** it is fullish, but still sharp, and in Italy's **Alto Adige** it is light and crisp – both good bistro jug wines. As 'Johannisberg' in **Switzerland** though, it can be surprisingly rich, yet without heaviness. But it is at its vigorous best in **Franken** in Germany. There is a unique sap and substance to Silvaner here, along with a refreshingly stiff acidity. Typically the wines are broad, dry, earthy, tenacious; yet freshly satisfying too, and the best have both elegance and class. In a Franconian *weinstube* one wet winter evening I had the following: bratwurst, sauerkraut, caraway-seed bread and cellar-cool young Silvaner – simple but incomparable! (Juliusspital, Wirsching, Castell.)

ABOVE *Rutherglen, Victoria in Australia. North Eastern Victoria makes mahogany hued, fortified liqueur Muscats that reek of caramel and raisins, are intensely sweet, liqueur smooth and extraordinarily fine considering their sugar concentration. They age for many years in large old wooden barrels, like these at Chambers winery, before being blended to different quality levels. Other names to look for are Morris, Stanton & Killeen and Baileys.*

*See also

CO_2 prickle **22**

muscat tasting *153*

oak-age **48**

shrivelled grapes **43**

uncomplicated & food **160**

ABOVE *Switzerland: vineyards in the Valais, many of them steeply terraced, where Chasselas flourishes to make full yet delicately racy wines known locally as Fendant.*

Chasselas (Fendant, Perlan, Gutedel)

Although a little Chasselas is grown in France (Alsace, Pouilly-sur-Loire, Savoie) and it is fairly widely planted in Eastern Europe, the wines are for the most part ordinary.

In **Switzerland**, however, it accounts for nearly 40 per cent of total wine production, and produces well-made, smooth, polished wines. The cantons of Valais (where the variety is known as Fendant) and Vaud produce the bulk of Chasselas, with Geneva (where it is called Perlan) a distant third. The grape makes fairly neutral flavoured wine, whose suppleness is exaggerated in most cases by malolactic fermentation*, and whose freshness is retained by a little CO_2 spritz*. Oak rarely figures.

The dry, sun-trap **Valais** vineyards produce wines which often combine fullness with a racy delicacy (B Rouvinez, R Gilliard). The **Vaud** wines tend to be more minerally (H Badoux). Those from **Geneva** are fresh and elegant, but lighter.

Petite Arvigne

An indigenous Swiss grape, grown exclusively in the Valais, especially between Martigny and Sion. The wines are dry, with the weight of a white Rhône or a full Mâcon, but the best have a firm to vigorous acidity, a honey and vegetal bouquet reminiscent of mature Chablis, and a slightly peppery character. Occasionally, off-dry to sweet wines are made from shrivelled (*flétri*) grapes, without the benefit of noble rot (R Favre, R Gilliard, B Rouvinez, Provins).

Marsanne (Ermitage)

A white grape from the Rhône Valley, also grown, in very small quantities, in Australia, California, and in Switzerland, where it is known as 'Ermitage'. It makes deep-yellow wine, high in alcohol, low in acid (and thus often slightly thick-textured). It has a bouquet of ripe peaches, almond kernels and sometimes a suggestion of pear drops or nail varnish. **Northern Rhône** whites are rare, but today most Hermitage, Crozes-Hermitage and St-Joseph are made from 100 per cent Marsanne (Chapoutier's Chante Alouette, Grippat's Hermitage and St-Joseph). In the Goulburn Valley, **Australia**, are Chateau Tahbilk: a taut, off-dry, honeysuckle and lemon wine that needs ageing time; and Mitchelton: full, generous, oaky. **Switzerland**'s 'Ermitage' is typically broad, soft and smooth.

Roussanne

Roussanne, too, comes from France's **Rhône Valley**. It is a better-quality grape variety than Marsanne, but is more demanding and less reliable to grow, and therefore rarer.

Roussanne makes wines of similar dimensions to those of Marsanne, but with more spine, and generally with more complexity too, both across the palate, and in bouquet, which, when mature, smells of roasted nuts, hay, and almond kernels. Jaboulet's white Hermitage, Chevalier de Sterimberg, is usually 50 per cent Roussanne, 50 per cent Marsanne, and Château de Beaucastel's white Châteauneuf-du-Pape is a weighty, almost viscously rich 80 per cent Roussanne.

Furmint

Furmint is the principal grape (along with the fragrant Hárslevelü and Muskotály, a variety of the finer Muscat Blanc à Petits Grains) of Hungary's Tokaji wine. The town of **Tokaj** lies at the foot of the Tatra Mountains in Hungary's northeastern corner. Here, bell-shaped, volcanic hills drain into the Bodrog River whose proximity to the vineyards creates the misty autumn conditions so perfect for the development of noble rot*. Tokaji is the oldest 'nobly rotten' wine, dating from the mid-1600s.

Furmint produces a juice naturally high in acid, making a full, stiff, spicy, dry style; but its ageworthy, sweet, noble rot- (*aszú*-)based Tokajis are its real gems. The sweet wines are amber-hued, redolent of orange zest, caramel and raisin, whose liquorous sweetness is offset by a mordantly fresh acidity and a distinct, fiery spiciness. They are vital, spirited, ardent reflections of their Magyar origins (Royal Tokaji Wine Company, Disnókö, Oremus).

Tokaji's alcohol level is typically 11–13%, and it comes in a range of styles: Tokaji *szamorodni* (literally 'as it comes') – dry (*száraz*) or sweet (*édes*), according to the grapes picked; Tokaji *aszú*: qualified by 3, 4, 5 or 6 *puttonyos*; or Tokaji *eszencia*. *Puttonyos* – grape pickers' hods – were the traditional measure of about 25 kilos of mashed, nobly rotten grapes added to 136 litres of dry base wine. This mixture is left to steep for a couple of days and then pressed off the pulpy skins prior to a slow second fermentation in barrel. The more 'putts', the sweeter the wine.

Scheurebe (Sämling 88)

Scheurebe is a Riesling x Silvaner cross, with the benefits of excellent acidity, a good depth of flavour and a distinctive aroma, combining grapefruit zest and raw blackcurrants, apparent in both its dry and sweet wines. Sweet wines, however, are what it does best.

In the **Pfalz** in Germany, and at Illmitz, on the shores of the **Neusiedlersee** in Austria, it makes beautifully defined, vividly juicy, nobly rotten Beerenauslese- and Trockenbeerenauslese-style wines, as well as Eisweins. If these wines are not quite as racily fine as the best Riesling versions, they are considerably cheaper (Kracher, Opitz).

Welschriesling (Riesling Italico, Laski-, Olasz-Rizling)

A variety that has nothing to do with Germany's great Riesling grape, but which has the advantage of retaining a lively acidity in warmer climates. It makes light, refreshing, floral, dry to off-dry wines in **Slovenia** (Olasz- and Laski-Rizling), in Styria and Burgenland in Austria and in Collio in northwest Italy.

In Burgenland, the **Neusiedlersee**'s large expanse of water regularly provides the conditions for noble rot, and some fine Beerenauslese and Trockenbeerenauslese wines result around Rust (Opitz, Kracher).

ABOVE LEFT *The thick, woolly mould that develops in the cold, damp underground cellars where Tokaji matures. It clings to ageing bottles and walls alike.*

ABOVE RIGHT *Refurbished cellars at Oremus, reflecting the recent investment in, and revival of Tokaji. The newly bottled wines will eventually acquire the monk's hood and cowl of fungus seen on the three old bottles on the left. To the right are glass carboys containing the indescribably sweet, barely fermentable eszencia, viscous free run juice from the aszú grapes before they are mashed.*

*See also

Savagnin

Savagnin is best-known in the **Jura** in eastern France, where it is mainly used for *vin jaune* (yellow wine). This is made by fermenting the Savagnin grapes dry before putting the wine in partly filled barrels to acquire a film of *flor* yeast, rather like that which covers fino sherry (*see* illustration below). However, *vin jaune* is not fortified. The *flor* prevents any oxidation as the wine slowly evaporates and concentrates over six years. It emerges with a yeasty pungency to smell, and a dry, piercingly sharp lemon and walnut flavour. Time (plenty…) softens it to a honey and melted-butter bouquet, and a mellowed, caressing, lemony fineness to taste.

BELOW Flor yeast lying on the surface of a partly full barrel of vin jaune in the Jura, France. This is the same sort of yeast that forms on fino Sherry in southern Spain. It develops a waxy coating which allows it to float and form a surface film, thus protecting the wine from oxygen, and permitting long barrel-ageing without spoilage.

Müller-Thurgau (Riesling-Silvaner, Rivaner)

Early to ripen, high-yielding and generally bland to taste, Müller-Thurgau is widely planted in Central Europe. It is perhaps best-known for making Liebfraumilch* in **Germany**, from grapes grown mainly in Rheinhessen, the Pfalz or Baden. When well made and drunk young, it smells of box hedge and elderflower, but any bottle age rapidly confers the smell of rotting vegetation, amongst others. This sort of wine is usually off- to medium-dry (sweetened with *Süssreserve*) and not unpleasant. But you rapidly get beyond its limited appeal! Its early-ripening characteristics make Müller-Thurgau attractive in cooler-climate wine regions such as America's Pacific Northwest, New Zealand and England. It is often crisper and clearer from these areas, with extra acidity giving the wine a bit of freshness and definition. Germany's **Franken** is the source of the best expressions of the grape: elegant, steely, lemony wines with both breadth and weight (Juliusspital). That bucks the standard image!

Grüner Veltliner

Grüner Veltliner is a variety indigenous to Austria, where it accounted for nearly 40 per cent of all the vines grown in the late 1990s. It is mostly found north of the Danube, in the **Weinviertel** of Lower Austria.

The bulk of Grüner Veltliner is inexpensive, deliciously juicy, clean and fresh dry wine, often with a touch of spritz*, and marked by the grape's telltale white pepper. And it should be drunk as young as possible. Finer wines, deeper, firmer, more perfumed, come from around Mailberg and Retz, close to the border with the Czech Republic.

But the true aristocrats (in Burgundian terms 'fine Premiers Crus', as opposed to the bulk of 'good village' wine) hail from the Wachau. Here the wines often taste of the minerally soils, and, whether vivid, bone-dry lightweight *Steinfeder*, pure, steely middleweight *Federspiel*, or full-bodied, deep, dry, yet succulent *Smaragd*, these are wines of real class. And the grape occasionally makes lovely bottles of intensely sweet, fresh, grapey-clean Eiswein*.

Neuburger

Neuburger is grown throughout Austria (except for Styria), but is at its best in the **Wachau**. Its wines are generally full-bodied, often a little wanting in acidity, with good examples being attractively broad, supple and peachy (Viognier with less alcohol?). The finest can be remarkably racy (Nikolaihof, Hirtzberger, S Donabaum);

Assyrtiko

Greece has a number of white grape varieties which have the enormous appeal, in my view, of being relatively light in alcohol and naturally fresh in acidity. They are at their highly individual best without any new oak*, which, when used, quite obliterates their originality.

Probably best of all is Assyrtiko, the grape which makes **Santorini** on the island of that name. It has a vivid acidity, and, in spite of a typical alcohol content of barely 12.5% (oh joy!), it is often saturated with flavour. A dry, palate-searching, gently lime-scented wine, clearly marked by a peppery spiciness from the island's volcanic soil. Whether light, or more concentrated, it impresses without having to shout its message. Boutari's range is excellent.

Moscophilero

Moscophilero makes a delicate wine called **Mantinia**, the name of the high, cool plateau in the central Peloponnese in Greece where the grape flourishes. It is notably light in alcohol, around 11.5%, but high in floral, musky fragrance. Often delightfully clean and sharp to finish, like Assyrtiko it doesn't need to be strong to be good. Its finest examples, though, are bone-dry, complex, zesty wines of considerable class and character. Of the limited range I have tried, the Boutari wines are again amongst the best. I love the resonance of the name, and want to try many more of these wines!

Rhoditis

Rhoditis is another grape that performs better at high altitude, especially in the wines of **Patras** from the northern Peloponnese. Whilst it doesn't have the distinction of Assyrtiko or Moscophilero, when grown high up it keeps its acidity and makes lightly fragrant, crisply fruity wines, not unlike good Muscadet, but with more scent and sinew. At lower altitude, it produces wines that are somewhat fuller, still fresh, but more supple. Fuller is relative. In almost any other vinous context we would call them light. Kourtakis makes particularly good examples.

Robola

Unique to the Greek island of **Cephalonia**, Robola makes strong, dry, vivid, lemon-zest-imbued wines that combine power with finesse.

Savatiano

Grown mainly in **Attica**, Savatiano is the grape of Retsina. Like many of Greece's other important white varieties it tends to be lowish in alcohol; unlike them it is generally rather soft and bland. It benefits from being blended with Assyrtiko or Rhoditis. Or, indeed, from being seasoned with the Aleppo pine resin, which gives Retsina its name and imbues its wine with a cooling, resinous edge, the scent that sits forever in the Mediterranean air.

Torrontes

Torrontes is making a name for itself as a lively, perfumed wine, with a scent reminiscent of both Muscat and Gewurztraminer. At its best from high altitudes in Argentina. Like Gewurztraminer, it seems to lose its scent rapidly once the yields become at all overgenerous. At which point it simply tastes hot and empty.

ABOVE *Retz, in the Weinviertel, Lower Austria. Particularly fine and scented versions of Grüner Veltliner come from this northerly region of Lower Austria, close to the Czech Republic.*

*See also

eiswein **43**
new oak **48**
spritz **22**
tasting liebfraumilch **152**

Malvasia (Malmsey)

Malvasia is a fairly complex family of grapes, which, apart from Madeira's Malmsey (*see* pp114–15), is most associated with Italy. Malvasia is grown throughout **Italy**, but is especially linked with Latium and Tuscany, and with the Trebbiano grape (*see* below). It naturally produces wines that are low in acidity, high in sugar and relatively neutral in flavour, at least for dry wines. And for dry wines it usually benefits from being blended with the more acidic Trebbiano. Grown at high altitude, or with low yields, it can make dry wines of vigour and tenacity, if no great complexity. Its high sugar potential means it lends itself well to sweet wines, of which **Madeira**'s Malmsey and Tuscany's Vin Santo are the most illustrious. Vin Santo (holy wine) is made from dried (*passiti*) grapes*, principally Malvasia and Trebbiano. It ferments and ages slowly in small wooden barrels for several years to emerge as a golden wine of varying degrees of intensity and sweetness (Avignonesi, Isole & Olena, Felsina).

Trebbiano (Ugni Blanc)

Italy's most widely planted grape, Trebbiano is responsible for a vast amount of Italy's whites. It is best-known blended with Malvasia to make Frascati and Orvieto. There is a large number of Trebbiano clones (Trebbiano di Soave, di Lugana, di Romagna, and so on), some of which can make wines of character. But most of what one encounters is from high-yielding, neutral-flavoured grapes, with the sole virtue of a lively acidity. Well-made Frascati and Orvieto might be described as having a pleasantly refreshing blandness.

Garganega

Garganega is grown, above all, in the **Veneto**, where it is the chief grape used for making Soave. Good Soave is a straightforward, smooth, dry, graceful wine, with an apple and pear aroma, usually given a bit of extra bite by Trebbiano. The top wines – from low yields and fine sites – can have considerable substance and length below their elegantly smooth, creamy surface (Anselmi, Pieropan). Recioto* di Soave is made from semi-dried grapes: raisiny to smell; fine, grapey, medium-sweet to very sweet wines.

Prosecco

Prosecco is grown largely in the **Veneto** in Italy and used for Prosecco di Conegliano or Prosecco di Valdobbiadene. These are dry to off-dry sparkling wines; light, fresh, appley and delicately frothy. They have none of Moscato's scent, but the best are delightfully fragrant, almond-imbued wines, less acidic and more delicate than Champagne. The finest are called Cartizze – a subdenomination of Prosecco di Valdobbiadene (Carpenè Malvolti, Mionetto).

Verdicchio

Verdicchio is chiefly associated with the **Marches** on Italy's Adriatic coast, and with the wine called Verdicchio dei Castelli di Jesi. Verdicchio has considerable quality potential, but varies in style a great deal. The grape has good acidity, and the wine styles vary from those that resemble a lively, unoaked Mâcon, to compact, sinewy, characterful whites, with a strong peach and almond fruit core as well as an earthy, volcanic flavour (Umani Ronchi especially).

Vermentino (Rolle)

Encountered predominantly in Sardinia, Tuscany and Liguria. **Sardinia**'s Vermentino can be crisp and refreshing if it comes from grapes grown high in the hills, where the nights are cold, even if the days are warm. From the Italian mainland, most famously the precipitous slopes of the **Cinque Terre**, it is a deliciously fresh crustacean wine, not unlike good Muscadet. Ambitious versions are bone-dry, full, and mouth-coatingly scented.

Cortese

Cortese is best-known, and most publicised, for Gavi, also for Cortese dell'Alto Monferrato – both from southeast **Piedmont**. Much Gavi seems overrated, but at its light (11–12% alcohol) best, it is mouth-wateringly dry, lemon-fresh, and deliciously vivid (La Giustiniana, Cà Bianca).

Vernaccia

Vernaccia makes a dry, steely, clean, but rather neutral wine as Vernaccia di San Gimignano in **Tuscany**. And also a much more individual, forceful, nutty wine of 15.5% alcohol in **Sardinia**'s dry, *superiore* versions of Vernaccia di Oristano. These wines age for several years in barrel, under *flor**.

Albariño (Alvarinho)

A high-quality grape in northwest Spain, Galicia especially, and, across the border, in Portugal's Minho region.

Spain's **Rías Baixas** wines have become deservedly popular beyond the Spanish border. Although some versions can be fairly full-bodied and strong, most (and for me the most attractive) are the lighter versions. Pale, floral-scented, delicate dry wines, usually lemon tinged and with a touch of spritz*, crisp yet smooth (Martín Códax, Murrieta, Pazo Bayon). Oak is anathema to them, but that doesn't prevent a few producers from trying it on!

Minho in Portugal makes its finer, fuller Vinho Verde or 'green wines' (green in the sense that they are for drinking young*), from Alvarinho and/or Loureiro. These are usually more slender in style and often off-dry, at least for the export market.

Loureiro (Loureira)

A fine, quality grape, Loureiro makes some of the best Vinho Verde (*see* above) in **Minho** in Portugal. Loureiro has more bite and less alcohol than Alvarinho, yielding wines that are more acutely dry. Sogrape's Quinta de Azevedo is particularly good.

Verdejo

Verdejo is the principal white grape of **Rueda** in Spain's Castilla-León. It produces wines of excellent quality: full, dry, flavoursome, and often cedary to smell, even without oak contact.

Arinto

The mainstay of **Bucelas** in Portugal, Arinto is a richly textured but bone-dry and crisply acidic wine. Aged Arinto from **Bairrada** can smell surprisingly like the butter, toast and honey aromas, and have the lean purity of flavour of mature, unwooded Hunter Semillon.

Bical

Another Portuguese variety from **Bairrada** and **Dão**, Bical's high acid means it is mostly used for sparklers. But some table wines have a quiet class to them. Dry, delicate, filigree wines, reminiscent of a dry Mosel Riesling, but with less acid. And the best can occasionally age like good Riesling too (Casa de Saima, Caves Aliança, Quinta da Bageiras).

ABOVE *Rías Baixas, Galicia in northwestern Spain. Albariño vines on traditional pergolas made from local granite. The leaf canopy here is deliberate and protects the grapes when the weather is hot.*

*See also

dried grapes **42**

drinking with food **161**

flor *78*, **110**

recioto **42**

spritz **22**

5. red grapes and their wines

ABOVE *Chilean Malbec, super ripe, evenly ripe and in perfect health.*

NB: *to find a particular grape variety, consult the index.*

Getting a handle on quality

How do you measure quality? It is never easy. But for so-called noble varieties (Burgundy's Pinot Noir, for instance), with practice you can develop a 'feel' for the approximate quality calibration provided by good examples of Burgundy's four-tier hierarchy: 'generic', 'village', 'Premier Cru', 'Grand Cru'. In a nutshell: 'generic' level wines (£–££ – *see* p118): simple, pleasant, brief. 'Village' (££–£££): straightforward, some length and aftertaste. 'Premier Cru' (£££+): more aromatic, greater flavour variety, sustained middle-palate and long finish. 'Grand Cru' (beyond the price scope of this book): pronounced scent, great tenacity of taste in the mouth allied to considerable clarity,

subtlety and aromatic persistence. A similar approach applies to Cabernet-based wines using generic Bordeaux (£–££), *cru bourgeois* (££–£££), lesser classed-growth (£££+) and first growth (again, beyond the price scope of this book).

The demarcation lines are inevitably imprecise, but the general concept is helpful as a guide to quality, value and a sense of 'what fits where'. France is useful as a reference because the complete quality spectrum exists, along with a couple of established hierarchies: Burgundy (Côte d'Or) and Bordeaux (Médoc). Good French wines, at each level, illustrate the distinctions well, and the broad quality categories have stood the test of time. I suggest New World parallels where practical. (*See* pp26–7, 30, 126–28,144–46.)

cabernet sauvignon

Cabernet Sauvignon is a most adaptable traveller, easy to grow, easy to vinify and with a telltale blackcurrant bouquet that everybody loves. With a tannic edge always there in one form or another, its wines range from fresh and simple, to the rewardingly aristocratic.

Cabernet Sauvignon is made round the globe: as a successful varietal wine in warmer climates; blended with Merlot to temper its rigidity in cooler environments; and as part of numerous other blends, to give fruit core, class and bouquet to less showy grapes. Cabernet's berries are small and thick-skinned, with abundant colour, tannin and acid. These strong characteristics mean that, unlike Pinot Noir, it is a forgiving and adaptable grape to vinify in the winery. And it takes to oak with relish.

These attributes also give its wines the constitution to age over long periods; and in Cabernet's case the ability to age is a real advantage. Its best wines have the potential to develop a complex array of flavours along with fine textures and a superb bouquet.

It is precisely this attractive bouquet and strong constitution that makes Cabernet such good blending material. For it rarely loses its cassis character – a signature smell which seems to be attractive to practically everybody, and which blends agreeably with the aromas of all sorts of other grape varieties. But so strong is its sweet, blackcurrant personality, that a little goes a long way in a blend, and all too often it masks the individuality of the less familiar grape(s).

One of its few disadvantages is that, easy as it is to grow, it is a late ripener, and therefore not ideal for cooler regions. And its very vigour as a plant means that its leaf canopy* needs careful managing in warm climates or vigorous soils, to avoid excess herbaceousness in its wines.

European Cabernet Sauvignon

Bordeaux is the home of Cabernet Sauvignon, and its favourite location is the so-called 'left bank' – the Médoc and Graves regions to the left of the Gironde Estuary and Garonne River (*see* p168). Cabernet prefers the gravelly soils of the left bank where the heat-retaining pebbles help it ripen, and where, therefore, most vineyards are Cabernet dominated.

All claret (red Bordeaux) is a blend of grape varieties. This is partly in order to spread the risk of one variety failing in the unpredictable maritime climate, but more because a blend of varieties makes a better wine here. Cabernet Sauvignon is too austere and charmless on its own in the Bordeaux context. A typical Médoc

BELOW *Pauillac, Bordeaux: looking east, past Château Latour's large dovecote, across the Gironde estuary, to the 'right bank'. The best claret is very expensive, but good alternatives are the châteaux's 'second' wines. These are made from batches that don't make the selection for the top wine. A third of the price, but by no means a third of the quality. 'Third' wines, like Latour's 'Pauillac', are real value in the claret context.*

Top wines to taste

Bordeaux, France
Châteaux: Latour; Léoville-
Las-Cases, Léoville-Barton;
Margaux, Palmer

California, USA
Dominus, Ridge Montebello,
Opus One, Phelps' Insignia

Australia Penfold's Bin 707

RIGHT *St-Julien in the
Médoc, Bordeaux. This is
classic 'left bank' gravel
soil, on a fairly marked
'mound' (you can barely see
the St-Julien church steeple)
which gives good drainage,
retains warmth well because
of the pebbles, and which is
what Cabernet Sauvignon
thrives in. When you taste
left bank claret, and
visualise the gravel soil, you
will find it difficult not to
taste its earthiness* too!*

BELOW *The Napa Valley,
California, with the peaks of
Stags Leap in the distance.
Much of California's most
elegant and consistent
Cabernet comes from here.*

wine will contain two-thirds Cabernet,
plus Merlot to put flesh on its bones, a bit
of Cabernet Franc to add perfume to its
raw blackcurrant essence, and maybe a little
Petit Verdot.

You will need a specialist book to guide
you through Bordeaux properly (*see* p159);
but here are some style sketches of the main
communes to get you started. 'Classed-growth'
Médocs* (*see* p30) have become very expensive,
but their 'second' wines (*see* caption p83) are a
good, and much less pricey alternative. These
are indicated here by °, followed by other
classed-growths, and/or local *crus bourgeois*.

Much of **St-Estèphe** is quite clayey and the
style tends towards the fruity, but robust and
chewy (Pagodes de Cos°, Dame de Montrose°;
Potensac, Tour-de-By, Charmail, Lavillotte).
Pauillacs, on heavy gravel, have the highest
proportion of Cabernet, making rich, muscular,
spicy wines (Latour's Pauillac, Carruades de
Lafite°, Tourelles de Longueville°, Pibran).
St-Julien, on a finer gravel, makes what many
consider to be the ideally proportioned middle-
weight claret, less strong and tannic than
Pauillac (Reserve de Léoville-Barton°, Lady
Langoa°, Amiral de Beychevelle°, Fiefs de
Lagrange°, Du Glana, Lanessan). **Margaux**,
on lighter sand and gravel, is more delicate,
and often particularly fragrant (Pavillon Rouge°,
Cantemerle, d'Angludet, Labégorce-Zédé).

South of Bordeaux itself, **Graves**, on fine,
thin gravel, tend to be more supple and open-

textured than the Médocs, with a marked,
finely earthy flavour (Clémentin de Pape-
Clément°, Parde de Haut-Bailly°; La Louvière,
Bouscaut). Contradictions will abound, but
all will have, to some extent, claret's tannic
dryness, its earthy aromas behind Cabernet's
blackcurrant fruit, and more or less new-oak*
vanilla according to status.

Cabernet Sauvignon is permitted in the **Loire**,
but rarely used there because it ripens less
regularly than Cabernet Franc. It is also part of
the blend of many South West wines: **Buzet,
Bergerac, Frontonnais, Madiran**. It is used to a
limited extent in the **Languedoc**, but it doesn't
much care for the soils, so Mas de Daumas
Gassac (70 per cent Cabernet Sauvignon) is
unusual in this respect, a good, aromatic wine
since the 1990s. Cabernet blends well with Syrah
in cooler parts of **Provence,** giving a sweet, cassis
centre to Syrah's peppery austerity (Domaine de
Trévallon, Château Routas 'Agrippa').

Austria makes occasional, tannic, minty
Cabernets, and the variety is successfully
blended with St George in **Greece,** as well as
being the principal grape in Greece's rich, supple,
oaky Château Carras. Eastern Europe suffered
from the political instability of the 1990s, but in
Bulgaria Domaine Boyar's Shumen, Iambol and
soft, juicy, cold-maceration Blueridge wines are

good. Villány is the best source in **Hungary**, and Gere is its quality flagship. **Italy**'s Cabernet stronghold is in the northeast, where for a long time it was thin and herbaceous in character. But today there are numerous, if limited-quantity, light, scented, and stylish wines in the Alto Adige (Letrari, Löwengang, San Leonardo). And Cabernet is increasingly used (10–20 per cent) in Tuscany to sweeten the Sangiovese pill, (Avignonese's I Grifi, Antinori's Tignanello).

Spain makes a small amount of good-quality pure Cabernet Sauvignon, above all in Catalonia (Raïmat, Enate, Jean León, Torres' Gran Coronas (££ – *see* p118) and Mas La Plana (£££)), also from the Marqués de Grignón in Toledo. But it is mostly used for blending: very successfully as the principal constituent, with Tempranillo and Merlot, of many Navarra (Guelbenzu, Ochoa, Chivite, Castillo de Monjardín), and as a small, but significant,

part of many wines in or near Ribera del Duero (Protos, Abadia Retuerta).

New World Cabernet Sauvignon

The majority of **California**'s Cabernets are 'varietal', but those with a high proportion of Merlot and/or Cabernet Franc – Bordeaux style – are called 'Meritage'. They haven't caught the imagination of the wine-buying public because most Cabernet here is ripe enough, and thus supple enough, not to need much blending.

There are good-quality wines made right across the state, but the southern Napa Valley stands out for consistency of quality, elegance of style, and value for money. As with Merlot, the wines are riper and sweeter to taste, and usually smoother in feel, than their Bordeaux counterparts. Estancia, Rodney Strong, Beringer Knights Valley and Beaulieu Vineyards are particularly good (£–££); Phelps, St-Supéry,

LEFT *Peñafiel castle in Ribera del Duero, Spain. Cabernet Sauvignon is a good blender, though with its strong personality a little goes a long way, as is the case here, where it regularly partners Tempranillo in modest proportions.*

Cabernet Sauvignon at a glance

Colour: generally deep.
Alcohol: medium to high.
Acid: fairly high.
Tannin: high.
Aroma characteristics: clear, strong; often marked by new oak vanilla/cedar/coconut. *Cool-climate/less ripe fruit:* herbaceous, mint, eucalyptus, tomato, bell pepper, green olive, red berry, raw blackcurrant. *Warmer-climate/riper fruit:* ripe blackcurrant, cassis, blackcurrant jam, licorice.
Bottle age bouquet: sweet, cooked mulberry, cassis, cedar, sometimes a fine earthiness.
Styles:
• light, fresh, herbaceous.
• firm dry middle weight.
• rich, tannic, oaky.

BELOW *Erràzuriz Winery, Aconcagua Valley, Chile, with part of the Andes foothills in the background, and its top vineyard, Don Maximiano in front. It is a first rate source of Chilean Cabernet and Merlot. One reason for the minty/ herbaceous flavour in many of Chile's red wines is a pronounced day/night temperature contrast that comes from cold air slipping down off the Andes at night. During very cold nights the ripening process slows, and the methoxypyrazine flavour compounds (source of the herbaceous aromas) remain in the grape longer, even whilst the sugar ripening continues. That it often seems even more pronounced in Merlot than Cabernet, may well have to do with much Merlot being Carmenère!*

Niebaum Coppola, Shafer and Ridge Santa Cruz Mountains (££–£££). For a top-quality, contrasting *style* comparison, line up Napa's Spottswoode, Silver Oak, Beringer Private Reserve (same £££+ and vintage). Fresh restraint, oaky extravagance, muscular intensity; all at a similar – Médoc classed-growth – quality level!

In **Washington State** there are numerous first-rate Cabernets and Cabernet blends. In style, they are often concentrated, but without being bulky; 'cooler' in flavour than California, less drily tannic and earthy than Bordeaux, and for the most part they are attractively textured. Start at ££ for good quality. Staton Hills, Hedges, Covey Run and Château Ste-Michelle are excellent value; Columbia Winery's Red Willow, L'Ecole No 41 and a sumptous Woodward Canyon 'Canoe Ridge' are splendid £££ wines.

Chile's Maipo Valley is the country's best Cabernet location. It is mostly a varietal wine, being soft enough to need no Merlot cushion, and usually a touch less herbaceous, less plummy and flowing, but a bit more tannic than Chile's Merlots (*see* pp93–5, and margin caption opposite). Carmen, Erràzuriz, Concha y Toro, Casablanca, Casa Lapostolle are particularly good value at ££. Across the Andes, **Argentina**'s Mendoza climate is continental and desert-like, in contrast to Chile's cool maritime character. Its Cabernets have an almost tarry concentration, a wonderfully natural,

soft, fleshy texture and a sweetly ripe, cassis flavour. When they don't toughen them and dry them out with new oak*, that is, a sad tendency the higher up the price and quality ladder one goes! (Catena for class throughout the range, Infinitus, Altos de Temporada).

Australia's Cabernets are as varied in style as its Shiraz. And Shiraz, rather than Merlot, is often successfully blended with Cabernet to make a richer, fleshier style. (But I do wish many winemakers felt less obliged to add what is a clearly 'perceptible' acidity, for stability rather than taste!) Much is very good pure Cabernet, Coonawarra making some of the most elegant wines. No lack of force, mind you, but more finesse, and a touch of *terroir, see* pp129. (Wynn's Black Label, Orlando's St Hugo, Chapel Hill – part McLaren Vale). Victoria's Cabernets are drier, cooler, more vigorous and more minty (Mount Langi Ghiran, Coldstream Hills and the very fine Yarra Yering No 1). For me, Mudgee has the most promising Cabernets in New South Wales, even better than its Shiraz: soft, round, compact, mulberry sweet wines (Montrose, Thistle Hill, and Huntington – in a class of its own). Orange is potently cool-climate (Reynolds, Rosemount). And from Western Australia there is a typically high incidence of sheer class in varying styles (Moss Wood, Vasse Felix, Cullens, Leeuwin, Plantagenet, Howard Park). They age beautifully and gracefully too.

Cabernet in **New Zealand**'s cool climate is a 'tough' varietal choice, hence there is much 'softening' with Merlot. But if a thread of natural acidity and a eucalyptus overlay generally remind us we are in a cool climate, there are now many well-balanced, fresh, harmonious wines. Hawkes Bay (Te Mata's Awatea, Matua Valley, Villa Maria, Vidal, Trinity Hill, Te Awa's Longlands, Montana's Church Road), and Waiheke Island (Goldwater, Te Motu, Stoneyridge – very good, very pricey).

South Africa's Cabernet hit rate remains low. Bordeaux-style blends are better than varietals. Generally a leaner style, but some good examples, mostly at the more expensive end (Warwick, Klein Constantia, Saxenburg, Verdun's Theresa, Simonsig's Tiara, Kanonkop's Paul Sauer).

pinot noir

Good Pinot Noir has a uniquely seductive combination of perfume, sweetness, silkiness of texture and overall delicacy. But wherever it is made, be it Burgundy or Bío-Bío, the success rate is exasperatingly low. Which is probably why, when it really is good, it seems sensational.

Pinot Noir is a thin-skinned grape, moderate in colour, low in tannin, high in acidity. And, with limited matter in its skins, the majority of its wines are relatively delicate. This means that it has a much narrower range of possible styles than, say, Syrah or Cabernet Sauvignon. For it simply doesn't have the substance to hide or balance manipulation or excesses of any kind: high yield*, over-extraction*, too much oak*. Its transparency reveals them all too easily.

Pinot Noir doesn't usually have much tannin, and thus relies on its acidity for definition on the palate. Excessively ripe, and/or without this freshness, it becomes just a soft, jammy red. To retain acidity it needs a coolish climate, and in such conditions it holds out the promise of at least occasional paradise. Too cold and it responds with aromas of mint, dill, tomato, white pepper, and herbaceousness. (*See* the margin caption on this page for Pinot Noir's aroma characteristics when content.)

European Pinot Noir

Pinot Noir from **Burgundy**'s Côte d'Or in France is rightly held up as a paradigm, though for consistency it is no better, or worse, than any

LEFT *Pinot Noir's name derives from the pine cone shape you see here. Its young wines have the keen yet juicy succulence of red cherries. After a few years in bottle its bouquet migrates from the suave scents of the orchard to the more primitive smells of the countryside proper: an evolution from fresh red fruit, via coffee, caramel and leather, to the more rural odours of vegetation, leaf mould, mushrooms, the farmyard, well-hung game.*

RIGHT *Burgundy. This slope is part of the limestone 'spine' that surfaces to a greater or lesser extent across Burgundy, from Chablis down to Pouilly Fuissé. Here we are on the Côte de Nuits, looking over Chambolle Musigny towards Vougeot and Vosne Romanée in the distance. The flat land is mostly 'village' quality, up the slopes 1er and Grand Cru.*

Pinot Noir at a glance

Colour: pale to medium.
Alcohol: moderate to high.
Acid: high.
Tannin: low, fine.
Aroma characteristics: pronounced, subtle; all too easily masked by excess new oak. *Cool-climate/less ripe fruit:* mint, tomato, dill, herbaceous, redcurrant, red cherry, raspberry. *Warmer-climate/riper fruit:* floral, 'smooth', ripe red cherry, black cherry.
Bottle age bouquet: undergrowth, leather, leaf mould, mushroomy, vegetal, 'gamey', as in well hung wild game.
Styles:
• light, crisp to sharp.
• medium-bodied, fresh but smooth.
• silky, scented grandeur.

other Pinot Noir region. It will infuriate often, and delight occasionally. The detailed, monastic complexities of Burgundy's wines are well beyond the scope of this book, so consult those recommended on p159. But you can get a basic idea of various styles by comparing wines from different communes, at a similar price level (ideally £££ – *see* p118). And a feel for quality differences by comparing wines from the same producer at village (££) and Premier Cru level (£££+); *see* page 82.

Côte de Nuits reds, on more iron-rich soil, are generally fuller, firmer, spicier and more minerally in style. A few comparative signposts might be: Nuits-St-Georges: earthiness, tannic muscle (L'Arlot, Chevillon, Gouges); Chambolle-Musigny: perfume, delicacy (Ghislaine Barthod, H Lignier); Gevrey-Chambertin: firm, spicy elegance (Rousseau, B Clair, D Bachelet). **Côte de Beaune** reds, on more limestone soils, are perceived as lighter, 'fruitier', more supple and quicker to mature. Savigny-lès-Beaune (Bize), Santenay (Pousse d'Or), and Auxey-Duresses (M Prunier) fit the image of the lighter styles, as does Volnay in a very perfumed way (Lafarge, Angerville). But to confound the generalisation, try a Pommard (Armand, J-M Boillot) and taste

the muscularity from its clay-rich soil! The **Côte Chalonnaise** is a good source of less expensive red burgundy: **Mercurey**, robust and earthy (M Juillot, Meix Foulot); **Givry**, more delicate (Joblot, L'Espinasse).

Generally, wines of large merchant houses such as Jadot (fairly solid red style) and Drouhin (more restrained) will be more easily available.

Almost all red burgundies will have an edge of acid and tannin, and a faint earthiness of flavour which is rare in Pinot Noir outside Europe. In **Champagne**, Pinot Noir is mainly used for sparkling wine. In the **Loire**, Sancerre (Vacheron) and Menetou-Salon make light, delicately earthy, fragrant wines to drink young. **Alsace** Pinot Noirs are mainly unoaked, and range from pale and fresh to plump and generous. Pinot from **Switzerland** (as Blauburgunder or Klevner) plays the major part in the blend of Dôle, and yields smooth, sweet, pepper-scented and faintly herbaceous, gently minerally wines in the Valais, Neuchâtel, Geneva and Zurich. **Italy** makes a little (as Pinot Nero), at its best as a pure, floral, delicate wine in the Alto Adige in the northwest (Hofstätter, F Haas). **Austria** produces tiny amounts of increasingly good Pinot Noir in Burgenland (Stieglemar). **Germany** has a surprisingly large amount – the best are light, lively, silky and classy too (Pfalz: Lingenfelder; Franken: Fürst; Ahr: Meyer Näkel; Baden: KH Johner). Soft, plummy Pinots come from **Eastern Europe**, especially from Dealul Mare in Romania.

New World Pinot Noir

California's good Pinot Noirs are less sharp-edged than those from Oregon or New Zealand, less dry (from tannin and acid) and earthy than those from Burgundy, and in general full, sweet and silky, with very little tannin. Cooler areas

LEFT *Rippon Vineyard, Central Otago, New Zealand.*
As far as I know this is Pinot Noir's most southerly outpost with spectacular scenery as you can see. Locations like this are known as 'lifestyle' wineries! Central Otago is just one excellent region for Pinot Noir in New Zealand, but Rippon is regularly one of the best.

such as Russian River, Carneros, Santa Maria and Santa Ynez valleys in Santa Barbara seem most consistent. **Russian River** wines are fullish, supple, classy and stylish with little or no herbaceousness (Rochioli, Williams-Selyem); **Carneros**, where much Pinot is for sparkling wine, makes scented, graceful wines, with a lovely purity of ripe, cherry fruit (Acacia and, especially, Saintsbury). **Santa Barbara** wines are deep and juicy, often with a slight dill-like, herbal note (Sanford, Au Bon Climat, Foxen). The best from **Monterey** are some of California's most 'serious' Pinots: muscular wines with more tannin and *terroir* flavour (Chalone, Calera); but Estancia's Pinnacles is an excellent-value lighter Monterey.

Oregon's coastal climate, to the west of the Cascade Mountains, is cooler than Burgundy, and its numerous Pinot Noirs are often marked with a touch of cool-climate mint. They are generally lighter in flavour, less sweet and smooth, and brighter in acidity than those from California. They are also less consistent. But the best have a delicacy which is close to similar styles from Burgundy. Rex Hill (£), Drouhin's basic wine (£££) and Cuvée Laurene (£££+) give a good idea of the region's style and potential. Amity, slightly rough-hewn but characterful; Eyrie, fine, subtle, lacy; Cristom, Chehalem, Bethel Heights and Ken Wright are all excellent sources.

New Zealand is another source of top-quality, cool-climate Pinot Noir, overall similar in style, range and flavour spectrum to Oregon's wines. And today, in the best wines, their crisp acidity and herbaceous hint, are usually balanced by real richness of fruit and smooth textures. Marlborough, Martinborough, and Central Otago are the key sources. Martinborough (the winery) remains the best widely available benchmark (££), and it still manages to make many other local Pinots look clumsy. There is also a fine, ample Reserve Martinborough in the best years, 'Premier Cru' (*see* p82) quality by Burgundy's standards; as are Cloudy Bay, Dry River, and the oaky Ata Rangi (all £££–£££+).

In **Australia** most of the finest Pinot Noirs come from Victoria, where Yarra Valley is the most consistently successful region. Good wines also come from Mornington Pensinsula and Geelong in Victoria; from Orange (Cannobolas Smith), Margaret River (a richly seductive Devil's Lair), Adelaide Hills (Lenswood), and piquantly cool from Tasmania (Pipers Brook). For a quality cross-section, and to see how deliciously rich, sweet and generous the best Yarras are, line up Green Point (£), Tarra Warra (££) and Yarra Yering or Diamond Valley (£££). All are lovely examples of true Pinot Noir, richer than New Zealand; less warmly ripe, on the whole, than California.

South Africa's Hermanus in the cool Walker Bay area has the two wines which demonstrate that South Africa can make good, clear, sweet and faintly peppery Pinot Noir (Hamilton Russell, Bouchard-Finlayson). **Argentina** seems mostly too hot for Pinot (except, maybe, for the Río Negro) and whilst Chile makes a few decent, black cherry, pepper and olive examples (Cono Sur), they are nowhere near the good value represented by its Merlots.

ABOVE *The beautiful Santa Ynez Valley in Santa Barbara County, California; with the lovely Californian poppy in flower. This cool region makes some of California's best Pinot Noir. Sanford's, especially, is deep and juicy, yet delicate and subtle too. Very Pinot Noir that is!*

Top wines to taste

Burgundy, France
La Tâche (Dom Rom Conti)
Chambertin (Rousseau)

Victoria, Australia
Mount Mary

*See also

high yield **36**
oak **46,48**
over-extraction **46,50**
tasting 5 **140**

syrah/shiraz

Syrah – or Shiraz – is the only major grape variety which regularly appears under one of two accepted names. This fact reflects a clearly perceived polarity of benchmark styles – the more restrained French Syrah, and the more flamboyant South Australian Shiraz.

Syrah/Shiraz is increasingly popular, and increasingly widely grown around the world. It has the advantage of numerous guises which are quite distinct from the Cabernet/Merlot group of wines, and it flourishes, if in very different ways, in many countries. It needs warmth to ripen properly, but even in cooler climates where it doesn't get super-ripe, it makes wines that are attractively aromatic, albeit rather too austere for some tastes.

In its cooler, less fully ripe, Syrah expression, the grape makes a moderately coloured wine, bright, redcurrant fruit to smell and taste, with marked pepperiness, a suggestion of mint or green olives, brisk acidity and firm, dry tannin. In a warmer climate, and/or from low yields,

RIGHT Côte-Rôtie, in the Northern Rhône. Pale, rocky, schistous soil on steep slopes. Here you can see the bottom of the local individual 'wigwam' or inverted 'V' staking onto which the vines are tied, and on to which vineyard workers cling for support on precipitous slopes. You can see the 'top' of the post on p73.

fully ripe Shiraz is profoundly coloured, black-fruit-scented, richer, softer and sweeter to taste, with its tannin better covered and its pepper spice less to the fore. Shiraz is, however, prone to overcrop*, and then, as with Merlot, it is pallid in colour and neutral in flavour.

European Syrah

Syrah's original, and continuing, benchmark is the **Northern Rhône** in France, where, although a percentage of white grapes is permitted, Hermitage, Côte-Rôtie, Crozes-Hermitage, St-Joseph and Cornas are, in practice, varietal wines. By comparison with warmer areas of Australia, California and South Africa, the Northern Rhône is temperate, and its wines tend more to the cool-climate model. Whilst good examples have more density and fruit core than most Southern Rhône wines, above all they have elegance, finesse and definition; along with a marked tannin! Generally they are firmer in acid, naturally drier and often more minerally in flavour than their New World counterparts.

There are barely 40 miles (60km) between Hermitage and Côte-Rôtie, but the wines they produce are very different. **Hermitage** is inkier, denser, with more fruit extract, more cassis-like to smell and taste, especially when mature. And with a more muscular tannic frame (Jaboulet, Chapoutier, Chave, Delas, Vidal-Fleury). **Côte-Rôtie** is usually paler in colour, more fragrant and smoky to smell; less fruit-rich, but more aromatically elaborate. And often more delicate

and less tannic to taste (Guigal, Rostaing, Barge, Champet, Jasmin). The last three producers use very little new oak, and their aromas, alongside the cassis, can be more 'rustic': rubber, pan-singed meat, venison, game; especially with a bit of bottle-age. Guigal is notable for using very ripe grapes and a high proportion of new oak, making softer, richer wines.

Good **Cornas** potentially has the darkest colour and purest Syrah blackcurrant essence of all – alongside its pepper and tannin. Alas, it is all too rare (Clape, most classic; Colombo, most modern; Jaboulet, Michel, Domaine de Fauterie). **Crozes-Hermitage** and **St-Joseph** are both slighter versions of Hermitage, from less well-exposed sites. And many are light, fresh, peppery reds, to drink young. The best (Jaboulet's Thalabert and Graillot's La Guiraude) are close to lesser Hermitage, but their tannins are coarser, their aromas and length less pronounced. Two cooperatives – Tain, for Crozes; St-Désirat, for St-Joseph – are both reliable sources. A good-quality 'trio' comparison would be a lesser Crozes (£–££ – *see* p118), Thalabert from Jaboulet (££), and a Jaboulet or Chapoutier Hermitage (£££+), ideally from the same year.

Syrah is well known as an 'improving' grape, providing class, core and backbone to Grenache-based **Southern Rhônes*** (*see* p102). This advantage has led Syrah to spread right across southern France. Here it is blended with Cabernet Sauvignon in **Provence** (Château Routas, Domaine de Trévallon); with Grenache and Mourvèdre, sometimes as the main constituent, in **Coteaux du Languedoc** (Granges des Pères, Château de Lascaux), **Pic St-Loup** (Domaine de L'Hortus), **Faugères**, **St-Chinian**, **Côtes du Roussillon**, **Minervois**, **Corbières** and **Collioure** (*see also* Mourvèdre*).

Spain boasts one good, if often dry and oaky, example from Toledo (Marqués de Griñón). In **Switzerland** it is a Valais rarity, rich and blackcurranty, Northern Rhône-like but smoother (R Gilliard). **Italy**'s Syrahs come mainly from Tuscany: taut, elegant, black peppery, cool-climate wines; refined but austere (Fontodi's Case Via, Isole & Olena's L'Eremo).

ABOVE *Best's of Great Western in Victoria. The sign here makes the point that the phrase 'New World' is just useful shorthand for what is, vinously, not European! Best's have been making fine, plummy Shiraz here for some time.*

New World Shiraz and Syrah

Australia's Shiraz styles are hugely diverse, but its particular, original Australian archetype is from **South Australia**: ripe blackberry, black cherry, oak vanilla, brown sugar and liquorice aromas to smell; warm, dark-chocolate sweet, mouth-coatingly rich*, fruit-saturated and pepper-spiced to taste; seductive, heady, elemental. Typically McLaren Vale! (Wirra Wirra, Chapel Hill, Haselgrove, d'Arenberg.) These are a few stars, and of course there are lighter wines too. Barossa wines are similar, the best combining density and richness with elegance (Melton, Rockford, St Hallett). Coonawarra is a cooler area, whose wines have more mint, pepper and restraint (Wynns, Penfold's Bin 128).

True cool-climate wines come from **Victoria** – the Yarra Valley, Grampians and Pyrenees. These are more Rhône-like: taut, fine, distinctly peppery and mint-edged (Yarra Yering, Taltarni, Langi Ghiran, Dalwhinnie). **New South Wales** makes soft, leathery wines from the Hunter Valley; quietly spoken, powerful styles from Mudgee (Huntington, Montrose, Rosemount); and, so far, one superb, polished, perfumed Syrah-style from Orange's warmer western slopes (Canobolas Smith).

The fewer **Western Australian** Shiraz are in a harmonious, moderately cool style, less flamboyant than South Australia, less peppery than Victoria (Plantagenet, a star; Cape Mentelle).

Syrah/Shiraz at a glance

Colour: medium to inky.
Alcohol: moderate to high.
Acid: moderate to lively.
Tannin: high, firm.
Aroma characteristics: distinct; takes well to new wood, especially when fully ripe.
Cool-climate/less ripe fruit: redcurrant, raspberry, green olive, mint, white pepper.
Warmer-climate/riper fruit: black pepper, blackberry, blackcurrant, licorice, smokiness.
Bottle age bouquet: cassis, pan-singed meat, leather, coffee, burnt rubber, brown sugar, caramel, raisins.
Styles:
• light, brisk, peppery.
• rich, elegant, tannic.
• dense, ripe, powerful.

*See also

mourvèdre **104**

overcrop/yield **36**

richness & food **162**

southern rhônes **102**

tasting 7 **148**

BELOW *Roussillon in southwestern France. The Agly valley floor is a 'choppy sea' where the soil is schist and limestone dominated, and any slope an opportunity for a vineyard. Syrah is very much at home here and figures increasingly in good quality Côtes du Roussillon. The scenery has a wild, chaotic, rugged beauty. The 'building' you can see, is the Château de Queribus, an extraordinary 13th century refuge of the Cathar religious sect, some 730 metres (2,400 ft) up the mountain, and with incomparable views of the Pyrenees and surrounding district.*

California's plantings of Syrah are small by comparison with those of Zinfandel, Merlot or Cabernet. But it is easy to see why there is a growing appetite for it. Styles vary greatly, the best having some of the Northern Rhône's grace and elegance, with a fuller, sweeter taste and less tannin, but without the power and thickness of, say, South Australia: ie, mostly 'Syrah', rather than 'Shiraz'! Slightly cooler areas seem to do best: Edna, Santa Ynez and Santa Maria valleys on the **Central Coast**; Carneros and Mendocino on the **North Coast**. Cambria (Santa Maria), Qupé (Santa Barbera), and Fetzer's Bonterra (Mendocino) are good ££ examples. Cline and Havens are rich, silky, classy, black-peppered Carneros wines, Alban's Reva is a superbly textured Edna Valley Syrah (all £££+).

Washington State's quantity of Syrah is tiny, but the promise of the best is clear: dry, yet ripe, succulent medium-weights, with clear black-pepper coolness. Côte-Rôtie seems a useful reference (Columbia Winery's Red Willow, Duck Pond). Lesser wines are more herbaceous.

South Africa's volume is small, and both style and quality are still inconsistent. But, indicating Australia as the preferred model, they are now increasingly called Shiraz. In the late 1990s there seemed to be huge improvements, with noticeably richer, riper fruit (Graham Beck's The Ridge, Bellingham, Kanu, Boschendal).

Chile is experimenting with Syrah (Errazuriz). But **Argentina** is currently much more successful, with many particularly good-value wines in the £–££ range: strong, dark, juicy and smooth (Villa Atuel, Terralis, Flichman, La Chamisa), often with a touch of green olive atop the jammy ripe fruit. Luigi Bosca and Viña Alicia show both the ambitions and potential of Luján de Cuyo with classic Rhône-like constitutions, but a softer texture and sweeter fruit. Great potential.

New Zealand is determined to make fine Syrah. Its wines are like Northern Rhône styles in a cool year: light, crisp, clear, red-fruited, peppery, savoury wines. Te Mata's Bullnose leads; plus Stonecroft, Fromm and Babich.

merlot

Merlot is the friendly noble red grape. It is lower in acid, softer in texture, sweeter in flavour and ready to drink sooner than Cabernet Sauvignon. For a world in a hurry, with limited cellaring facilities and used to instant gratification, these are no mean advantages.

Merlot is a larger, thinner-skinned grape than Cabernet Sauvignon, making wines that are higher in alcohol, lower in acid, less tannic, and thus drinkable with pleasure earlier. It matures before Cabernet, an advantage in cooler climes, and it is also happier in colder, heavier soils in which Cabernet struggles to ripen.

The softness of Merlot's texture is echoed in its smells and tastes, which, when fully ripe, are a smooth, blueberry-blackberry-plum character. It takes readily to new oak, which adds a buttery, creamy topping to its dark fruit. If it is less 'complex' than Cabernet Sauvignon, its sensuality and drinkability more than make up for a perceived lack of intellectual challenge!

European Merlot

Outside Bordeaux, Merlot is widely planted throughout **South West France**, as part of the blend in Bergerac, Duras, Buzet, Cahors and Marmandais, and increasingly as simple, fruity Vin de Pays in the Midi generally.

In **Bordeaux**, Merlot accounts for more than half the red grapes, twice as much as Cabernet Sauvignon. And most of this is on the so-called 'right bank', unofficial but useful shorthand for the vineyards to the 'right' of the Gironde Estuary and Garonne River as you look at a map (*see* p168). Here it is the primary ingredient in the vast majority of wines. Merlot-based clarets* are drier-textured, less sweet to taste, and 'earthier' than most of their New World counterparts, and generally less overtly oaky.

The best-known Merlot-based prototypes of Bordeaux's right bank are St-Emilion and Pomerol. A typical **St-Emilion** wine will be

ABOVE *Pomerol, Bordeaux: on the right bank, whose cool, clay-dominated heart is ideal for the Merlot grape.*

LEFT *A close up of the clay soil in Pomerol, heavier textured than the gravelly soils of the left bank, less well drained when it rains, but holding the water better in drought conditions. Swings and roundabouts!*

Top wines to taste

Bordeaux, France
Châteaux: Pétrus, L'Evangile
Conseillante, L'Eglise-Clinet
Ausone, Magdelaine

California, USA
Duckhorn, Ridge Santa
Cruz, Pahlmeyer, Havens
Reserve, Newton

one-half to two-thirds Merlot, the balance being Cabernet Franc, sometimes with a touch of Cabernet Sauvignon. They tend to be light- to medium-bodied, fresh, dry, gently tannic wines. Once they get beyond their primary fruit stage they smell of melted butter, mown grass, fruit cake, with the local earthiness* behind. The affordable wines are 'straight' St-Emilion, and the satellite commune wines (*see* p168) to its northeast (Tour du Pas St-Georges, Maquin St-Georges).

Pomerols usually contain more Merlot, up to three-quarters, and are generally richer, warmer, fleshier wines with more fruit core, more cassis to smell, and with an exotic spice and truffle character in maturity. Pomerol is never cheap, so look for the lighter wines (De Sales, Clos René, L'Enclos) and **Lalande de Pomerol** (Siaurac, Haut Chaigneau, Des Annereaux).

Excellent Merlot-based, right-bank, value wines are found in: **Premières Côtes de Blaye** (Haut Sociando, Charron, Segonzac); **Bourg**, more solid (Roc de Cambes, Haut Guiraud); **Fronsac** (Richotey, Fontenil, Mazeris, Carles); **Canon Fronsac** (Charlemagne, Moulin Pey Labrie); and **Premières Côtes de Bordeaux** (Carsin, Constantin). But consult a specialist book for detailed advice on Bordeaux (*see* p159).

Ticino, in southeast **Switzerland**, makes a speciality of Merlot wines: ranging from light, fresh, stainless-steel-fermented wines to classy,

softly rich and faintly minerally, lighter Pomerol styles (Tamborini, Valsangiacomo). **Italy**, too, is a plentiful source of Merlot, the best coming from the northeast, Trentino-Alto Adige (San Leonardo), the Veneto and, especially, Friuli, whose wines are slender, juicy, perfumed examples. Not surprisingly, Tuscany makes fine, plush Pomerol look-alikes when they are not over-oaked; Avignonese's Desiderio is splendid.

Spain's limited amount of Merlot comes mainly from the northeast, largely a straightforward, juicy, berry-fruited style: Raïmat (Costers del Segre); Ochoa and Castillo de Monjardín from Navarra; Torres' Atrium and, more serious, the tongue-twisting Can Rafols Dels Caus from Penedès. Much of **Eastern Europe** makes soft, plum- and strawberry- fruited Merlot when the grapes are allowed to ripen sufficiently. Made around Villány in **Hungary** and, notably from 1999 onwards, from Domaine Boyar at Shumen and Iambol in **Bulgaria**, especially its Blueridge range.

New World Merlot

Merlot has become so popular in **California** that plantings increased more than tenfold between 1985 and 2000. During the 1980s it was often a strong, tannic, bell-peppery bruiser. Today it makes some of the state's most consistently drinkable wines – the best being softer, smoother and sweeter-flavoured than the Bordeaux model. Much ordinary, if pleasant wine comes from high yields in the Central Valley (Lodi, Modesto), but the whole state produces good Merlot, with cooler Napa and Sonoma doing particularly well.

There is abundant opportunity for making 'trio' quality comparisons here. Any cheap Central Valley wine (£ – *see* p118) will do as the first wine. Benchmark bottles at ££ would be Clos du Bois, Estancia, Fetzer Barrel Select, all smoothly plummy wines from Sonoma. And you are spoilt for choice at £££: Havens Reserve and Shafer are sleek, elegant Napa wines; Beringer is also good. With so much that is so good on offer, no wonder its popularity! Southeast **Washington State** is also clearly an excellent location for Merlot. Lesser versions

BELOW Washington State, USA: the bleakly beautiful, dramatic junction of the Walla Walla (left) and Columbia rivers on a frosty morning. Merlot has a great future here, would that they made more of it.

ABOVE *Hawkes Bay, New Zealand. The local landmark of Roys Hill in the background, and in front the flat, free draining shingly soils west of Hastings where Gimblett, Ngatarawa and Mere Roads are locations we will hear more of. Given the right clones, vineyard management, and sites, this looks like being prime Merlot country.*

are often red-berry in style, with a touch of herbaceousness. But the better wines are a particularly harmonious expression of the grape: soft-textured, yet fresh; blueberry and blackberry in flavour, with an elegant balance, crisper and tauter than California, closer to Bordeaux in style (Columbia Winery, Columbia Crest and Château Ste-Michelle, Canoe Ridge, Hogue, Hedges, Woodward Canyon, L'Ecole No 41.)

Chile makes very individual Merlot. One reason is the marked difference between day and night temperatures*, another is that much, maybe two-thirds, of Chile's 'Merlot' has turned out to be Carmenère (also known as Grande Vidure), a related, but clearly different-tasting grape. It has more colour, less acid and less

tannin than Chilean Merlot (making darker, softer wines). And, unless very ripe, it keeps its herbaceous characters: herbal, bell-peppery, sweet-sour tomato cum soy sauce. And that's the smell of most of Chile's Merlot – in a most attractive way. Rapel Valley seems particularly well-suited to the variety and there are first-rate wines at all levels: the basic and reserve wines of Casa Lapostolle, Cono Sur and Concha y Toro; and, from the Maipo Valley, Carmen. Fresh, juicy consistency and value!

Across the Andes, in Mendoza, **Argentina** makes less Merlot, and in a different style. The wines have little herbaceousness, less acidity, more alcohol and often more tannin. They are sweet to smell, sometimes to the point of jamminess, warm, ripe and generous to taste (La Rural, Weinert, Altos de Temporada).

There is little **South African** Merlot, and much is still dry and lean. The good wines vary enormously in style: fresh, supple, red-fruity from Paarl and Stellenbosch, probably the best sources (Warwick, Vergelegen, Morgenhof, Uiterwyk). And smooth, ripe, fluid (Benguela Current); strong and potent (Spice Route, Sejana) from the hotter, western Cape.

Australia also makes little varietal Merlot, but Henschke, Petaluma and Katnook are good from South Australia in a ripe, open, medium-weight plummy style. **New Zealand**, on the other hand, shows real promise for the variety, especially in Hawkes Bay. The 1997 and, especially, the '98 vintages were a revelation; I tasted several '98 Hawkes Bay cask samples for blending that would have done credit to a middle-rank Pomerol – rich, ripe, fleshy, ample wines. New Zealand Merlots to try: Esk Valley, Te Awa, Unison, Red Metal, Sileni, Sacred Hill, Kumeu River – basic wines, and reserves where available.

Merlot at a glance

Colour: medium to dark.
Alcohol: fairly high.
Acid: low to moderate.
Tannin: moderate, supple, but *can* be tough.
Aroma characteristics: moderate; marries very well with new oak. *Cool-climate/less ripe fruit:* red berry fruit, bell pepper, mint, eucalyptus, bruised leaf, green olive. *Warmer-climate/riper fruit:* blueberry, blackberry, ripe plum, violets, jam.
Bottle age bouquet: caramel, fruit cake, butter, mown grass, mushroom, truffle, leather, exotic spice, cassis.
Styles:
• light, fresh, soft.
• pliant, juicy medium-weight.
• full-bodied, rich, sleek.

LEFT *Sottoceneri, Ticino, Switzerland. A rare parcel of flat land in this most southern part of fine Merlot country.*

*See also

day/night temp *86*
earthiness *145*
tasting 6 *144*
claret *144*

nebbiolo

Top wines to taste

Piedmont, Italy
Barbaresco: Bruno Giacosa,
Angelo Gaja's Sori Tildin
Barolo: Giacomo Conterno,
Aldo Conterno, Elio Altare

Nebbiolo wines are most individual. They often combine a distinctly forbidding structure of acidity and tannin with a scent and flavour of remarkable delicacy. Modern winemaking is rounding off the rougher edges, but not to everybody's satisfaction!

BELOW *California: Bien Nacido Vineyard, in Santa Maria Valley, Santa Barbara. Here you can just see a trial patch of Nebbiolo on the left of the hillside. An experiment by the ever curious Jim Clendenen of Au Bon Climat, perhaps more in hope than expectation. There are trials elsewhere too: Erràzuriz in Aconcagua, Chile; Viña Alicia in Lujan de Cujo, Argentina; Brown Bros. in Victoria, Australia. The tannin always obliges, not so the perfume!*

With rare exceptions (*see* margin caption), Nebbiolo is limited to northwest Italy, **Piedmont** in particular. Here it is the grape used to make Barbaresco and Barolo, east of the Tanaro River and, respectively, north and south of Alba. It also makes tiny quantities of Gattinara, Ghemme and Carema in northern Piedmont (where it is known as Spanna), and Valtellina in Lombardy (where it is called Chiavennasca).

Nebbiolo ripens very late, and gets its name from the autumnal *nebbia*, mist or fog, that blankets the Piedmontese landscape by the time Nebbiolo is ready to be picked in late October.

Typically the wines are high in alcohol, high in acidity and with an abundant, fine-grained, but very dry tannin*; and its moderate colour (there is not a lot of pigment in the skins) develops a brick hue after only a few years.

The aroma of young Nebbiolo emphasises its sweeter, more fruity side: cherries, plums, violets; with maturity it develops smells of tar, oil, truffles, woodsmoke. These have given rise to the well-known shorthand: 'tar and roses'.

Barbaresco's image is of a somewhat lighter, more 'feminine', more rapidly maturing wine than Barolo. But, if there is a kernel of truth to this, individual vineyards and winemaking styles soon blur the distinction.

Communes and *crus*

In the past, producers would tend to blend the grapes from their different sites to make generic Barolo or Barbaresco. But recent interest in 'cru' wines has resulted in a greater awareness of subtle differences of style and quality between individual vineyard sites, and of Nebbiolo's ability, like Pinot Noir, to transmit them. These sites are often, if unofficially, called *crus*, by association with Burgundy.

Broader, perhaps more easily perceptible, differences are those between communes, in Barolo especially: La Morra and Barolo itself make lighter, more perfumed wines, which mature earlier; Monforte d'Alba, Serralunga d'Alba and Castiglione Falletto produce wines of greater richness, power and austerity. As with Bordeaux and Burgundy communes, these can be useful generalisations when trying to make sense of local variations in style.

Barolo and Barbaresco (£££+ – *see* p118) are pricey wines, the *crus* particularly so. A more

affordable start, for most pockets, would be Nebbiolo d'Alba (££), a lighter and more accessible Nebbiolo style. They come mainly from Roero – west of the River Tanaro, opposite Alba (Ratti, Prunotto, Ceretto, Bruno Giacosa).

Tradition versus innovation

Good, traditional, 'classic' Barolos or Barbarescos are not in any way 'thick'. Rich, yes, but with a transparency of flavour closest to that of fine red burgundy. And their impression of volume is due more to a mouth-filling scent, than to a concentration of fruit as such. Considering their power and firm, dry tannin, there is a surprising delicacy of balance, an unexpected subtlety of taste and aroma, to these great wines. That is one of the main reasons for the controversy over new methods of winemaking. For Nebbiolo's subtleties are easily overwhelmed, their distinctive, original qualities easily suppressed.

Traditionally the wines macerated for a long period on the skins, and were aged in large, old Slavonian oak or chestnut tuns. They were relatively pale in colour, with no new-oak flavours and the wines were certainly pretty astringent for many years. The new approach aims at more colour, greater fruit, and softer textures. Admirable aims as such, achieved mainly via much shorter skin contact* (sometimes using the Australian method of running the wine off the skins after a few days and finishing the fermentation in barrel*); and a shorter period in wood – and that oak being *new*. And this certainly makes good wine. What follows is a blind tasting note of mine (written knowing I was tasting Piedmontese wine). It encapsulates the debate: 'Inky purple; a thick, sweetly oaky nose, but with the tarry character of mature Nebbiolo behind; a rich, supple, fleshy wine, almost unctuously textured; concentrated, dark, sweetly ripe, spicy black cherry fruit, and fine length. Excellent quality, and very appealing. But seems

RIGHT *Piedmont, Italy; looking due west from Monforte d'Alba to the Alps and Mount Viso. The region gets its name from its location at the 'foot of the mountains'.*

ABOVE *Piedmont, Italy: Barolo castle at sunset, late November, after the vines have lost their leaves. Truffle time! Looking at the complexities of the landscape, you can see why there is such interest in individual 'cru' wines. But price, and pitiful quantities mean that for most of us 'straight' Barolo will have to do, or a good Nebbiolo d'Alba. I won't complain though.*

like Australia rather than Piedmont.' It was a ten-year-old, new-wave Barolo. Good wine? Yes. Good Nebbiolo? That's the issue. Because, good as it is, you can make this style of wine in many places. But the unique, traditional Piedmontese characteristics are only produced in this one location!

Innovation has indeed polished many old-fashioned Barbaresco and Barolo. And a balance which preserves but enhances their character rather than engulfs it is surely the ideal mean. Good traditional sources are the cooperatives in Barolo (Terre del Barolo) and in Barbaresco (Produttore del Barbaresco); and the individual producers Aldo and Giovanni Conterno, Ratti, Ascheri, Marcarini. Notable modernists are Altare, Scavino, Clerico. And somewhere between in terms of taste style are Sandrone, Grasso, Pio Cesare, Prunotto. Compare them.

Nebbiolo at a glance

Colour: moderately dark, browns rapidly.
Alcohol: high.
Acid: high.
Tannin: high, very dry.
Aroma characteristics: distinctive; subtleties easily masked by excess new oak. *Cooler-climate/less ripe fruit*: scented, floral, red fruit, red cherry, strawberry, white pepper. *Warmer-climate/riper fruit*: rose petal, black cherry, plum, violets, minerals.
Bottle age bouquet: sweet, scented, roses, tar, mineral oil, truffles, woodsmoke, leather.
Styles:
• full, crisp, aromatic and drily tannic.
• powerful, scented, dry-edged, yet delicate and fine.

*See also

barrel-fermentation **46**
skin contact **46**
tannin & food **162**
tasting 5 **140**

other red grapes

Constraints of space preclude a more extensive listing of all the following grapes, a number of which might fairly be considered as 'major': Sangiovese and Tempranillo, for example. A few of the pages have something of a national feel to them, but for a more precise listing, consult the index.

Sangiovese

Sangiovese is **Italy**'s most common grape, and central Italy is its heartland: Tuscany (Chianti above all), Umbria and the Marches. It is generally of moderate colour, medium-bodied, and high in acid and tannin. Its austerity can be softened by blending with a small amount of local white grapes or the mellow red Canaiolo, but today a little Cabernet Sauvignon* often does the job.

The nose of good Chianti is smoothly fragrant, reminiscent of rose petals, quality cold tea, and faintly oily. To taste, it is naturally crisp, and dry-edged with a cherry-sweet fruit. A 'cutting' wine, to be enjoyed with food. Inexpensive Chianti is light and vivid, to drink young. Good

Colli Senesi is a marked step up and real value (Falchini, Villa Sant'Anna). Chianti Classico and Chianti Rufina are the most reliable; fresh, dry, scented, elegant wines, often a touch bitter-sweet (Volpaia, Fontodi, Badia, Felsina, Grati, Antinori). Morellino di Scansano and La Parrina are also Sangiovese-based, as are the more truffly, concentrated and aristocratic wines of Brunello di Montalcino (Costanti, Barbi) and Vino Nobile di Montepulciano (Dei, Carpineto), whose *rosso* wines are less expensive versions.

Varietal Sangiovese is also found in modest quantities in **California** (Seghesio, and Fetzer's Bonterra). In **Argentina**, it is mostly quaffing wine; occasionally made in **Australia** (Montrose).

RIGHT *Flaccianello vineyard of Fontodi in Chianti, Italy; a so called 'Super Tuscan' because it is 100 per cent Sangiovese and thus doesn't qualify, legally, for Chianti. (Other prototype Super Tuscans are Sassicaia: 100 per cent Cabernet Sauvignon, and Tignanello: 80/20 per cent Sangiovese/Cabernet Sauvignon). Flaccianello is one of the most successful; firm without being astringent and not unreasonably priced. Many though are absolutely parched by excess new oak*. One of the justifications given is that new-oak ageing is supposed to displace grape tannin, a result that rarely seems to be born out, by my gums at any rate. Wickedly astringent is the more likely effect.*

Barbera

Widely planted throughout Italy, Barbera has good colour, low tannin, but high acidity. The acidity is a virtue in hotter climates such as those of Argentina, California and Australia. It performs best in Italy's **Piedmont**, especially in its southeastern corner, as Barbera d'Alba, Barbera d'Asti and Barbera del Monferrato.

Despite its much-mentioned acidity, well-made wines are usually lively, rather than sharp, and the low tannin gives them an easy, supple texture. Unlike many varieties native to Italy, its modest tannin and its unindividual flavour profile mean that it takes to ageing in small, new oak barrels with excellent results. Just as well, because much ambitious attention has been focused on Barbera since Nebbiolo became so expensive. Good examples are delicious: rich, smooth, vivid, the best also having considerable flesh, elegance and perfume. Barbarous? Nonsense! (*See* Nebbiolo for producers pp96–7).

Dolcetto

Dolcetto is another essentially **Piedmontese** variety. Its profile contrasts with Barbera's in that it is low in acid, and high in both colouring matter and tannin. Skin contact is thus usually relatively brief in order not to extract too much tannin once the colour has been drawn. Low acid notwithstanding, the basic wines are usually briskly fruity, the best being smooth, vibrantly juicy, black cherry and bitter almond gulpers, dangerously 'moreish'! They are mainly to drink young, though a few serious, oak-aged wines benefit from a year or two in bottle. Look for the good Barolo/Barbaresco producers.

Montepulciano

Montepulciano* is grown in eastern and southeastern Italy, but is at its best in the **Abruzzi** and the **Marches** (Rosso Conero), where plenty of sugar but moderate tannin and acid make an early-drinking, easily accessible style. Although much Montepulciano d'Abruzzo can be rather rustic, low yields and good winemaking produce a splendid, dark, softly rich, fleshy wine with a complex, mulberry warm, slightly peppery taste.

New oak? Yes, but with care: Illuminati's oaked wines often seem excessive; Valentini and Umani Ronchi judge their oak perfectly.

Lagrein

Lagrein is a high-colour, low-tannin grape from **Trentino**. Rosé wines are called *kretzer* or *rosato*; and the dark reds *dunkel* or *scuro*, reflecting the area's Austro-Italian duality. Good *rosatos* are full and scented, *dunkels* abundantly fruited, the best ageing a few years (Lageder, Niedermayr).

Lambrusco

From Emilia-Romagna. Look for a cork, not a screw cap! Then this grape produces a scented, frothy, red-cherry fruited wine to confound your prejudices. *Secco* is dry (Cavicchioli, Casali).

ABOVE *Every good wine book warns you not to confuse Montepulciano the town in Tuscany (in the picture here) with Montepulciano the grape, grown widely in southeastern Italy. I have made precisely that confusion, as this was* supposed *to be a picture from the Abruzzi, where particularly good Montepulciano comes from! However, I trust this will now have clarified the matter well and truly for you!*

BELOW LEFT *Just a lovely picture of Italian red wine demi-johns. I wish it could have been bigger.*

*See also

cab sauvignon **83**
montepulciano names **54**
new oak/grape tannin **46,48**

Corvina

Corvina is the main constituent of **Veneto**'s Valpolicella and Bardolino (*see* caption, left). A noble grape of considerable finesse, its virtues are those of scent, freshness and low tannin. But it lacks backbone and is therefore blended mainly with Rondinella – for colour, tannin and extract – and 'stretched' (many would say) with the pale, smooth Molinara.

Valpolicella is vastly more interesting than Bardolino. It comes in four versions, the 'normal' light red, *amarone*, *recioto* and *ripasso*. The standard wine is light in alcohol (11–12%), cherry-scented, and red-fruit fresh. *Amarone** is a dry wine, high in alcohol (14–16%), fermented from air-dried grapes into a bitter-edged, damson- and almond-flavoured wine, with a fine, filmy texture and great aromatic scope. *Recioto** comes from shrivelled grapes, not fully fermented, and is a rich, raisiny, bitter-sweet wine, in some ways port-like but lower in alcohol. *Ripasso* is a finished wine re-fermented on the sweet *recioto* lees to give complex, off-dry, faintly bitter-sweet flavours. Wonderful wines, many fine producers: Masi, Tedeschi, Boscaini, Allegrini, Quintarelli, Speri.

Teroldego Rotaliano

Teroldego Rotaliano is a highly individual grape, unique to **Trentino**. It is deeply coloured, densely flavoured, with a lively acidity and soft tannin. Good Teroldego has a supple texture and a real charge of blackberry fruit, sometimes slightly gamey (Foradori – outstanding, Dorigati, Sebastiani).

Nero d'Avola (Calabrese)

Sicily's red speciality, Nero d'Avola is light, fresh and vividly fruity at the cheaper end. However, finer versions are packed with strong, ripe black cherry and plum flavours; warm, mouthfilling, heartwarmingly delicious wines.

Corvo is the brand name for a good range (Duca Enrico especially); Regaleali (name and brand) is the best producer.

Negroamaro

The native grape of reds and (good) rosés from Italy's Puglia heel: Brindisi, Squinzano, Salice Salentino and Copertino. Vivid, juicy wines; warm, sweet, smooth, gently spicy, often with the faint sloe 'bitterness' of the grape's name. Occasional *amarone* style: Graticciaia. (Taurino, Vallone, de Castris, Conti Zecca.)

Aglianico

Aglianico is the splendid indigenous grape that makes **Basilicata**'s Aglianico del Vulture (Paternoster, D'Angelo, Martino); and **Campania**'s Falerno del Massico (Villa Matilde) and Taurasi (Mastroberardino). Smooth, fresh, limpid basic reds; elegant, tasty, remarkably complex and appetising top wines.

Sagrantino

Dark, tannic, sugar-rich Sagrantino, from **Umbria**, makes Montefalco Sagrantino: impressively potent dry reds. And, as *passito*, a powerful, bitter-sweet *amarone* style. (Antonelli, Adanti.)

Gaglioppo

Gaglioppo makes **Calabria**'s Cirò: strong, sweet, tarry, dry-edged wine full of character and individuality (Librandi's Duca San Felice).

Cabernet Franc (Bouchet)

Cabernet Franc is paler, less tannic, less structured than Cabernet Sauvignon, but its virtues are its raspberry and redcurrant fragrance, and its fineness of texture. In **South West France** it is usually part of a blend, adding scent and aromatic complexity wherever it is used: Bergerac, Côtes de Duras and Côtes du Frontonnais, for example. In **Bordeaux** it is used more in St-Emilion*, Fronsac, Bourg and Blaye than in the Médoc*, resulting in lighter, fresher wines where it appears in a high proportion.

Pure Cabernet Franc is at its finest in the **Loire**. Here the grape often has a faintly herbaceous aroma, allied to a fine chalkiness. Good Saumur-Champigny is a light, supple wine, mouth-wateringly fresh, positively surging with raspberry and cassis fruit (Couly-Dutheil Hureau, Filliatreau). Chinon makes a richer, more refined, scented and complex style (Joguet, Raffault, Baudry); while Bourgueil, often stiffened with a little Cabernet Sauvignon, has both sinew and tannin (Druet).

Northeast **Italy** makes fragrant, grassy examples, and though it is rare as a varietal in the **New World**, a handful of wines show just how good it can be: Yorkville Cellars, Vita Nova (California); Hogue (Washington State); Warwick, Bellingham (South Africa); Vasarelli, Cowra Estate, Heritage (Australia).

Malbec (Auxerrois, Cot)

Malbec shines in Cahors in France, and in Argentina. **Cahors** must be made of a minimum of 70 per cent Malbec, Merlot making up the balance. Its old-fashioned, 'black' wines were dark, strong, forceful and chewy. But that rustic character has recently become more civilised: riper grapes, a touch of new oak, more careful winemaking. Its best wines still have sinew and vigour aplenty, but with plummy fruit, and elegance, too (Triguedina, Gaudou, Lamartine).

Argentina's rendering of Malbec is different. Between 800 and 1000 metres (2600–3300ft) on the foothills of the Andes in Mendoza, Malbec is an altogether fleshier wine, often raisiny ripe, smelling of jam, tar and leather, and full of soft

blackberry and bitter chocolatey fruit. Catena (Argento and Alamos Ridge) and Valentin Bianchi make good-value, inexpensive Malbecs, and the new Terrazas winery has a consistently classy, ready-made trio for quality comparison: Alto (£ – see p118), Reserva (££) and Gran Malbec (£££).

Tannat

Tannat is effectively limited to **Madiran** in South West France, and to Uruguay in South America. Madiran is normally 40–60 per cent Tannat, with Cabernet Franc and Merlot adding scent and mollifying its abrasiveness. As the name suggests, tannin is the grape's most obvious feature, though most Madiran today is less astringent than it used to be. Noticeably earthier in flavour than Cahors, its top wines now have a dark, fine-textured, minerally elegance (Montus Bouscassé, Meinjarre). Uruguay's have a brisk Northern Rhône-like quality, and less tannin than most Madiran (Pisano, Toscanini, San Juan, Zaranz).

Négrette

Négrette is blended with Bordeaux varieties, and increasingly with Syrah, in the **Côtes du Frontonnais**. These wines are the antithesis of Cahors and Madiran. Fresh, gently flavoury, supple, scented, medium-weights, with a touch of pepper and a gentle blackcurrant fruit. They slip down a treat! (Bellevue La Forêt, Le Roc).

ABOVE *Argentina. Nicolas Catena's vineyards in Tupungato, Mendoza, high up in the Andes foothills. A perfect location, it seems, for fleshy, good-value Malbecs. And Catena's are amongst the best, at every quality level.*

RIGHT *France: Châteauneuf-du-Pape in the Southern Rhône. The most famous of Grenache's homes, with some of the famous large, oval 'galet' stones visible. These conserve the day's heat and keep the grape ripening at night, to produce the heady levels of alcohol typical of good Châteuneuf.*

BELOW *A view from the estate of Castillo de Monjardin in Navarra, Spain. The winery makes innovative blends of traditional varieties such as Tempranillo, with Cabernet, Merlot and Pinot Noir, for example.*

Tempranillo (Tinto Fino, Tinta Roriz)

Tempranillo is a Spanish grape making wine throughout much of north and central **Spain**, as well as **Portugal**. Typically its wine has plenty of colour along with moderate acidity and tannin. It is usually part of a blend, which can – in mature examples of Rioja at least – taste remarkably like good Pinot Noir: fresh, sweet, smooth, scented and relatively delicate.

It is best-known as the major component in **Rioja** (along with Garnacha, amongst others), where traditionally its sweet, cherry flavour has been strongly marked by the vanilla character of American oak*. In the past, much Rioja seemed stripped of both colour and fruit by spending too long in wood. But today's best producers are making a wine with more fruit emphasis, less oak dryness; as well as an increasing proportion of juicy young (*joven*) wines with little oak ageing.

To get a feel for the grape and its quality range you could line up Torres Coronas (£ – see p118), Barón de Ley Reserva (££) and Marqués de Murrieta Prado Lagar, La Rioja Alta Viña Ardanza or Marqués de Riscal Gran Reserva (£££) – all first rate. Ochoa, Guelbenzu and Chivite in **Navarra**, and Los Llanos from

Valdepeñas in central Spain, are other producers of Tempranillo-based wines to look out for. **Ribera del Duero's** high-altitude vineyards make Tinto Fino (Tempranillo) with more colour, black-cherry concentration, acidity and muscle than Rioja. And it is also successfully blended with Cabernet Sauvignon and Merlot (Flor de Pingus, Pesquera Crianza, Bodegas Reyes).

Grenache Noir (Garnacha Tinta, Cannonau)

Grenache – usually as part of a blend – produces a wide range of wine styles, from fluid, peppery, dry reds to thickly rich, fortified wines, most of these along a broad swathe running from southwestern **France** to northeastern **Spain**. **Southern Italy** (Sella & Mosca, Sardinia), **South Australia** (Melton, Mitchell, Henschke, Gramp, D'Arenberg) and **California** (Alban, Bonny Doon) are other quality sources.

The grape's typical attributes are a dark colour (which tends to brown rapidly), high alcohol and low acidity. Many **Southern Rhône** reds will have a high proportion of Grenache, blended with Syrah, Mourvèdre, Carignan and Cinsaut, amongst others. And the wines show Grenache's distinct white-pepper aroma, along with smells and flavours of raspberry, liquorice, aniseed, and a sweet, warm, peppery, mouth-filling power. Most of them seem to taste best without any new-oak ageing. **Côtes du Rhône-Villages** (especially from the villages of

Cairanne, Rasteau and Beaumes-de-Venise), then a step up to **Vacqueyras** and **Gigondas** (Domaine Cayron, and St-Gayan), and finally **Châteauneuf-du-Pape**, all generally represent good value for money. Try Clos des Papes, Château de Beaucastel, Janasse, Vieux Télégraphe and Clos du Mont-Olivet for good, traditional Châteauneuf, and Château La Nerthe's Cuvée des Cadettes for a new-oaked version.

Between the heady Southern Rhône reds and the sweet, fortified splendour of Banyuls from the southwest tip of France is an increasingly quality-oriented belt of elegant, aromatic wines based on Grenache, Syrah* and Mourvèdre*. Mas Julien (Coteaux du **Languedoc**), Mas Champart (St-Chinian), Mas Crémat and Domaine Gauby (Côtes du **Roussillon**) are some of the well-known leaders.

Banyuls and **Maury** are sweet, fortified wines – usually pure Grenache – now made in two styles: the traditional, deliberately 'oxidative', version, and, since the 1980s, a more modern, early bottled style (*see* margin caption). In **Sardinia**, Sella & Mosca's Anghelu Ruju is a fine Cannonau: richly raisiny and faintly medicinal, in the 'traditional', long-cask-aged style.

In northeast **Spain**, Garnacha is usually the major component in the red wines of **Navarra** (with Tempranillo). But the steep, rocky, schistous slopes of **Priorato** are where, blended with Cariñeña and Cabernet Sauvignon, it reaches its potent, inky, tannic and minerally acme – at prices which are the very inverse of the vines' derisory yields here (Costers del Siurana's Miserere and Clos de l'Obac, and Alvaro Palacios' Les Terraces).

Carignan (Cariñeña, Mazuelo)

Carignan is essentially a good blender, especially in Languedoc-Roussillon, and Penedès and Priorato in northeast Spain. It is the original mainstay of **Corbières** and **Minervois** – the quality of which is now much improved by more Syrah and Mourvèdre in the blend. Low yields from old bush vines can make special wines (Gauby, Vacquer in Roussillon) but these are exceptions.

ABOVE *Mas Amiel in Roussillon, Southern France. Traditional Maury is a fortified, 100 per cent Grenache wine: rich and sweet, with strong raisin, dried fig and caramel flavours. It spends a year outside in these 70-litre bonbonnes, before ageing in large old wooden casks for 5, 10, 15 years. Since the mid-1980s, 'to cater for a younger market', it has been making a wine more akin to vintage port, freshly fruity and tasting of ripe black cherries; and aged in bottle, not in wood: 'Vintage' Maury! Banyuls is similar, with its 'vintage' wine called 'Rimage'.*

Gamay

Gamay is at its light*, fresh, faintly peppery, strawberry-fruited best in **Beaujolais**, though there is also plenty of thin, acid Beaujolais that does little credit to the grape or the region. It's good too, if headier in style, in **Switzerland**, as a varietal wine in Geneva, and as a blend with Pinot in the Vaud (Salvagnin) and the Valais (Dôle). Widely planted in central France, and the upper **Loire**, with refreshing, redcurranty results.

Carbonic maceration is a fermenting technique closely associated with early-drinking Beaujolais. The fermentation begins with bunches of intact grapes in a CO_2-saturated atmosphere, resulting in a partial fermentation within the grape. This gives good colour, 'fruity' flavour, little tannin and its typical bubble gum, banana aromas. The ten Beaujolais 'Crus' (*see* p169) make more individual wines, of which Régnié and Chiroubles are the lightest, Morgon and Moulin-à-Vent the most structured – often to keep and age a few years (Duboeuf for a quality range, and availability).

Pinotage

South Africa's crossing of Pinot Noir and Cinsaut. The latter was originally called 'Hermitage' in the Cape, hence the name. Styles vary from plump, supple, juicy and unwooded (L'Avenir, Neetlingshof), often with a slightly 'acetone' nose; to rich, velvety and oaked (Kanonkop, Stellenzicht). **New Zealand** has some good examples, too (Te Awa).

*See also

american oak **48**

light/fresh & food **160**

mourvèdre **104**

syrah **91**

tasting 5 **140**

Mourvèdre (Monastrell, Mataro)

Mourvèdre is known as Monastrell in **Spain**, where it is widely planted; and, sometimes, as Mataro in **California** and **Australia**, where it is relatively rare. A small, thick-skinned grape, its wines have real individuality: high in alcohol, tannin, acid, and often 'high' in bouquet, too. A key feature is its nose, usually described as 'meaty', gamey, leathery; though to balance this somewhat primeval character there is also its fine fruit aroma of blackberries.

In **France**, Mourvèdre is grown all around the Mediterranean coast. As part of a blend, it provides fruit core, complexity and structural sinew to Grenache's* rather loose, peppery warmth in Châteauneuf-du-Pape, and blends with Syrah* in the **Languedoc**: Pic St-Loup, Faugères, St-Chinian; and Collioure in **Roussillon**. The finest French expression,

though, is in Provence's **Bandol** – wines of elegance, concentration and great perfume (Tempier, Pibarnon). In **Spain**, Monastrell is prominent in the Levant: Valencia, Alicante, Yecla, Jumilla. But yield is often high and, as yet, potential is barely realised except for an occasional potent, juicy, medium-sweet 16% alcohol red (Olivares). **California** makes small quantities of first-rate Mourvèdre: rich, dense, fine-textured and scented wines; less tannic, and accessible sooner than their French counterparts (Jade Mountain, Cline, Ridge, Phelps).

Baga

Baga is indigenous to, and widely planted in, **Portugal**, and notable, in particular, for its thick skin and dry, grippy tannins – second only to Nebbiolo! Best from **Bairrada**, its wines have an excellent centre of slightly bitter plum fruit, along with length and complexity within the slightly severe texture. Given time, well-made examples mature into firm, elegant, perfumed, faintly earthy wines, not unlike good Margaux (Luis Pato, Casa de Saima, Sogrape Reserva).

Touriga Nacional

Rare, top-quality varietal, Touriga Nacional is usually part of a blend, for port and table wines in **Portugal**'s Douro and Dão. Low-yielding, it produces deep, rich, tannic, structured and classy wines. Increasingly fashionable as a varietal table wine (Quinta do Crasto, Ramos Pinto, Quinta de Pellada). The great temptation is to over-oak them.

Touriga Francesa

Top-quality **Portuguese** grape. Used mainly in port, where it is a good foil for Touriga Nacional, being more delicate, fleshy and supple. It has a particularly fine, floral scent.

Zinfandel (Primitivo)

Grown throughout California, Zinfandel also appears in tiny quantities in **Australia** (Cape Mentelle), **Chile** and **South Africa**; and in southern Italy, along with Negroamaro, it is Puglia's most important red grape. Although, famously, it has been known to produce every style from pale rosé 'blush' to dark, sweet port-like wines, what it regularly makes best are characterful dry reds. More consistent than its styles are its lively acidity, its 'briary' nose (as in the faintly resinous aroma of the wild rose) and 'brambly', blackberry flavour (also rose-related) when really ripe.

In **California**, much straighforward, quaffing wine is sourced around Lodi in the Central Valley, but the cream comes from Sonoma, especially the old, stony river-bed soils of Dry Creek. There are numerous specialists: Ridge, Ravenswood* (rich, powerful, muscular), Nalle, Seghesio, Rosenblum (deep, generous yet elegant). An interesting comparison would be Ravenswood's Vintner's Blend (£ – see p118), Fetzer Barrel Select (££) and a top Seghesio or Rosenblum (£££).

In the heel of **Italy**, Primitivo is best known in Puglia as Primitivo di Manduria, with wines ranging characteristically from warm, juicy, supple table wines to fine, naturally sweet, *amarone* styles at 16% alcohol and more. Wherever it is made, excess oaking easily overwhelms its Zinfandel personality.

St Laurent

St Laurent is grown widely in **Eastern Europe**, but is an **Austrian** speciality in Neusiedlersee and Burgenland. Similar characteristics to Pinot Noir: pale colour, red-cherry scent, fresh acidity and little tannin. Low yields and subtle oaking make for fine red burgundy look-alikes (Umathum, Nittnaus, Stift Klosterneuburg).

ABOVE *100 year old Zinfandel vines at Kenwood, Sonoma, California. Sonoma seems to be the best overall source for this characterful grape variety, and Kenwood make a couple of good, and widely available versions.*

Blaufränkisch (Lemburger)

Blaufränkish is moderate in colour, with fair tannin, lively acidity and redcurrant to blueberry flavour. Simple versions are Gamay-like, more serious ones juicily aromatic. Oak easily dries them out. Best from Burgenland and Neusiedlersee in **Austria** (Igler, Triebaumer, Kollwentz) and Württemberg in **Germany** (Drautz-Able).

Zweigelt

Zweigelt is by far the most planted **Austrian** red grape, especially in Burgenland and Neusiedlersee. There are a few 'serious' wines, but it is mostly enjoyed for its bags of fruit and wonderful quaffing character (Pöckl, Umathum).

Dornfelder

Germany's third most planted red grape, Dornfelder, makes dark, generous, vivid wines, which take well to oak ageing. Finest in the Pfalz (Siegrist) and Württemberg (Drautz-Able).

Melnik

Melnik is grown around the town of Melnik, in **Bulgaria**, near the Greek border. Robust, potent wines, with a dry, peppery, Southern Rhône style. Generally finer than Mavrud (*see* below).

Mavrud

A Balkan grape, Mavrud comes mostly from Assenovgrad in **Bulgaria**. Tannic, muscular and chewy, often rustic from inadequately ripe fruit. Currently, prospects better than performance.

*See also

grenache **103**
ravenswood **162**
syrah **91**

Xynomavro

Xynomavro is Greece's most planted red grape variety – best-known for its wines from the northern Greek appellations of **Naoussa** and **Goumenissa**. The name means 'bitter-black', and if a few of its wines are indeed made in a dark, tannic, tarry mould, most are friendlier than the name suggests. Deep in colour, relatively full-bodied and fairly high in acid, but without a lot of tannin, they often have the red-cherry character on the nose and the lively sweetness of flavour to taste reminiscent of young Pinot Noir. And whilst not particularly high in alcohol, their fullness and warmth seem to recall Châteauneuf-du-Pape. An interesting cross! Naoussa ages well, developing Burgundian characteristics of game and undergrowth. Boutari's Grand Reserve is a benchmark.

Agiorgitiko

Also known as St George, Agiorgitiko is Greece's second most widely planted red grape. Its wines come from Nemea, near Corinth, in the eastern Peloponnese. As is often the case in Greece, the style of wine it makes depends greatly on the altitude of the vineyard, with grapes from higher sites, between 450 and 650m (1500–2000ft), making the best-balanced wines – not too much alcohol and with a fresher acidity.

    Nemea produces plenty of light, smooth rosés, but more typically a full, ripe, soft-textured, plummy wine, sometimes with a Côtes du Rhône-style pepper, and usually with cherry-sweet fruit. Numerous good sources: Semeli, Lazaridis, Boutari, Achaia Clauss. Particularly distinctive is George Skouras' Megas Oenos ('Great Wine'!) from Argos, where old-vine Agiorgitiko is blended with 10–20 per cent Cabernet Sauvignon. The result is a stylish medium-weight wine where neither new oak nor the Cabernet Sauvignon dominate unduly.

Limnio

Originally from the island of **Limnos**, Limnio is largely limited to Halkidiki and Thrace in northern Greece. Here it flourishes on the slopes of Mount Meliton on the middle of Halkidiki's three digit-like peninsulas. This is the location of Domaine Carras, and of the top Carras Limnio, (blended with 10 per cent Cabernet) – a soft, dry, warm, herby wine. The hallmark of Limnio is its herbal quality, a most individual bay leaf and sage aroma cum flavour. A character which shows itself in a particularly elegant manner in Constantin Lazaridis' Amethystos from Drama, Thrace; a long, crisp, elegant, ripe-fruited, savoury and herb-tinged wine.

Mavrodaphne

Meaning 'black laurel' or 'black bay tree'. Mavrodaphne is a speciality of **Patras** in the Peloponnese, where it produces deeply coloured wines. The best-known is Achaia Clauss's lightly fortified (15–16% alcohol) sweet, raisiny dessert wine, aged for many years in large old-oak barrels. There are also rich, dark, dry Mavrodaphnes.

Mandelaria

Widely planted in Greece, Mandelaria makes dark, strong, heady and often tannic wines, most frequently used for blending. Perhaps best-known as a principal ingredient in **Crete**'s Peza, and in the straightforward Chevalier de Rhodes.

Refosco

Refosco is rare. Makes a fine, individual Ktima (domaine) Mercouri red in the **Peloponnese**: dense, sweetly ripe, softly spicy wine. Delicious.

BELOW Domaine Carras' slightly oddly named 'Côtes de Meliton' vineyards on the central Halkidiki peninsula, Greece. Carras makes fine Limnio and Cabernet wines; the latter his most well known, especially to those outside Greece. It was John Carras who hauled Greece into the 20th century of wine by founding this vineyard in Sithonia in the mid-1960s.

sparkling wines

The best Champagne remains an unchallenged quality reference for sparkling wine, but the 'middle-ground' is fiercely contested, with many New World bubblies looking particularly good value for money.

Putting the bubbles in

Carbonisation is the cheapest, and simplest, way to make sparkling wines. CO_2 is pumped into finished wine in the way that soft, fizzy drinks are made – only used for the most basic wines that don't warrant a costlier process.

For better-quality wines, most other sparkling wine methods involve **two fermentations**: the first produces the 'base wine', the second the bubbles. Italy's Asti and exquisite Moscato d'Asti* undergo only one, partial fermentation in pressurised vats, thus preserving the wine's own sweetness and, above all, its muscat perfume.

Champagne method

The Champagne method involves six essentials.
1 First fermentation: in vat, furnishes a variety of base wines that will be blended to a desired style and quality.
2 Second fermentation: in bottle, is induced by adding to this blend a measured amount of sugar and yeast. The well-mixed blend of wine, sugar and yeast is then bottled. The 24 grams per litre of sugar, once fermented, are sufficient to raise the level of alcohol by just over 1% to 12–12.5%, and to produce a CO_2 gas pressure of 5–6 atmospheres in the bottle, three times the pressure in a car tyre! (It is gradually absorbed over time: *see* p137.)
3 Ageing on lees: once their sugar is exhausted the yeasts die and form a deposit – the lees.

Leaving the wine in contact with this, from a few months to several years, gives it a richer flavour, as well as time to soften.
4 Riddling: the yeast residue needs to be removed for the wine to be bright. The bottle is gradually turned and elevated from its horizontal position to the vertical, but upside down, so shifting the yeast into a shallow heap in the neck. Riddling was originally done by hand for each bottle over several weeks, but it is now more usually carried out *en masse* by computer-activated machines (giropalettes) over a few days.
5 Yeast lees removal (disgorgement): still in its inverted position, the neck of the bottle is immersed in freezing brine until a slushy plug of iced wine covers the yeast. The bottle is then up-ended, the temporary crown cap removed and the yeast plug expelled by the wine's pressure.

BELOW *Champagne's underlying layer of pure chalk, usually offered as a principal reason for the finesse and perfume of its wines. Most vineyards have a layer, of varying thickness, of cultivated topsoil above the chalk.*

6 Topping up and addition of sugar (dosage): when replacing the wine lost during disgorgement, and just before the cork is inserted, a small amount of sugar is also added, up to 15 grams per litre for 'brut' wines – the vast majority. This takes off the edge and softens the natural acidity of many sparkling wines.

Tank method

This is also known as *cuve close*, or the Charmat method. The essential stages are the same as the Champagne method, but from second fermentation everything takes place on a large scale in pressurised vats, including lees ageing, filtration, dosage and bottling. The process is less costly, and therefore better suited to less expensive wines and to bulk production.

Quality

The bubbles or 'mousse': sparkling wines have an extra dimension, their bubbles. These are the essence of their appeal, but they are not easy to describe. Criteria for assessing the mousse* are the size of the bubbles and how long they last. Coarse sparklers are aggressively bubbly and the seemingly large bubbles disappear rapidly. The best wines have a mousse which feels both small-bubbled, fine and creamy, and will continue to refresh and thrill for as long as you keep the wine in your mouth.

The wine: the bubbles blur our view of the wine itself, like looking at an image through frosted glass. But in terms of quality, the same criteria apply as to all wines: look beyond the bubbles for depth of flavour, how the wine holds up across the palate, for scent and persistence of finish.

Sparkling wines and styles

True Champagne rarely has a strong flavour as such, that is not its point. Blended, sparkling wine is made in this coolish, northerly climate precisely because the grapes ripen irregularly, and because as still wines they tend to be too mean and acidic for comfort. The appeal of good Champagne lies in its delicate, racing texture, its appetising edge and the way it refreshes and perfumes your palate.

The Champagne region is planted with three-quarters red grapes – Pinot Noir and

BELOW TOP LEFT Pinot Noir grapes being pressed, and yielding a pale rose coloured juice. Most of this colour will be lost during vinification.

BELOW TOP RIGHT Juice from different grapes and vineyards is fermented, and kept, separately. These wines are the 'base' wines which will be blended to a desired style, the cuvée, in the spring following the harvest. This is what Henri Krug is doing. The main aim is replicate the house style as closely as possible.

BELOW BOTTOM LEFT These detailed proportions will be mixed on a large scale, according to the quantities of wine available. To this new blend will be added a measured amount of yeast and sugar to produce the second fermentation. The small motor and propeller you can see aids both the large scale blending of the cuvée, and the mixing in of the wine, yeast and sugar.

BOTTOM RIGHT This still wine blend is bottled and sealed with a crown cap. Once the second fermentation, in bottle, is complete, the yeast die from lack of nutrients (sugar) and fall to the lower side of the bottle, forming the deposit you can see.

RIGHT *Anderson Valley, Mendocino, California. North of Sonoma, the climate here is cool and often foggy, the soil thin and rocky. It is ideal for making the light, crisp base wines for quality sparklers. No wonder that Roederer elected to plant here for its Californian operation.*

Pinot Meunier – and a quarter white, Chardonnay. Although Pinot Meunier accounts for nearly half the total plantings, Chardonnay is planted in nearly half of the top sites, for it produces a wine of great finesse, with a particularly fine-textured mousse. But on its own it tends to be lean, so it is complemented in Champagne blends by the softly fruity Pinot Meunier, and by the breadth and richness of Pinot Noir.

The rule is that a blend of the grapes is more complete than single-variety wines, as tasting the 'base' wines always confirms. And the exception that proves it, is a handful of exquisite *blanc de blancs*, pure Chardonnays, such as Pol Roger's Chardonnay, and Dom Ruinart! *Blancs de noirs*, black grapes only, can often be good value, cheaper Champagnes because they have a 'fat' that *blanc de blancs* at that price level rarely have. Pure black grape Champagnes at the top end are rare, because, without Chardonnay's freshness and tension they tend to be ponderous.

Personal non vintage favourites, in contrasting styles, are Veuve Clicquot (cushioned richness), Pol Roger (finesse, elegance) and Bollinger (weight, sinew). Bruno Paillard and Charles Heidsieck are two of the best value non vintage. **France** produces numerous other Champagne-method sparklers, which are now called *crémant*, a term previously used to indicate a lower pressure mousse. The best are light, fresh, gently sparkling wines, from (amongst many) Saumur* in the Loire (Langlois-Chateau, Bouvet-Ladubay), Alsace, Limoux near Carcassonne, and Burgundy. Cava describes wine made using the Champagne method in **Spain**. Most Cava comes from Penedès in Catalonia, where it is dominated by two firms, Freixenet and Codorníu. Much is pleasant enough but rather bland, often with a combination of pear-drop smells and earthy flavours. Codorníu's Raïmat, 100 per cent Chardonnay sparklers, are excellent, if atypical! **Italy**'s sparkling gems are its light, fragrant muscats from Asti in Piedmont; some of Lombardy's Chardonnay-based Franciacorta can be nutty and elegant (Ca' del Bosco, Bellavista). Most Prosecco, from Veneto, is a gentle, frothy, faintly almondy fizz.

The Champenois aggressively sue any use of Champagne-related words (as in *méthode Champenoise*) for wines not from Champagne. Fair enough. But many don't seem to mind using their own, intimately Champagne-associated brand names to promote their New World sparklers. At best it's called eating your cake, and having it! Perhaps we shouldn't carp, because many of the best non-European sparklers are collaborative ventures with Champagne houses: Mumm's Cuvée Napa, and Roederer Estate's Anderson Valley Brut/Quartet in **California**; or Domaine Chandon (Green Point for export) and Montana's Deutz in **Australia** and **New Zealand** respectively. For a crisper Australian style, from Tasmania's cooler climate, try the vintage Jansz Pipers River and Pirie, foils for Cloudy Bay's rich, yeasty Pelorus from Marlborough in New Zealand. **South Africa**'s top sparklers are Krone Borealis, Simonsig's Kaapse Vonkel and Graham Beck; whilst Nyetimber shows **England**'s promise.

BELOW *Sparkling wine just looks better in a flute, or a tall glass of some kind where you can see the bubbles rising in a prolonged column.*

sherry

Fino sherry, manzanilla in particular, has for some time been the most inexpensive fine wine you can buy. It is one of the rare cases where fashion and image (sherry fails on both counts) are noticeably to the aficionado bibber's advantage!

Jerez, in the southwestern extremity of Spain, has a hot, dry Mediterranean climate. The local *albariza* soil, a beautiful bright white (whence *alba*) chalk, is, however, sufficiently retentive of what rainfall there is, to make for practical viticulture. This soil, *flor* yeast, and unhurried *solera* time combine to make something special out of what is otherwise a rather dull wine grape.

The sherry grapes

Three grape varieties are permitted. The relatively neutral Palomino accounts for over 95 per cent of production, whilst tiny quantities of Pedro Ximenez and Moscatel, often partly sun-dried or 'raisined', are mainly used to make various types of sweet wine for final blending.

How sherry is made

Fermentation: all sherry starts life by being fermented dry, until a level of between 11% and 14% alcohol is reached. Indeed all sherry remains dry unless it is sweetened.

Fortification: for fino or for oloroso? Before being fortified, all newly fermented sherries are divided into these two broad categories according to their basic style, itself a reflection of the vineyards they come from. This is because they will need to be fortified to different levels of alcohol according to which category they fall into. Lighter, fresher styles will follow the fino route. This requires the presence of the surface yeast know as *'flor'*, which will not develop comfortably above 15.5% alcohol. Fuller, softer wines will become olorosos, and will be fortified up to 18% alcohol before going into barrel and into a solera (*see* p111). The barrels, or 'butts' as they are known, are not completely filled, in order to allow a gentle oxidation to take place over time.

Flor*: is known as a 'surface' or 'film' yeast because its waxy coating means that it floats on top of the wine. It occurs naturally in Jerez, developing best on wines of about 15.5% alcohol. As it needs air to flourish, fino barrels are only about four-fifths full, allowing the yeast to grow into a crinkly white skin. *Flor* produces fino's unique characteristics: it protects the wine from oxygen, keeping its colour pale; it feeds on traces of residual sugar, making it bone dry, with a unique, tangy bouquet.

BELOW *Dazzlingly white, water retentive, 'albariza' chalk soil in Jerez, Spain. This is what makes fine wine viticulture a practical possibility in a region that would otherwise be far too dry and hot. It holds the water, sponge like, for the root systems below the surface, and forms a hard crust in the sun which helps prevent excess evaporation underneath.*

How the *solera* system works: the aim
of a *solera* is to produce wines of consistent
style and quality. It is a form of controlled
blending based on the principle that young
fortified wine added slowly to older, more
mature and concentrated wine will take on
the characteristics of the older wine. (In the
case of fino wines the addition of younger wine
also keeps the all-important *flor* nourished.)
Solera is the term for a stock of such wines
in cask that are roughly a year apart. As the
oldest wines are drawn off for final blending,
so the casks are replenished from the previous
year. The system relies on no more than
a third of a cask being withdrawn per year.
The oldest *soleras* – those with the largest
number of vintages – will have been based
on the finest young wines initially, and will
be the most concentrated and scented.

Blending: as with port and Madeira, blending
to a house or brand style, and sweetening
where required, is the basis of the sherry
industry. This final product is made up from
a large palette of *soleras*.

Sherry styles

Fino manzanilla (*see* p156): is the palest,
lightest, most piquantly refreshing of finos –
drinkable, indeed, as table wine. Hidalgo's La
Gitana and Argüeso's San Léon are both widely
available and inexpensive benchmarks.

Fino: from further inland is fuller in style,
with less bite. The best is Tio Pepe from
González Byass; also good are Domecq's La Ina
and Garvey's San Patricio. Finos should be no

more than 15.5% alcohol, and, when opened,
drunk within a day or two.

Amontillado: true amontillado (as opposed
to a medium-dry commercial blend) is a fino
which has continued to age, but no longer
under its cap of *flor*. With more exposure
to oxygen these wines are darker in colour with
an aroma of melted butter and walnuts. They
are bone dry, penetratingly pungent and full
of personality. Valdespino's Don Tomás,
Barbadillo's Principe or González Byass'
Amontillado del Duque, for example.

Palo cortado: is a very rare beast sharing
the 'cut' of an old amontillado and the soft
scent of an old oloroso. Valdespino's Cardenal
is worth seeking out.

Oloroso: these sherries, based, as they are
initially, on broader, fuller wines and not
shielded in cask by *flor*, are darker, softer,
rounder wines than either finos or amontillados.
They are often noticeably fragrant – oloroso
means 'fragrant' in Spanish. Williams &
Humbert's Dos Cortados is a first-rate dry
oloroso, Sandeman's Imperial Corregidor,
González Byass' Apostoles and Matusalem
increasingly sweet versions. Emilio Lustau's
Old East India is a soft, luscious, grapey-sweet
oloroso. Syrupy sweet PX or Muscatel,
part-fermented then boiled down, impart the
colour and sweetness to these sweet olorosos.

PX (Pedro Ximénez): is occasionally
produced as a dark, thick, syrupy wine in
its own right. I am not alone in considering
it best used as a distinctive topping to good
vanilla ice-cream!

ABOVE *The port of Sanlúcar
de Barrameda, Andalucia,
Spain. Proximity to the
Atlantic ocean, onshore
breezes, higher rainfall and
a cooler local climate mean
that the vineyards close to
Sanlúcar produce the
lightest and driest of all
sherries, under the thickest
layer of flor. The finos here
are known as manzanilla.
This is one of Mick Rock's
many splendid photographs.*

Top wines to taste

Emilio Lustau: Almacenista
sherries
Valdespino: Don Tomás,
Cardenal, Coliseo
González Byass: Tio Pepe,
Amontillado del Duque,
Apostoles, Matusalem
Williams & Humbert: Dos
Cortados

*See also

flor **78**
tasting 9 **156**

port

Top wines to taste

Vintage ports from 1970 would be perfect: Taylor, Fonseca, Graham, Dow; 1977 Fonseca, Dow, Warre. 20 Year Old Tawny: Fonseca and Niepoort.

A thick black-purple liquor, with a prolonged, fiery, mouth-coating charge of tannic, peppered, liquorice and blackberry sweetness. A pale mahogany wine, raisin-scented, delicately sweet, satin-smooth.... These extremes are both top-quality ports: young vintage, and aged tawny.

RIGHT *Longstanding, traditional, narrow terraces at Taylor's Quinta de Vargellas in the upper Douro, Portugal. This only became accessible by road within the last 20 years!*

BELOW *The mouth of the Douro River with Oporto (right) on the north bank, and Vila Nova de Gaia on the south. Much port is still aged in Vila Nova in cool 'lodges', where it avoids the danger of 'Douro bake'.*

Protected by the Serra do Marão mountains from the Atlantic-generated moisture (in contrast to the lush, green Minho, Vinho Verde country) the upper Douro's arid, schistous soils and precipitous slopes bake for much of the year – as do the grapes they yield.

The port grapes

Port is not a varietal wine. Like Champagne, its best wines consist of a blend of complementary grapes. Amongst the dozens of legally sanctioned varieties, four of the best are Touriga Nacional (rich, muscular, low yielding), Touriga Francesca (refined and particularly fragrant), Tinta Roriz (the fresh, cherry-scented Tempranillo) and Tinta Barocca (potently high in sugar).

How port is made

Most port is red, and the key to its making lies in extracting as much colour and tannin as possible from the skins during the brief

fermentation period (24–48 hours). This brevity is essential because once the must has reached 5–6% alcohol, fermentation must be stopped, by fortification, in order to retain enough sugar for the wine to be sweet.

Fermentation and extraction: the grapes may still be trodden in old-fashioned lagares for the best wines (*see* margin), but the majority are fermented in sealed autovinifiers, which use the pressure created by the fermentation gasses to circulate the must and so effect the extraction. Mechanical treading devices are the latest innovation.

Fortification: port is fortified to between 19% and 21% alcohol by the addition of neutral grape spirit of 77% vol. In practice this means blending one part grape spirit to four parts partly fermented wine. The resulting level of alcohol kills the yeast and stops the fermentation.

Pressing: the wine pressed from the skins is blended back into the free-run wine.

Ageing: the various wines will then be aged according to their quality and destined style. Most is matured in old wooden barrels called pipes (550–620 litres), where the wine is racked, topped up regularly, and blended as required.

Port styles

Ports vary according to whether they are matured in wood or in bottle, and whether they are a blend of different years or a single vintage. The vast majority of ports are wood-aged blends – ready to drink when bottled, 'throw' no deposit and don't improve in bottle.

Basic ruby and tawny: 2–3 year old wines, blended to a style and price. Mostly bland, but good ruby wines (Smith Woodhouse, Dow, Cockburn, Skeffington) have juicy fruit and the requisite touch of fire and pepper.

Premium ruby and Vintage Character: 3–5-year-old wines from better grade fruit. Vintage Character is a premium ruby that is neither single vintage nor vintage in character. In the Premium ruby category Warre's Warrior and, especially, Graham's Six Grapes are a good

introduction to genuine port characteristics: peppery bouquets, depth of fruit, sinew, grip and warmth.

Late Bottled Vintage (LBV): single vintage wines. If bottled at six years, after fining and filtering, they throw no deposit. Traditional LBVs are bottled at four years, improve in bottle and need decanting. Considering the 'vintage' category, many LBVs are disappointing. Graham, Niepoort, Quinta do Noval, Taylor and Quinta de la Rosa usually have the extra savour, refinement and length.

Aged tawnies: 10, 20, 30 and 40 years old. These wines come from the same vineyards that produce Vintage port. Long barrel-ageing gives them polish, class, concentration and subtlety – *see* title paragraph p112. Fine 10 and 20 year olds, from Fonseca, Graham, Taylor, Niepoort, Dow, Poças and Ferreira, represent some of the best value of all ports.

Vintage: accounts for less than one per cent of all port production. 'Declared' only in the greatest years, and made from the best of the estate's own and purchased grapes, Vintage port is bottled after a couple of years in wood, and then needs 15–20 years to harmonise, lose its rawness, mellow in texture and sweeten in bouquet. Single Quinta Vintage wines are made by the well-known houses in 'lighter' years. These are from the grapes of one estate, with similar qualities of scent, richness, complexity and persistence to 'declared' wines, but on a less grand scale. Ready to drink sooner, at 12–15 years, and at under half the price of declared vintages, they are excellent value: Taylor's Vargellas, Graham's Malvedos, Warre's Cavadinha, Dow's Bonfim and Niepoort's Quinta do Passadouro are all good; as are independent Single Quintas, such as Quinta de la Rosa and Quinta do Crasto.

ABOVE *Traditional 'treading' of port grapes in large cement 'lagares'. This is still used for many of the best wines. Here the grapes are still being trodden in the far lagar, whilst the run off is taking place in the closer one; the point at which the partly fermented must is 'run off' into containers holding the fortifying spirit.*

NB decanting – *all vintage port contains abundant colouring matter and tannin, part of which precipitates out during ageing in bottle, forming a substantial deposit. For this reason it needs decanting*.*

*See also

decanting **138**
tasting 9 **156**

madeira

Top wines to taste

15 Year Old, Colheita, Old Solera or Vintage from: Blandy, Cossart Gordon, Henriques & Henriques, Lomelino, Rutherford and Miles, Leacock. All rare!!

Madeira is a most improbable wine – shot through with an acidity as sheer as the island's cliff faces, heated to a degree that would destroy any other wine, commercially anachronistic. And yet, for intensity of scent and savour, and value for money, quality Madeiras are without peer.

BELOW Funchal, Madeira. In the 18th century Madeira began to be shipped to the Indian subcontinent. Often barrels of wine were used as ballast, making a 'round trip', and subjected both ways to gradual, but extreme, temperature variations. It was discovered subsequently that these very wines aged with great beauty and complexity, so leading to the development of a more deliberate, controlled and practical method of heating the wines: the estufa system.

Some 400 miles (640km) west of the Moroccan coast and 300 miles (500km) north of Gran Canaria, Madeira is the visible remnant of an extinct volcano. A small (35 x 24 miles/ 57 x 23km) island of dramatically fissured rock breaches the Atlantic from its ocean bed nearly 4 miles (6km) below, and quickly rises to a peak of over 1,850 metres (6,000 ft). Much of this subtropical island is still covered in the forest that gave the place its name: Madeira, meaning wood.

Madeira grapes and their styles

Five grapes are used in the production of Madeira: four aristocrats, Sercial, Verdelho, Bual and Malvasia*, and one able *bourgeois*, Tinta Negra Mole. Madeira's viticultural history is too complicated to cover here, but of its 3,000 acres (1,250 or so hectares) of vines, barely two-thirds are used to make fortified Madeira, and of that, sad to say, 90 per cent is wine made from Tinta Negra Mole, and a derisory 10 per cent from the noble quartet.

Madeira and European law: European Union law decrees that if a grape variety appears on a wine label, the wine must be made from at least 85 per cent of that grape. As only the four noble grape varieties are permitted on Madeira labels, and given that they make so little of these wines, most Madeira has, perforce, to be described on its label by the style associated with one of the four noble grapes. The various styles are mentioned in brackets below, after the relevant grape name.

Sercial: (labelled as 'dry', in practice off-dry): grows its best quality when ripening slowly on the northern side of the island. The palest, driest of Madeiras; austere, tangy, with a piercingly lemony cut, and, given age, a fine, nutty scent.

Verdelho: (labelled as 'medium-dry', in practice medium-dry to medium-sweet): the other principal north coast variety; a more caramel-tinged vigour, still with an incisive acidity, but more mellow than Sercial.

Bual: (labelled 'medium-rich', medium-sweet to taste): grown on the south coast, the rarest of the noble grapes. A moderately rich wine whose medium-sweetness tempers its acidic edge. Smokily aromatic, subtly butter- and caramel-flavoured; at its best my favourite.

RIGHT *Two faces of Madeira, the north and south coast. The shadier northern side of the island is cooler just to look at, chilled as it is by north westerlies, and with its shingle constantly pounded by the surf. This is where the best Sercial and Verdelho grow, you can just make out the little hamlet of Seixal (a possible origin of the name Sercial) in the distance.*

BELOW RIGHT *Looking down the Girao cliff face on the south coast is a warmer, and headier, experience. 580 metres (1,900ft) below you can see Malmsey growing in a sea level hot spot, and half way up, on a giddyingly inaccessible outcrop, is a parcel of Bual.*

Malvasia, called Malmsey: (labelled 'rich', sweet but not intensely so): mainly grown on low-level hot-spots on the south coast. Richly sweet, and though the characteristic acidity tugs beneath the surface, this is the most immediately appealing of all Madeiras.

Tinta Negro Mole: is a relatively neutral grape which, according to when and whence it is harvested, can be broadly vinified to imitate any of the four styles described above.

How Madeira is made

Fermentation and fortification: Madeira is fortified with neutral grape spirit, which is 95% alcohol, to arrest fermentation at a point which will leave the amount of residual sugar* for the desired style, though the level of sweetness in lesser wines may also be adjusted later.

Controlled warming: immediately after fortification, Madeira is deliberately heated in an *estufa* (meaning a 'hot house'), in a slow oxidative process which only such high-acid wines can withstand. This gives Madeira its particular caramelised-sugar flavour, and, thus 'innoculated', renders it almost immune to oxidation after opening. (*Estufa's* origins are described in the caption p114.) Today the cheapest wines are kept between 40 and 50°C (104 and 122°F) for the legal mimimum of three months in large vats heated by stainless steel coils. Finer wines, destined for longer ageing, are heated more gently in barrel, either in centrally heated rooms or, for the best wines, in naturally sun-warmed attics (*canteiro*).

Ageing: subsequently, all Madeira is aged in old wooden barrels before being blended to a style and price. A minute proportion is destined to become 'Vintage' Madeira after a legal miminum of 20 years' barrel-ageing.

The quality hierarchy

Madeira's quality ladder is: 3 Year Old, 5 Year Old, 10 Year Old, 15 Year Old and then Vintage. Almost all 3- and many 5-year-old wines are of relatively expensive banality that gives little hint of the challenging beauty, drama and crystalline clarity of flavours that time confers on the nobly varietal 10- and, especially, 15-year-old wines. Today's best and most widely available Madeiras come from two companies: Henriques & Henriques, whose style is concentrated and vigorous across the range. And the Madeira Wine Company, who make Blandy's (rich and polished), Cossart Gordon (with more delicacy and finesse) and Leacock (somewhere between).

If, individually, Madeira wines seem expensive, remember you can keep returning to the pleasure of an opened bottle for months without its spoiling. Relish and treasure them before they disappear!

ABOVE AND FAR LEFT *A glance at any of these pictures shows the pressure there is on usable land on this small island. And bananas, buildings and tourism have been a more pressing priority than vines!*

*See also

malvasia **80**
residual sugar **42–3**
tasting 9 **156**

in the glass

7. the tastings

how to use the tastings

Do this course on your own and it will reward you, but it lends itself to larger numbers with clear advantages in cost, as well as in the exchange of ideas. A group of three to four people would be perfect!

Course structure

Synopsis: the course is summarised on p159, also in the summaries concluding each tasting. Consult p5 for the list of essay topics.
• Nine tastings, comprising 35 selected wines.
• Nine topics either specifically related to tasting, or short essays which consider a few key arguments arising from some of the most regularly discussed subjects relating to wine.
• Selected wines cover a price range of approximately £3–20/$5–30 per bottle.
• The 'ideal' wines are selected as mainstream examples to illustrate the principal characteristics of wine, and to provide illuminating contrasts of style and quality.
• In order to provide a sound foundation there is a progressive approach, limiting the aspects to be compared and absorbed at one go.
• As the course proceeds, certain instructions/observations are taken for granted, and the specific questions become more demanding.
• Throughout the tastings there is regular reinforcement of previously covered techniques, questions and perspectives.

Aims of the tastings

1 To provide a practical grounding in the essentials of tasting technique.
2 To show a representative selection of the most important wine styles and grape varieties from around the world.

3 By raising numerous issues and asking a wide variety of questions, to show you how to think about wine.

Tasting structure

Each tasting includes elements of:
• Tasting technique: the means to seeing what there is to see, reading the signals so to speak.
• Grape variety/wine styles: a cross section of major grapes and wine styles.
• Influences on wine other than grape: country of origin, vineyard site, winemaking.
• Value questions: interpreting what you have tasted; assessments relating to style, quality, preference, value for money, wine and food.

Each tasting consists of:
• A heading: a thought to consider, related to wine in general and to the particular tasting in question.
• The specific aims of the tasting.
• Wines to purchase: a table listing the ideal wines for the tasting, with an indication of origin (*see* maps), price, style and alternative wines.
• Buying advice: more specific guidance on the selection of appropriate wines.
• Suggested serving temperature.
• The detailed tasting exercises.
• Cross references to the main text.
• At the end, a summary of the principal points covered.

Tasting method

• **Discovery** by comparison is the essence.
• The basic method is to compare specific aspects of selected wines, with a particular purpose in mind, then to make sense of those **comparisons** by asking various questions.
• The point made early on is not to have too many variables to **consider**.
• Initially you consider just one aspect at a time, gradually building up a pattern of **observation**.
• The chosen aspects will reflect what is appropriate for the particular wine(s) and what suits the course **sequence** at that juncture.
• As you become more confident you will notice more anyway, and ask your own **questions** in addition, as you go along.
• The 'rhythm' of comparison is always 'to and fro', left to right first, then the other way round. Tasting subsequently in reverse order is often even more **revealing**.
• In this way you will learn an approach to tasting which includes a methodical **technique**, a set of reference wines and a vocabulary with which to describe them. You will also build up criteria for judging, along with a variety of questions to ask. As every good journalist knows, the real insight comes from knowing which questions to ask in the first place.

Preparation

• Consult the ideal wines list and buying advice carefully and then purchase the best 'ideal' or 'alternative' wines you can afford at the given price indications. It is a false economy to stint here! You can learn much from exemplary wines, whereas you will learn little from poor examples.

   The alternative wines will offer you similar, if perhaps less precise, comparisons.
• Section 2 in this book, a good wine merchant and various reference books suggested in Further Reading will all help. In spite of guidance there will be a 'hit and miss' purchase element occasionally. Don't worry, the comparisons will still be useful.
• Respect the price differentials as far as possible.
• Suggested serving temperatures for white wines are on the cool side as they tend to warm up rapidly in the glass.
• Make yourself a tasting sheet with plenty of room to note your impressions. The date, full names of the wines and their price will be useful references. You can simply head each section, as you go along, with: Appearance: wine 1, wine 2; Nose: wine 1, wine 2… etc.

Using the tastings to best effect

• Read the aims, ideal wines list and buying advice first to orientate yourself.
• The serving order is very important, left to right as indicated that is.
• Amount to serve: 3–3.5cl is about right, a generous half inch or a centimetre in a tasting glass.
• Instructions as to what to do are in bold type. My comments, to compare with your tasting impressions, follow in standard type.
• Rest and have a dry biscuit/water as you require, but not in between immediate wine comparisons.
• At the end of each tasting, check you have absorbed the essentials by reading the Summary.

Symbols and abbreviations

£, ££, £££
£ = £3–6/$5–10, ££ = £6–12/$10–20,
£££ = £12–20/$20–30, £££+ = £20–30/$30–50.
Alcohol
low = 5–10% vol,
medium (med) = 11–13% vol,
high = 13% and above.
(Always very approximate.)
Acid
low, moderate (mod), high, along with various acidity adjectives.
Tannin
low, light, moderate (mod), high.
+
for alcohol, acid, tannin, indicates likely to be on the higher side.
++
for grape varieties, indicates a blend, only main grape(s) indicated.

practicalities

A checklist of essential, desirable and luxury items for seated tastings

Essential
- A white background: plain white paper!
- Corkscrew: I find the Screwpull or the Pulltaps the best.
- Glasses: three or four per person, one for each wine, plus a water glass. ISO glasses are probably the most practical tasting glasses (*see* p13). Whatever you use, they should all be the same.
- Spittoons: one per person, or at least one between two. Any receptacle will do: jug, mug, beaker....
- Water: whatever is neutral and takes your fancy.
- Dry biscuits or plain bread.
- Jug and torch or candle for decanting.
- Writing materials.
- Kitchen roll: ...accidents will happen!
- Access to a fridge.

Desirable
- Foilcutter (1).
- Wine thermometer: for observing both room and wine temperature.
- Drop-Stop pourers (2): prevent any dribbles.
- Rapid Ice sleeves: kept in the freezer, the most practical means of chilling whites (*see* p125).
- Wine Saver inert gas (6): food-grade nitrogen to preserve unfinished bottles of still wine.
- Vacuvin (3): an alternative method for preserving unfinished still wine, but inert gas is best!
- Sparkling wine cap (5): for preserving unfinished bottles of sparkling wine.

Luxuries
- Daylight simulation bulbs/artist's bulbs (7): for true colour comparisons.
- Decanter(s): because they look nice!
- Champagne-cork grip (4): for weak hands.

Preparation
Avoid perfume and tobacco-smoke saturated clothing; many people find them off-putting in a tasting context.

Room temperature: start on the cool side if the room is likely to warm up rapidly. About 20°C (68°F) is ideal.

Wine temperature: each tasting has instructions relating to the wines in question.

Chilling wine: mainly whites (starting with the wine at a 'room' temperature of 18–20°C (65–68°F), and to chill by about 10°C (50°F):
- Ice bucket with ice and water: quickest – and messiest – method: a bottle of wine loses about 1°C every 2 minutes for the first 20 minutes.
- Rapid Ice sleeve: almost as quick and more practical: chills about 1°C every 3 minutes (*see* illustration p125).
- Your freezer: the wine loses 1°C every 4–5 minutes. Set a timer lest you forget....
- Your fridge: the slowest means by a long way, especially if constantly opened. Count on 3–4 hours for what the other methods achieve in 30 minutes!

Warming wine: mainly reds. Avoid direct heat such as open or electric fires as they heat excessively and unevenly. Buckets of warm water are acceptable. Standing the wine in an appropriately warm room in advance is much the simplest.

basic tastes and wine structure

These exercises remind you where your own sweet-, acid- and bitter-sensitive taste-buds are. They demonstrate the complex tastes and textures of alcohol, as well as how they function in wine. And they illustrate, albeit in a crude way, the basic structure and balance of elements in a white wine.

First you need to prepare three water-based mixtures, using sugar, lemon juice and vodka (*see* below). These you will then taste individually, and in various blends.

Serve the mixtures in four glasses, left to right: water; sweet (sugar); acid (lemon); alcohol.

Individual tastes

Sweet: have a sip of water, then taste the sugar solution, distributing the mixture well round your mouth.

Most people register sweetness* in two places, at the tip of the tongue, and at the 'taste-bud-dense' areas at the

How to prepare the mixtures

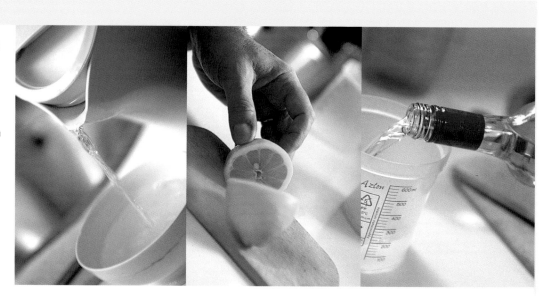

Ingredients (will serve ten):
25 grams/3 heaped teaspoons caster sugar
2 medium-sized, ripe lemons
¼ bottle (18.5cl) of branded vodka, about 38% vol (supermarket ones are often too sweet)
3 litres of still water

Equipment:
Boiling water
Measuring jug, ¾ litre minimum
Fine sieve
Sharp knife
Weighing machine or large teaspoon
Small bowl
Marked, empty plastic bottles, for the solutions.

For the tasting you will need:
4 tasting glasses
A spittoon
A few water biscuits
Paper to record your notes

Sweet mixture:
25 grams/3 heaped teaspoons of caster sugar + ¾ litre water.

Measure the sugar into a bowl, add enough boiling water to melt. When cooler, tip into the measuring jug and add water to make 75cl in total.

Acid mixture:
juice of 1–1½ lemons + ¾ litre water.

Cut and squeeze the lemons, sieve the juice, add water to make 75cl in total.

Alcohol mixture:
¼ bottle (18.5cl) of vodka + approximately 60cl water.

Measure the vodka, dilute with water to make 75cl in total.

back of the tongue, near your rear molars (*see* diagram, right). But many people also find they can taste sweetness over much of the tongue; it is not a very localised sensation.

Acid: taste the lemon juice solution.

Acidity* *is* a localised taste, you are likely to notice it clearly at the sides of your tongue. This makes it easy to focus on. The way in which it lingers also explains how acidity supports and defines the finish/aftertaste of a wine.

Alcohol: alcohol has a complex mixture of tastes and textures.
1 Consider its tastes first.
Take a sip, work it well round your mouth, and make sure you swallow a little. You should taste both a general **sweetness**, and a clear quinine **bitterness** at the back of the tongue. If you are unsure about the sweetness, have a sip of water first and taste the alcohol* immediately after for a comparison. That should make it clear.
2 Now consider the textures, the 'feel' of alcohol. Have a sip of water first, and taste the alcohol immediately after. How does it feel different from the water?
There are three sensations which distinguish it:
• **Weight** or **thickness**, a palpable viscosity which differentiates it from water. This gives wines their attractive 'body'. Return to the water and see how 'thin' and 'runny' it is by comparison.
• **Warmth**, which, when alcohol is high, can make wines taste 'hot'.
• A **spreading, carrying sensation** – you can feel alcohol coating the surfaces of your mouth. As such it distributes the flavours of wine all round your palate, and it also prolongs them.

NB: 'dry' white wines, especially, that have inadequate flavours to balance a high level of alcohol (13% and more) often taste somewhat 'sweet', and can be 'hot' and or 'bitter' in aftertaste as well.

Balance of tastes
Empty water glass and use for the following blends:
1 Mix the lemon and alcohol, 50/50: taste the pure lemon juice first, then the blend.
If you were in any doubt as to the 'sweetness' of alcohol, you won't be now. It moderates the acidity in a striking way.
Discard this mixture.

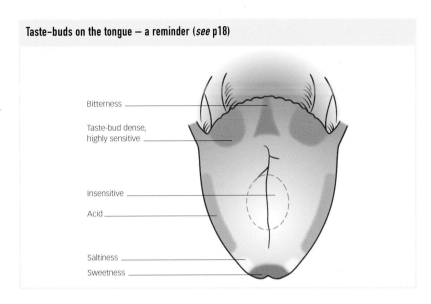

Taste-buds on the tongue — a reminder (*see* p18)

Bitterness

Taste-bud dense, highly sensitive

Insensitive

Acid

Saltiness

Sweetness

2 Mix the sugar and alcohol, 50/50: taste the plain sugar solution first, then the mixture.
Notice alcohol's own sweetness means there is no dilution of sweetness from the blending. Notice too how the alcohol 'spreads' sweetness round your mouth, and makes it linger after swallowing. Taste in reverse order to make the effect of alcohol even clearer. **Discard this mixture.**
3 Mix the lemon and sugar, 50/50: taste either the lemon or sugar solution first, then the mixture.
The way they neutralise and 'balance' each other to some extent is clear. Notice also how you can be aware of both tastes at once, or focus* your attention, at will, on either the 'sweet' or the 'acid' flavour, as you will do with wine's multiple flavours. **Retain this mixture.**
4 Add half as much again of alcohol to the lemon/sugar solution.
You now have a rather anaemic representation of a white wine: sugar is the flavour, the lemon represents the defining acidity, alcohol acts as you have just experienced.

BELOW LEFT *Colour code or identify your three mixture bottles, so as not to confuse the sugar and alcohol especially.*

*See also

acidity **20**
alcohol **21**
focus **16,23**
sweetness **20**

tasting 1

style and quality in dry whites

Wines vary in their make-up, like fruit. A good apple should be crisp and running with juice, sweet and sharp to taste. A good pear should be yielding, slightly granular in texture, softly sweet and scented. If they are good examples, one fruit is not better than the other, just different. So it is with wine.

Serving temperature:
6–8°C (42–46°F).

General procedure:
remind yourself on pp117–19.

Aims: this tasting teaches you the first steps in tasting technique and quality assessment. The comparisons will show what is meant by a 'noble' grape variety, Gewurztraminer* in this case, in contrast to less distinctive varieties such as Trebbiano* and Malvasia*, which go into Frascati, and Melon de Bourgogne, the Muscadet* grape. You will see how the balance* and style of white wines vary, especially in terms of alcohol* and acidity*.

Buying advice: all the wines for this tasting should be dry and unoaked. The main contrasts to look for are medium alcohol in wines 1 and 2, high in wine 3. Stick to the price differentials if possible (the alternative wines, Chablis and Alsace Riesling, are likely to be ££ rather than £).

Serve wines 1 and 2 left (Frascati) to right (Muscadet).

Appearance: wines 1 & 2

Check for clarity and brightness from directly above; describe the colour.

Both these young wines should be bright, and relatively pale.

Nose: wines 1 & 2

Compare the noses of both wines. Going from one to another will help you identify the differences. **Note intensity and specific aromas.**

If you find it difficult, don't despair! Both wines are made from grape varieties with little individuality of smell – usually light and fairly neutral, but hopefully clean and fresh.

Taste: wines 1 & 2

When you taste, take about 6–7ml of wine into your mouth, a large teaspoonful. Too little and you cannot taste properly, too much is unwieldy. Spit or swallow, as you like.

Taste for acidity 1: taste the two wines, left to right just to see the differences in acidity, focusing your attention on the upper sides of your tongue*, where you perceive acidity best. Which is sharper? Normally you would expect the Muscadet to have a bit more acidity than the Frascati. The Muscadet grape is naturally more acidic and the wine also comes from a more northerly latitude, from a cooler climate.

Taste for acidity 2: now taste right to left. If you were uncertain which was more acidic the first time, this order will make it clear.

Ideal wines	Origin	Grape variety	Price	Style			Alternative wines	
				alcohol	**acid**			
1 Youngest available Frascati	Latium, Italy	Malvasia/Trebbiano*	£	medium	mod+		1 Italian Soave	£
							Italian Pinot Bianco	£
2 Youngest available Muscadet	Loire, France	Muscadet*	£	medium	crisp		2 Petit Chablis, Chablis	££
							Alsace dry Riesling	££
3 1997/8/9 Gewurztraminer	Alsace, France	Gewurztraminer*	££	high	low		3 Viognier, France	££
							Gewurztraminer,	
							New World	££

This way round you will probably notice that the Frascati tastes softer than it did initially. This is because your palate is more used to acidity after several tastes, and because you are tasting a softer wine after a sharper one, which emphasises the difference. Remember, the very first taste at any session can be unreliable because your palate is not used to acid and alcohol! (*See* contrast effect p20.)

Taste for length as a measure of quality: if you are spitting, make sure you swallow a little wine first, as there are taste-buds in your throat too. (*See* p19.)
Taste 1 and 2 again, first left to right, then vice versa. This time concentrate on how long you continue to sense the presence of the wine in your mouth and throat after swallowing. Which wine lasts longer?
This persistence of flavour is referred to as the 'finish', or 'aftertaste'. If we like the tastes of a wine, the longer they last with each sip, the more pleasure we derive.

Thus length* is an important measure of quality. At a similar price level these two wines are likely to have similar lengths of finish, though the higher acidity of the Muscadet often makes it appear to last longer. (*See* p27.)

Taste for different balances and different styles: now go back and try the two wines again without focusing on anything in particular – just for pleasure. Which do you prefer? Can you say why?
These two wines are similar in that they are both light, dry wines, 'light' at only 11.5–12.5% alcohol, and 'dry' meaning that all the sugar in the grape juice has been fermented. But their balance* and their styles are slightly different. The Muscadet is crisper, 'drier'. Which you prefer here is a matter of personal taste. You may find the 'bone' dry Muscadet a bit too lean and sharp to be pleasurable, especially on its own; but this acidity is precisely what makes it such a refreshing foil to the briny juices of fresh oysters for example. Frascati, however, is often a deliciously easy apéritif on its own, as well as being very flexible with a wide variety of food.

Now serve wine 3 (Gewurztraminer) in the third glass, to the right of wines 1 and 2. (You may like to top up and refresh the first two wines at the same time.) Follow the same 'rhythm' of tasting with the Gewurztraminer.

Appearance: wine 3
Check the clarity, brightness and hue.
The Gewurztraminer may have a point less in brilliance than the first two, and it is likely to be a darker yellow. This may be because it is a year or two older, also possibly because the grape variety yields a deeper coloured juice.

Nose: wine 3
Describe the intensity and characters of the bouquet. How are they different from wines 1 and 2?
The nose is likely to be more intense, and easier to describe because its smells are more distinct. Gewurztraminer generally has a perfumed bouquet, recalling lychees, turkish delight and rose petals.

ABOVE LEFT *Colour is much easier to describe when you have two wines side by side to serve as reference points for each other.*

ABOVE RIGHT *Plain dry biscuits and/or water relieve the palate without distorting flavours. Use them when resting, but not between two wines you are comparing directly.*

*See also

acidity **20**
alcohol **21**
balance **31**
gewurztraminer **72**
length **27**
malvasia/trebbiano **80**
muscadet **75**
tongue **18**
'working' wine **19**

This distinctiveness means it is sometimes referred to as a 'noble' grape variety. This is not an official term, but one often used to refer to grapes which have a particular distinction, making them easily recognisable.

Taste: wine 3

Taste for acidity and alcohol again: remind yourself of the taste of 1 or 2, then taste 3. How does it differ from the first two wines? Focus on its acidity, its overall feel in the mouth and its flavour. You will notice that the acidity is softer. The overall impression of the wine in the mouth is fuller, smoother and warmer, the combined result of lower acidity and higher alcohol. This combination will also give the wine a slightly sweeter flavour, described as 'off-dry'.

Notice also the hint of spiciness from which the grape gets its name. Here again is a very different style of dry white wine; at the opposite end of the spectrum from the Muscadet for example (retaste after the Gewurztraminer to highlight the difference).

There is a rich, luscious quality to these wines that makes them attractive to taste, but maybe exhausting to drink by themselves. They are not refreshers in the manner of wines 1 and 2, but as a cool emollient to a mouth on fire from hot, spicy oriental cuisine they can seem an ideal choice.

A tasting technique comparison: take a sip of the Gewurztraminer and swallow it immediately. Concentrate, and note the impressions you get of the wine. Take a second sip, and this time work* the wine gently right round your mouth for several seconds, as though you were 'chewing' it. Swallow a little, and spit. Concentrate on your impressions again. What is the different effect of tasting the wine in these two ways? You should find that when swallowing immediately, you barely 'taste' the wine at all. Working it round your mouth means that you maximise the contact of the wine with your taste-buds and you will find all the sensations it has to offer magnified. For this reason, work the wine well round your mouth whenever you taste.

The Gewurztraminer costs twice as much as wines 1 and 2. You ought to feel at the very least that you are getting more sensations for your money, even if it is not your favourite of the trio. It should have a longer finish, with the fruit lingering at the back of your throat and its perfumes scenting your mouth.

Summary

In this tasting we have looked at the basic mechanical aspects of tasting, and considered the easiest means of measuring quality. We have seen that different grapes and origins produce different styles. There is no such thing as one ideal balance of wine. You will have a preference, but that is a different matter. And that preference may change according to your mood, the context, or the food.

wine and temperature

The temperature at which a wine is served makes a big difference to your drinking pleasure, and to whether or not the wine gives of its best. No question about that.

Once in the glass, wine is rarely static – it is usually warming up – and inevitably the serving temperature is a compromise between what is practical and what might be considered perfection. Furthermore, to judge by the way my wife and I fret over being served wines we consider too warm, and by the way friends of ours immediately wrap both palms round the glass we have just served them, personal taste plays no small part in deciding what is perfection!

You will also find your preferences vary according to whether it is summer or winter, and the food hot or cold. A relief, then, to know that you don't have to be too precise. Most wines will taste good, if slightly different, over a range of several degrees. The following are the basic principles:

Served colder

All wines:
• Smell less because the odour molecules vaporise less readily when cool.

White wines:
• Makes them more refreshing to drink, just as with water.
• Gives shape and definition to wines that are low in acidity.
• Masks sugar by delaying your perception of sweetness, making sweet wines less cloying.
• Reduces the burn of excess alcohol.
• Masks acidity by delaying your perception of it. (There is some disagreement over this amongst wine writers and scientists, but for me cold reduces the tartness of high acid whites. Try a crisp, dry white warm!)
• Makes sparkling wines less 'gassy' because the colder the wine, the less rapidly the CO_2 comes out of solution.

Red wines:
• Emphasises bitterness.
• Accentuates the astringency of tannin.

Served warmer

All wines:
• Smell more because warmth releases the bouquet more readily.

Red wines:
• Softens the astringency of tannin.

In the case of fine white wines, sweet or dry, there is a trade-off to be made between bouquet and freshness. To serve them too cold limits access to both flavour and the pleasure of a fine bouquet. But many people simply *prefer* their dry whites cold, and sweet whites very cold. In the case of red wines, the less tannic they are (and therefore the closer in structure to white wines) the cooler you can serve them, the more tannic they are, the warmer.

It is always easier to start with wines on the cooler side, as glass and wine can be rapidly warmed in the cup of the hand. If they are too warm when poured, the situation is irretrievable, except with ice cubes – OK only for lesser reds and whites in careless restaurants!

ABOVE *The Rapid Ice sleeve is the most efficient means of chilling wine; almost as quick as the freezer and less messy than the ice bucket. Fridge door is slowest.*

Serving temperature guide

A rough guide to serving temperatures: you must experiment, for your own tastes.

Wine type	°C	°F	
Full or tannic reds	17–19	63–67	Below 5°C (41°F) the
Medium reds, red burgundy	15–16	59–61	palate is anaesthetised,
Fine or full dry whites	11–15	52–59	much above 18°C (64°F)
Light, medium-dry whites	7–10	45–50	all wines lose bouquet,
Rich sweet whites	7–10	45–50	freshness and definition.
Champagne, fine sparkling	7–9	45–48	See p119, for advice on
Light, sweet whites	6–8	43–47	chilling or warming.
Sparkling	6–8	43–47	

tasting 2
terroir and quality in dry whites

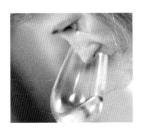

Some grapes have a singularity of aroma which makes their wines instantly recognisable, for that reason they are called 'aromatic'. Sauvignon Blanc is one of these. Here we contrast Sauvignon Blanc with Chardonnay. Both comparisons will show how important vineyard site – *terroir* – can be for quality.

Aims: this tasting presents a further step in tasting technique, and demonstrates that the vineyard site – *terroir** – where you grow your grapes can have an important impact on quality.

The comparison will show the different characteristics of two more noble grape varieties: Sauvignon Blanc*, the aromatic variety, contrasted with non-aromatic Chardonnay*. Finally, you will discover some of the effects of new oak on white wine.

Buying advice: wines 1, 2 and 3 should be unoaked, wine 4 should be oaked. It is important that the wine pairs are from the same grape and region, but different appellations. The second wine of each pair will be about twice the price of the first, maybe more in the case of the second white burgundy. Village and producer names matter here, consult the grape variety section, other reference books and a wine merchant you trust.

Serve wines 1 and 2 left (Sauvignon) to right (Sancerre).

Serving temperature:
8–10°C (47–50°F).

General procedure:
remind yourself on pp117–19.

Appearance: wines 1 & 2
Check both wines for clarity* and brightness.

Nose: wines 1 & 2
Compare the noses of both wines. Note down the differences in intensity, character and clarity.
These two wines are from the same grape, same region and made in the same way, but they come from different locations. Both should have the fundamental cool-climate Sauvignon Blanc characteristics of gooseberry, nettles, blackcurrant leaf… but wine 1, the Sauvignon de Touraine, is likely to be a slighter, more piquant, more pinched version. The Sancerre should be richer, more 'aromatic', maybe with more ripe fruit, and possibly with a stony, flinty undertone.

Taste: wines 1 & 2
Taste for depth of flavour and length of aftertaste: Taste wine 1 and concentrate on, and note your impressions of, two aspects –

Ideal wines	Origin	Grape variety	Price	Style		Alternative wines	
				alcohol	acid		
1 **Youngest available Sauvignon de Touraine**	Loire, France	Sauvignon Blanc*	£	medium	high	1 Inexp Sauv Blanc N Zealand, S Africa	£
2 **Youngest available Sancerre**	Loire, France	Sauvignon Blanc	££	medium	high	2 Premium Sauv Blanc N Zealand, S Africa	££
3 **Youngest available Mâcon Blanc**	Burgundy, France	Chardonnay*	£	medium	mod	3 Inexp unoaked Chard from almost anywhere	£
4 **1997/8/9 Côte de Beaune (St-Aubin, Auxey-Duresses)**	Burgundy, France	Chardonnay	£££	medium+	mod	4 Premium, oaked Chard from same area as 3	£££

the depth/breadth of flavour, and length of aftertaste or finish. **Taste wine 2 for the same aspects and note them down. Then retaste the other way round, wine 2 followed by wine 1, to confirm your impressions. Which has more flavour and greater length?**
Both wines will have a marked acidity*; that is the nature of Sauvignon Blanc, especially in a cool climate. But the Sancerre should seem richer and rounder, with more flavour and a longer persistence, altogether a more generous version of the first wine. This will taste even clearer on going back from the Sancerre.

A tasting technique comparison:
1 Take a sip of wine 2, the Sancerre, and work it gently round your mouth, swallow a little, spit. Note your impressions.
2 Take a second sip, and this time, as you taste, alternate between 'working' the wine (see p124), and drawing a little air through it, 'aerating'* it. (The easiest way to do this is to keep the wine at the front of your mouth, purse your lips as though pronouncing 'F' and gently to suck, rather than breathe, air across the wine.) Swallow a little, and spit. How do your impressions of the wine differ from the first taste?
Aeration helps release the wine's particles of smell and thus enhances your ability to 'taste' it. This is particularly true for wines with a strong aromatic component such as those made from Sauvignon Blanc. You should find that

doing this makes the wine come alive, 'turns it on', suffusing your oral cavity with a fine mist, a starburst of scents that you barely experience otherwise. And the more aromatic the wine, the more you will notice this. Beware of overdoing it, however, as it can also make alcohol and acidity appear more aggressive.

Taste for quality as revealed by aromatic intensity: this time taste wine 2 first, and then 1. Gently alternate between 'working' and 'aerating' the wine before swallowing a little, and spitting. Concentrate on how differently the two wines fill your mouth with their aromas.
This is likely to show up the qualitative differences between the two wines very clearly. After the Sancerre, the basic Sauvignon will taste thinner, slighter, leaner, even if aerating it brings out more flavour. The Sancerre should have not only more fruit, but a greater range of aromas, amongst which aeration should highlight a certain chalky, mineral character – often referred to as the *terroir** taste.

The essential difference between these two wines is where the grapes are grown. The best Sauvignon de Touraine will never have as much to offer as the best Sancerre. This is because its generic soils, sites and climates simply don't nourish the Sauvignon Blanc grape in the same way as they do in the much more specific locations of Sancerre, Pouilly Fumé or Menetou-Salon. It is this idea of *terroir*, *ie* that particular sites exalt the possibilities of particular grape varieties, which underlies

ABOVE LEFT AND RIGHT
These inexpensive, flexible and washable Drop Stops are the most practical means of avoiding drips when pouring slowly.

Middle-palate length: if you have the time and the inclination, either of these pairs will clearly illustrate middle-palate length as a measure of quality. *See* pp26–7,146.

the French, and other, appellation systems (*see* p54,129). **Now serve the second pair of wines left (Mâcon) to right (Beaune), and 'refresh' the first pair.**

Appearance: wines 3 & 4

Check the clarity, brightness and hue.

Nose: wines 3 & 4

Compare the wines carefully, noting the differences of intensity and characteristics.

There should be a marked contrast. Most basic, unoaked Mâcons will have straightforward fruit aromas: apple, melon, tangerine. The more senior white burgundy will probably smell predominantly of its new oak*: caramel, butter, vanilla and so on, maybe masking the Chardonnay 'fruit'.

Taste: wine 3

Consider the Mâcon *on its own* first. Gently work and aerate, and make a brief note of a) its balance of alcohol and acidity, and b) its flavours.

This should taste medium- to full-bodied, be round yet fresh in its acidity, and have simple, pleasing melon and tangerine flavours which mirror its nose.

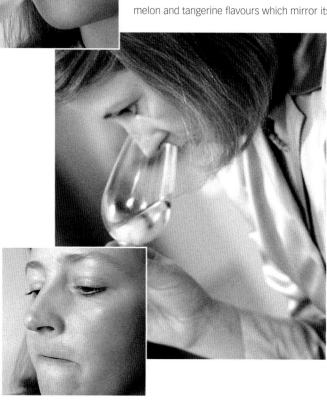

You will also find that aerating the Mâcon makes much less impact than aerating the Sauvignons. Chardonnay is less aromatic.

To put its acidity in context, briefly taste the Mâcon followed by the Sauvignon de Touraine.

You will see how much acidity the Loire Sauvignon has by comparison.

Taste: wines 3 & 4

Briefly retaste the Mâcon first to remind yourself of what it's like. Now taste the final wine, the second white burgundy, work, aerate, swallow a little, spit. Look in particular at the volume and variety of flavours, at the effect of aerating the wine, and at the length of finish. And compare them directly with wine 3, the Mâcon.

You will find similar types of difference as with the first pair of wines in terms of volume and variety of flavours*, and length of aftertaste. The Mâcon will taste 'simple' on going back to it, if still pleasing. You will also find that aerating wine 4 makes more difference than aerating the Mâcon. In particular it will bring out the oak 'aromas', and you may find that the oak also gives a more interesting 'key' to the wine's texture. The quality differences here reflect both *terroir* potential and oak influence. Oak cannot account for them on its own.

Other questions

As in Tasting 1, here we have grape varieties with very contrasting styles and characters, the Sauvignon briskly sharp and very aromatic; the Chardonnay more mellow, more obviously fruited, much less aromatic, but perhaps more immediately friendly. We consider their role with food in the next tasting. Meanwhile, ask yourself which of these four you *like* best*? Which do you think is the best *value*? The answers may well not be the same wine. And, of course, you may well feel you would want different wines for different occasions.

Summary

This time we have tasted clear quality differences again, as shown by depth and length of flavour. We have seen how aerating wine when you taste enables you to taste more completely and we have experienced what is meant by an aromatic grape variety. We have taken a first look at the influence of new oak, and at how vineyard location affects quality.

terroir

Terroir is the French word for soil. In the context of wine it has two very specialised meanings. The first refers to the influence of both the general and the specific environment in which the vine grows: the individual site and topography, soil and geology, general climate and specific weather patterns. The second refers to particular – and positive – tastes and qualities in the wine which are claimed to be the consequence of these environmental influences.

As a concept, *terroir* divides winemakers and winetasters because there is considerable disagreement as to what, if any, the connection is between the site and the wine. And, more importantly, whether it isn't possible to make just as good wine using the best possible practices in the vineyard and winery, but without the benefits of a special location. This is very similar to the nature versus nurture debate about you and me, and it is just as ticklish to resolve.

Those who possess a so-called privileged site – a 'terroir' – will insist that its 'nature' has the potential to imbue the juice of the grape, and subsequently the wine, with qualities of taste and texture that we value highly. And which a less-privileged site will never be able to match, however good the 'nurture' of winemaking.

Evidence to support the notion of *terroir*

In spite of considerable research there is little scientific evidence to show any correlation between specific soils and specific tastes or qualities. But what defies laboratory analysis is clear enough to our palates in some wines. What one might describe as the 'call of the soil' pervades the wine and reaches out to tug at your taste-buds and bewitch your sense of smell.

For proof of its existence one has only to taste in a good Burgundian or German cellar, to see that year in year out, in greater and lesser vintages alike, the same prime site consistently reproduces particularities of style* and quality*

which are noticeably different from those of its neighbours. Where the grape variety, vineyard practices and winemaking are exactly the same, *terroir* provides a convincing, if not yet scientific, explanation for those differences.

France's controlled appellation laws give geographically based names to her wines. These are founded on the idea, born of long experience, that certain combinations of soil, site and grape variety, *ie* certain *terroirs*, offer the potential to do better than others. Potential, because poor viticulture and/or winemaking can easily nullify the possibilities. But compare two good-quality Sauvignon Blancs from the Loire, and the best Sancerre or Menetou-Salon will always be better than the best Sauvignon de Touraine. Which is also a justification for the price differential.

Why *terroir* matters

Terroir matters because where it exists *terroir* offers the opportunity to create something special which, once sensed and enjoyed, we would feel poorer without. It matters because as consumers we are asked to pay more for such wines, and we should therefore demand more from them, and complain if they don't come up to scratch. It matters because winemakers* and winemaking practices can easily dominate and mask their qualities, and, given their uniqueness, that is tragic.

Is *terroir* important for all wines?

Absolutely not! For the vast majority of wines, especially the less expensive ones, what matters is simply good husbandry in any vineyard which will grow good wine grapes, followed by attentive winemaking. This combination produces the bulk of decent, juicy, regular-drinking wine; but the copious availability of standard, everyday wine is precisely what makes the *terroir* 'call' worth cultivating and cherishing.

ABOVE *Australia's most famous 'terroir', in Coonawarra*. This is a band of soil, approximately nine miles (15km) long by one mile (1.5km) wide, of deep limestone covered by a layer of red, 'terra rosa' soil.*

tasting 3

dry whites: old world v new world

An obvious comparison to make: Old World Sauvignon Blanc against New World Sauvignon Blanc. Like against like that is. Well, the comparisons are always interesting, but be wary of the conclusions you draw: the differences are often more telling than what the wines have in common.

Aims: this tasting introduces another tasting technique. By comparing Old World and New World wines of the same grape variety we can illustrate the profound effect of climate* on varietal character and wine style.

It raises the subject of how you decide what is 'typical'* for a given grape, looks at how temperature affects your impressions of bouquet and taste, and considers the influence of oak* again.

Buying advice: both the Sauvignon Blancs, wines 1 and 2, should be unoaked. Both Chardonnays should be oaked. Try to buy the Sauvignon Blancs at as similar a premium price as possible, but you may well have to pay a bit more for the white burgundy than for the New World Chardonnay. Look at the producer names I mention in the White Grapes and their Wines section, and, for the French wines, the same buying advice applies as on p126.

Serve wines 1 and 2 left (Pouilly) to right (N Zealand) – a generous helping this time (third of a glass).

Serving temperature:
8–10°C (47–50°F).

General procedure:
remind yourself on pp117–19.

Appearance: wines 1 & 2
Check the wines for clarity and brightness, and compare the colours.
With this pair you probably will see a difference in colour*. The New World wine, coming from a warmer climate and therefore with riper fruit, is likely to be a slightly darker hue.

Nose: wines 1 & 2
A tasting technique comparison:
1 Smell and compare both wines carefully *without* having swirled* them. Write down two or three adjectives for each (*see* pp12,14,66 if you want help with vocabulary).
2 Smell again, but this time give the glass a good swirl first and smell immediately, continuing to do so as the wine subsides. Note down what you smell this time. Are the aromas different?
Sometimes the differences will be marked, sometimes non-existent, but in order to maximise the number of sensations

Ideal wines	Origin	Grape variety	Price	Style		Alternative wines	
				alcohol	acid		
1 Youngest available Pouilly-Fumé/Sancerre	Loire, France	Sauvignon Blanc*	££	med	high	1 Premium Sauv Blanc Europe	££
2 Youngest available New Zealand Sauvignon Blanc	Marlborough, New Zealand	Sauvignon Blanc	££	med/high	high	2 Premium Sauv Blanc N Zealand, S Africa	££
3 1997/8/9 Montagny, Rully, St-Aubin	Burgundy, France	Chardonnay*	£££	med/high	mod	3 Village Puligny- or Chass-Montrachet, France	£££
4 1997/8/9 California Chardonnay	Napa Valley, California	Chardonnay	££–£££	high	mod	4 Premium oaked Chard, New World	££–£££

you can get from the wine, it is always worth trying both (*see* pp14–15).

The Loire wine will be more restrained than its New World counterpart and smell of the cooler side of the Sauvignon Blanc spectrum: sharp, nettly, gooseberry-like, and maybe (hopefully) with a minerally scent as well. The New World Sauvignon, especially if it is from New Zealand, is likely to be much more exuberant. The Sauvignon gooseberry will be there, but behind a ripe tropical and citrus fruit character.

Tasting reminders: remember the alternating rhythm of 'work – aerate – swallow a little' as you consider the wine before spitting.

Taste: wines 1 & 2

Taste for general differences 1 (left to right):
In the previous tastings you have made specific comparisons, one at a time, between acidity, alcohol, aroma, length of finish. This time make a more general comparison of style. The procedure is the same in that you will focus your attention on different aspects individually, but you will be implicitly addressing several questions at once. Given that this pair of wines is made from the same grape variety, pretty much in the same way, and at roughly the same retail price, what distinguishes one from the other? How would you tell the difference, if given them blind?

Taste left to right first, noting* down your impressions of the differences, maybe just as two short lists of adjectives.
This way round, you will probably be impressed by how much more of everything the New Zealand wine seems to have: a fuller alcoholic weight, a greater concentration of fruit, a more immediate rush of sensation in the mouth, a riper taste, and so on. But all the while with the clear Sauvignon Blanc characteristics that were apparent to smell. Notice again how aerating this grape variety in the mouth brings out its flavour.

Taste for general differences 2 (right to left):
This time do the same thing, again asking yourself what distinguishes one from the other, but tasting the New World wine first.
Most of your 'left to right' impressions will be reinforced. The Loire wine will taste lighter, most probably sharper and with less fruit impact. But when you aerate it, you should find the almost chalky, mineral aroma of the Loire wine gives it a dimension which its New World counterpart does not have. You may, or may not, regard this as a virtue; what is interesting is to *notice* the difference to begin with, and then to evaluate it.

Making notes: you could use this Sauvignon pair to practise making complete notes, and, especially, to see how clearly you can make your words reflect the differences between the wines, *see* p26.

ABOVE LEFT *When preparing your tasting sheet, be generous with the space between wines. To begin with you will probably want to use more rather than fewer words as you experiment and develop your vocabulary.*

ABOVE RIGHT *An oak barrel stave. The underneath will show varying degrees of toast.*

Now serve wines 3 and 4 left (Old World) to right (New World), but this time leave wines 1 and 2 *unrefreshed* to start with.

Appearance: wines 3 & 4

Check for clarity, brightness and compare colours.
As with the Sauvignon Blancs, and for the same reasons, the New World Chardonnay is likely to be somewhat more golden hued.

Nose: wines 3 & 4

For New World/Old World contrast: as with the first pair, smell the wines *before* swirling, and *after*. How do they differ?
You will probably find similar generic differences to those between the Sauvignon Blancs. Given a similar age, the California nose is likely to be riper and more tropically fruited (pineapple, mango, passion-fruit), with a more up-front caramel and vanilla oak. The white burgundy will probably be more discreet in its fruit (apple, melon, peach) and less 'sweet' in its oak character – overall drier and slighter.

Taste: wines 3 & 4

Taste for general differences (left to right first, then right to left): compare these two, making brief notes as you did with the Sauvignons, for overall

differences of style, asking yourself again: both being Chardonnays, what distinguishes one from the other? And how can you articulate that in words?
The differences to taste will largely mirror the differences of smell. And once again you will notice a more mouthfilling presence – riper fruit flavours and an overall more 'abundant' character in the Californian. Note how, by comparison with the Sauvignon Blancs, aerating the Chardonnays mainly highlights the oak, rather than any additional aromatic character from the grape.

A number of rapid nose and taste comparisons: go back to either, or both, of the Sauvignon Blancs, by now well warmed up, and notice –
How the nose is stronger and sweeter for being warmer, though it is may be less clear-cut.
and in comparison with the Chardonnays –
1 Their lack of oak to smell, and their 'fruit'-based aroma.
2 How much sharper they taste a) because they are now warmer, and b) because the Chardonnays have less acidity.
3 How much more 'aromatic' they are to taste on aeration.

Conclusion

The differences you smell and taste between these pairs of the same grape variety are above all a reflection of climate differences, of very ripe versus less ripe fruit, of a warmer 'New World' climate versus a cooler European 'Old World' one. And your preferences? In a direct comparison like this it is often easier to like the more immediate fruit of the New World wines. But that is not the same as saying the Old World versions are 'poorer', either as a wine, or as an expression of their grape. They are different. In the case of the Sauvignon Blancs, both are recognisably Sauvignon, but perhaps with the family likeness of cousins rather than siblings. And in terms of what is 'typical', both pairs of wines speak at least as much of their country of origin as of their grape variety. You need to judge them, initially at least, on that basis. You can also try to make more objective quality comparisons using some of the criteria suggested on pp26–28.

Summary

In this tasting, we have looked at the effects of smelling wine before as well as after swirling it in the glass. At the effect of warmer temperature on white wine, and at the combination of oak and Chardonnay again. But above all at the effect of climate on varietal character and wine style.

tasting technique summary

Appearance

Action 1: with the glass vertical, on a white background, view the wine directly from above.
Note clarity, brightness, depth of colour; any CO_2 bubbles or sediment.

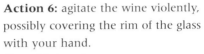

Action 2: with the glass tilted, view the wine at an angle, against a white background.
Note the principal hue – found at the 'core' of the wine – any colour nuances, difference in hue at the rim.

Action 3: holding the glass at eye level, look horizontally across the wine.
Note possible CO_2 bubbles sitting under the surface, and, after swirling, the viscosity.

Nose

Action 4: smell the wine without swirling it, either on the table, or by picking it up.
Note cleanness, intensity, varietal characteristics, oak quality, finesse and persistence of bouquet.

Action 5: give the wine a good swirl, smell immediately, continuing to do so as it settles.
Note differences from the motionless state, weightier smells, a possible progression of scents as the wine subsides, overall quality.

Action 6: agitate the wine violently, possibly covering the rim of the glass with your hand.
Note this is only necessary to encourage a 'dumb' nose to open up, or to confirm a suspected fault.

Taste

With simple wines you will be able to summarise them at one go; with the finest wines you will want to taste and retaste several times to experience all they have to offer.

Action 7: take a sip, about the size of a large teaspoonful, and work the wine all round your mouth; aerate, consider, swallow and/or spit.
Concentrate on the overall dimensions of the wine, making a rapid *quantitative* summary of the balance of alcohol, acid, tannin (in reds) and concentration of flavour.

Action 8: alternate between working the wine gently round your palate, aerating it and swallowing a little, for as long as the wine continues to hold your interest.
Concentrate this time on noting actual flavours, qualities and lengths. Look for the individual tastes, their intensity, variety and 'fruit' versus 'aromatic' character. Consider quality of texture, and the way in which the wine develops and holds up in the mouth (middle-palate length). Finally note the finish, its balance of 'scent' and 'fruit', and how long it persists.

Action 9: purse your lips and 'compress' the wine out with your tongue so as to produce a thin jet, accurate aim and no dribbles!

making notes

Why am I tasting this wine?

This is not as silly a question as it might appear. A tasting note requires a deliberate effort of attention, and, for the purposes of efficiency if nothing else, it makes sense to focus your attention so that you can concentrate on the issues which matter. These will vary according to the time available and the number and the type(s) of wine you are tasting. To give scant scrutiny to a fine, expensive wine which you will try only rarely is a wasted opportunity, whereas to write reams of adjectives about a basic quaffer may well just be a waste of time.

Two aspects to a useful note: **information** and **interpretation**, or the 'what?' and the 'so what?' These are quite different activities, and how well you can answer the questions in the second category will depend on how carefully you have tasted for the first. (*See* pp18–20.)

Information: this is the tasting note properly speaking, and answers the question, what is it like? It should be as objective, accurate and complete a description of the wine as possible, taking into consideration the limitations of time, space and quality. Simple wines merit a limited sketch, fine wines obviously deserve a more thorough coverage, but a minimum should include a summary of the wine's dimensions, along with an outline of its flavours, texture and quality. How to practise this is covered in detail in Section 1. (*See* pp25–6.)

Interpretation: decision time! A label and a price make implicit claims for every bottle of wine, and this is where you evaluate those claims based on the information your palate has just provided. Time, space and what you are trying to do will dictate which of the following questions you want to address:

• How much do you like it?
• How good is the wine, irrespective of what it is?
• How good an example is it of its type/grape variety/vintage/geographical origin?
• What are its particular virtues?
• What are its shortcomings?
• How does it rate as value for money?
• How ready is it to drink, and is it likely to improve with extra bottle age?

Shorthand: numerical scores, ticks, stars and so on – these can be a useful adjunct to help situate a written note, but if you rely on them as your primary, or only, means of assessment, you are likely to taste lazily.

• Directional arrows: a rapid means of indicating the state of maturity of a wine. (*See* margin illustrations p135.)
• Value for money initials: gv, fv and pv to indicate, respectively, good value, fair value and poor value.

If you find that you often need to taste rapidly – and efficiently – it is well worth experimenting and devising your own range of shorthand. One which will, when you look back at your notes, tell you more about the wine than the ticks, stars and scores on their own.

Château Sénéjac
1990
CRU BOURGEOIS
HAUT-MÉDOC
APPELLATION HAUT-MÉDOC CONTROLÉE

12 % vol.   ℮ 750 ml

COMTE CHARLES DE GUIGNÉ, PROPRIÉTAIRE-33290 LE PIAN MÉDOC FRANCE

PRODUCE OF FRANCE

MIS EN BOUTEILLE AU CHATEAU

BOX LEFT *Is the sort of complete note which requires time and careful attention, but which is well worth practising for the discipline it imposes and the insights it will bring.*

BOX RIGHT *Is the sort of note you might write when pressed for time.*

A complete tasting note

Wine: 1990 Château Sénéjac, Cru Bourgeois, Haut-Médoc

Essential details.

Place and date tasted:
London, 27th February 2000.

Appearance:
Clear, bright, dark red, with a brick rim just beginning to indicate some age.

Colour and evidence of maturity.

Nose:
Medium intensity bouquet; a plummy Merlot character along with a bit of Cabernet 'edge'; ripe cassis and Médoc earth after swirling, and just a hint of new-oak sweetness.

Varietal character, oak quality (if there).

Taste:
Supple, moderately concentrated, medium-bodied wine with a light, dry-textured tannin. Light, dry yet ripe fruited black and redcurrant flavour – Merlot flesh tempered by Cabernet freshness in character. Gently aromatic earthiness underlies; modest complexity and length across the palate, with good medium length of fruit and aroma on the finish.

Summary of the wine's dimensions. Flavour, aroma and texture characteristics.
Quality as indicated by middle-palate and finish.

Summary:
An exceptional Cru Bourgeois with the unusually fleshy texture reflecting the very hot 1990 vintage. Delicious and fully mature at ten years, but should drink beautifully for several years. A tribute to a great vintage and to the winemaking skills of New Zealander Jenny Dobson.

Performance within category and vintage.
Readiness to drink and future prospects. Any other thoughts.

A short tasting note

Dark red, brick rim; plummy Merlot nose + cassis and gravel. Supple medium weight, light tannin. Light, dry, gently earthy Médoc; ripe, fleshy, good length. V good Cru B.
gv ⟶

gv (good value), clearly for price x
⟶ *= drinking now*
↗ *= needs time*
↘ *= in decline, drink up*

You will invent your own shorthand too.

tasting 4
sparkling wines: style and quality

Curious things, sparkling wines: they are difficult to taste and describe, for the bubbles seem to get in the way! And though most of us will spend twice as much on a bottle of Champagne as we normally spend on a bottle of table wine, we probably pay it the least attention when drinking.

Serving temperature:
6–8°C (43–47°F).

General procedure:
remind yourself on pp117–19.

Aims: this tasting considers how to assess sparkling wine's* special feature – its bubbles, or 'mousse'*. It also looks at variations in sparkling wine style from different countries, examines how you can make quality distinctions in these wines, and finally considers relative value* for money amongst them.

Buying advice: you should pay roughly the same price for the Spanish cava and New Zealand sparklers, maybe a little more for the latter. For the Champagne you should pay one and a half times to twice as much as for the non-Champagne wines. Champagne prices vary enormously so shop around. 'Own brand' or High Street chain *blanc de noirs* (made only from the black grapes Pinot Noir and Pinot Meunier) are worth searching out for this comparison, they tend to be softer and richer.

Serve all three wines left to right (in the order of the illustration).

Appearance: wines 1, 2 & 3
Compare the colour of the three wines.
These are young wines and they should all be a pale yellow, the cava probably the palest, the Champagne the deepest

of the trio. Any suggestion of deep yellow or gold suggests the bottle has been on the shelf for some time and darkened with age.

Compare the bubbles.
From a visual point of view, the fizz is an unreliable indication of anything. After settling, the same wine, in three different glasses, may 'bubble' quite differently. CO_2 requires the trigger of microscopic air pockets to liberate its bubbles. These are found on dust particles and in pits and scratches on the glass surface, and they vary enormously from one glass to another (*see* p109).

Nose: wines 1, 2 & 3
Compare the three noses. Be wary of too much agitation as it encourages the sparkle to escape.
A lot will depend on how old they are, and that is so difficult to tell. Cava often has a combination of boiled-sweet, pear-drop fruit along with an earthy, minerally character; the New Zealand sparkler usually has a fresh, green-apple and citrus nose. In this sort of company Champagne usually stands out, sometimes with a bruised-apple aroma, usually with a noticeable yeastiness.

Ideal wines	Origin	Grape variety	Price	Style		Alternative wines	
				alcohol	acid		
1 Spanish cava NV	Penedès, Spain	Macabeo, Parellada++	£–££	medium	mod	1 Prosecco, Italy	£–££
						Inexp Aus sparkler	£–££
2 New Zealand sparkler NV	New Zealand	Chardonnay, Pinot Noir++	£–££	medium	lively	2 Loire Crémant	£–££
						S Africa sparkler	£–££
3 Champagne NV	France	Pinot Noir, Pinot Meunier, Chardonnay	£££	medium	lively+		

Taste: wines 1, 2 & 3

Taste for differences in style and quality: taste left to right in all of these exercises, and then vice versa. Please note to work the wine gently as usual, but you may not want to 'aerate' quite so much. There are sufficient bubbles already!

Taste for acidity: concentrate on the general feel of the wine in your mouth, and on the upper sides of your tongue. Note down an acidity adjective for each (see p20 if you want help here).
The acidity is likely to rise from left to right. The cava's will be the softest, it comes from a moderate climate; the New Zealand sparkler will have a livelier feel to it and the Champagne will have the most vigorous acidity. The last two both come from cooler climates, the Champagne especially. Tasting them the other way round will make the distinction even clearer.

Taste for mousse quality: you judge the bubbles by 'size' and 'time'; the smaller they feel, the more regular they are and the longer they last in the mouth, the better. The comparison will illustrate the differences.
The cava will probably seem frothiest, the New Zealand sparkler gentle by comparison. The Champagne will be the most aggressive to begin with, but its bubbles will probably last longest as you keep the wine in your mouth. Mousse quality has much to do with the quality of the base wine and the length of time the wine has spent in the bottle (see pp107–9).

Taste for length: look at how the bubbles and flavour 'hold up' as you savour the wine. Consider the fruit and aromatic persistence on the finish.
The acidity in the New Zealand sparkler and the Champagne will tend to give them a longer finish (see pp21,26–7), but notice how much more 'scent' the Champagne has in your mouth, and then leaves in its wake after you have swallowed.

More difficult and more tiring than tasting still wines, isn't it? After a rest, refresh the wines and just compare them generally.
The Champagne here should have the most to offer, it is the most expensive wine. But it is almost impossible to get tolerable Champagne at much under this sort of price. There are plenty of very pleasing sparklers from other parts of France, and especially from the New World, at half the price, like the Lindauer. Not the scope maybe, but for parties these alternatives represent real value.

Summary

Here we have seen how to judge the special aspect of sparkling wines: their bubbles; how their styles, like those of other wines, vary according to origin, and the virtue of scent as a feature, in Champagne especially. And what value non-Champagne sparklers provide.

ABOVE LEFT *Avoid swirling small samples of sparkling wine too much; you gradually lose the fizz by doing so, and the wine tastes flatter as a result.*

ABOVE RIGHT *The visual appearance of the bubbles is an unreliable guide to anything. How the wine 'sparkles' in the glass depends on numerous factors such as the cleanliness and smoothness, or otherwise, of the glass interior.*

decanting

Decanting is pouring a wine from its bottle into another receptacle, usually a glass decanter, but possibly into a jug, and then back into its own rinsed bottle – known as double decanting.

Why decant wine

The only *necessary* reason for decanting is when a wine has thrown a deposit in the bottle. If the wine is not separated from this sediment before being served it will look duller, and taste less pristine. The other possible reasons are to allow the texture of a tannic wine to soften and the bouquet to improve through rapid oxidation from contact with air. In each case the question arises of how far in advance of serving to decant (*see* p139).

Which wines to decant

Almost any wine, red or white, looks more appetising in a handsome decanter, and we are all influenced by appearance! But the vast majority of wines do not *need* decanting.

Deposit in a bottle

Substantial 'smudge' of deposit at the bottom of an old bottle of Châteauneuf-du-Pape, viewed with the bottle base held up to a domestic light bulb. This had been carefully taken from the cellar and stood up for two hours, most of the deposit settling within the first half hour.

Those that do are Vintage port, and fine red wines which are designed to mature for many years in bottle, principally those made from

RIGHT *Hold the bottle at the base and rest the neck on the decanter for a comfortable, steady fulcrum. Then manoeuvre the bottle so that you can see your light source across across the wine.*

deeply coloured, tannic grapes: Cabernet Sauvignon, Merlot, Syrah/Shiraz, Nebbiolo and Sangiovese. But the simple way to tell if there is sufficient deposit to warrant decanting is by holding the bottle base up to a light bulb. The Burgundian tradition is not to decant their reds, but if they are likely to be murky otherwise, many drinkers prefer to. Fine old whites can have a deposit too, they are then worth decanting to preserve their lustre.

How far in advance to decant

Blind tastings to try to decide this have been utterly inconclusive because individual wines vary so much. Unless you know how the wine behaves from previous bottles, the safest policy to follow is: the younger the wine, the less it matters how far in advance, several hours will not be a problem; the older the wine, err on the side of caution, and decant as late as is convenient. And convenience is often the deciding factor. If the wine needs to 'open up' it can do so very satisfactorily in the glass.

A lighted candle or bicycle torch behind neck or shoulder shows when the deposit appears as you pour, indicating when to stop (*see* photo left and below). Hold the bottle at the base, rest its neck on the decanter and 'slip' the wine down for gentle decanting of old or delicate wines with deposit (*see* above). The dregs can be filtered (muslin or coffee filter, though purists would say the paper can affect the taste), and used if not too muddy. A good 'splash' from a height will help awaken the bouquet and soften the tannins of a muscular youngster (*see* right).

LEFT *Gentle decanting: for old or delicate wines, just 'slip' the liquid gently down the side until you see the sediment start to appear.*

BELOW LEFT *Once you have begun decanting, pour steadily until the sediment appears, then stop.*

BELOW RIGHT *Vigorous decanting: this will most likely be for a young wine, in which case you won't need a light source. Pour so as to get a really good splash!*

tasting 5

style and tannin in reds

Red wines have an extra dimension – tannin – in addition to alcohol, acid and flavour. This means that they give us more to consider when tasting. It also means that, unlike white wines, we rarely drink them as apéritifs, because their tannin often needs to be tempered by food.

Aims: this first red wine tasting will examine colour* in red wine, and will introduce you to red wines of contrasting personality, in particular those made from the noble grapes Nebbiolo and Pinot Noir. You will see how we perceive tannin*, how different levels of tannin strongly influence the style of red wine, and how appropriate food* can moderate tannic astringency.

Buying advice: this group should not cause many problems, with the possible exception of the Nebbiolo. As usual, stick to the price differentials, and consult the Red Grapes and their Wines section for Rioja and Pinot Noir producers. The Nebbiolo should be without new oak preferably; any Nebbiolo substitute should have plenty of tannin and the Pinot Noir very little. Good, affordable Pinot Noirs of this type also come from New Zealand, from Victoria and Tasmania in Australia, from Oregon, and from the southern extremes of South Africa.

NB: you will need some good Parmesan (*Parmigiano Reggiano*) for this tasting, enough for a few shavings per person.

Serving temperature:
Beauj, Rioja and P Noir cool, 15–16°C (59–61°F); Nebbiolo warmer, 18–19°C (64–67°F).

Decanting:
check for deposit, decant if necessary, *see* p138.

General procedure:
remind yourself on pp117–19.

Tasting technique revision: you will have covered most of the techniques of tasting by now, and you might like to remind yourself of the sequence by looking at the complete summary on p133.

Serve wines 1 and 2, left (Beaujolais) to right (Nebbiolo).

Appearance: wines 1 & 2

Examine for clarity and depth from above.
Both wines are likely to be only medium depth, and may well look similar viewed like this, the Nebbiolo possibly a bit darker. But you will find that looking from above it is difficult to see the differences in actual hue, for that you need look at them with the glasses tilted.

Examine for differences in hue: holding the glasses by the stem and next to each other, tilt them away from you against a white background (*see* illustration p145). Note the core colour, and the

Ideal wines	Origin	Grape variety	Price	Style			Alternative wines	
				alcohol	acid	tannin		
1 Youngest available Beaujolais-Villages	Beaujolais, France	Gamay*	£	med+	lively	low	1 Any light, dry red	£
2 1996/7/8 Nebbiolo d'Alba	Piedmont, Italy	Nebbiolo*	££	high	high	high	2 Barolo or Barbaresco, Italy	££–£££
3 1997/8/9 Rioja or Tempranillo	Rioja, Spain	Tempranillo++*	£	med	mod+	light	3 Navarra Tempranillo, Spain	££
4 1997/8/9 Pinot Noir	Carneros, California	Pinot Noir*	££	high	mod+	light	4 Oregon, USA	££–£££
							Yarra Vally, Australia	££–£££

tint at the rim for each wine (*see* pp10–11 for details). Much easier to see the difference now, isn't it? The Beaujolais will be a pale, youthful purple/violet colour, the Nebbiolo more ruby, possibly even brick hued, because its colour matures and 'browns' rapidly.

Nose: wines 1 & 2

Compare the noses still, and after swirling. Concentrate, and describe the differences.
The Beaujolais will be light, and recall bubble gum, tinned strawberries, with a touch of pepper perhaps. The Nebbiolo will be fuller and more distinctive: sweet, smoky, tarry. Overall more aromatic, with a noticeably greater 'presence' in the glass.

Taste: wines 1 & 2

Taste for tannin 1: taste the two wines, left to right (Beaujolais first) just to see how different they 'feel' in the mouth, and in particular how they affect your gums. No need to pay attention to anything else at this juncture.
The Beaujolais should be light, simply fruity, maybe a little sharp from its acidity at this first taste, but relatively smooth. The Nebbiolo, however, along with a sharp acidity, is sure to grip your gums, 'fur them up', and give a strong impression of 'dryness'. This is 'astringency', the effect of tannin (*see* p22). It is typically marked in Nebbiolo wines. That's part of Nebbiolo's individual personality, but it does make them forbidding wines to taste on their own.

Tannin – a comparison with food:
1 Take a sip of the Nebbiolo, work it round your mouth briefly, swallow/spit. Note the general taste and 'feel' of the wine.
2 Then eat a piece of Parmesan first, and take a sip of the Nebbiolo immediately after. How does the wine taste different?
It will transform your impression of the wine. The forbidding astringency disappears as its tannin is neutralised by the cheese's abundant protein, and the Nebbiolo's fruit comes singing through. Tasted on its own, this forceful wine seems disagreeable, but with appropriate food it becomes delicious.

The Nebbiolo's strong flavour also matches the intensity of the Parmesan's taste; but the strength of this cheese will completely smother the lighter flavoured, almost tannin-free Beaujolais. Try it.

3 Try the Parmesan before tasting the Beaujolais to see what an unequal contest it is!

This is a simple illustration of two basic principles of combining food and wine:
1 Choose food and wine which broadly match each other's weight and flavour intensity.
2 If there is a strong individual flavour element (tannin in this case), then take that into consideration too. (For a more detailed explanation of this, *see* pp160–62.)

After a rest, some water and a dry biscuit, refresh the wines. Now taste them individually, just to see

ABOVE LEFT *Parmesan. It's remarkable what a bit of protein can do to transform the astringency of a tannic wine!*

ABOVE RIGHT *Decanting doesn't have to be into a fancy decanter, a jug is fine, especially if you are double decanting, ie decanting the wine off its deposit, rinsing the bottle, and pouring the clear wine back into the cleaned bottle.*

what they have to offer, noting their general proportions, flavours and lengths.

This pairing shows two wines at opposite ends of the red wine spectrum: a light and lively Gamay, relatively smooth, easy and fruity, a pleasant wine to quaff on its own or with simple fare; and a strong, firm, tannic rough diamond of a Nebbiolo wine which requires rich fare to make sense. Notice also the extra alcoholic warmth and aromatic aspect of the Nebbiolo on aeration in the mouth.

Now serve wines 3 and 4, left (Rioja) to right (Pinot Noir). Follow the normal tasting 'rhythm', comparing appearance, nose and taste.

Appearance: wines 3 & 4

Compare from above, and then tilted, as you did with wines 1 and 2.

Both wines are normally relatively pale in colour: with the glass no more than a third full you will probably be able to see the glass stem clearly. If you have a young, 'new-wave' Rioja, it may well be a bit darker, and more purple hued than the Pinot Noir.

Nose: wines 3 & 4

Compare them still and after swirling. Concentrate, and write down two or three adjectives to describe them. Going to and fro will help.

The most obvious difference here is likely to be the presence of clear oak vanilla on the Rioja. Both wines could have fruity black or red cherry notes to smell if they are young, along with more 'vegetal' characteristics if they have a bit of age. The Pinot Noir may also be more 'smoothly' sweet to smell.

Before tasting, go back and compare the noses of these two wines with those of the Gamay and Nebbiolo, in order to make the differences between the four grapes clearer.

Taste: wines 3 & 4

Whereas the first two reds, made from Gamay and Nebbiolo respectively, represent opposite ends of the red wine style spectrum, these two are much closer in style. Look particularly at differences in quality as revealed by tannin texture, and by length and scent; bearing in mind that you have probably paid a lot more for the Pinot Noir. Taste left to right to see the differences first, and then in reverse.

Neither of these will be strong wines. Good Rioja is both sweet and fresh – there is often a lemony hint to the acidity – with the oak clear to taste as well, and maybe causing a slightly 'dry' texture. The Pinot Noir is likely to feel 'fuller', without being 'stronger'. It will also taste sweet in its fruit, but it should 'perfume' the mouth more; and the 'feel' of good Pinot Noir is particularly silky. Because of its price the Pinot Noir should also be 'longer'. Notice how, when you go back to the Rioja, the 'dryness' of its texture is more apparent by comparison.

Finally, go back and taste the Nebbiolo.

This puts its tannin in perspective even more forcefully, doesn't it?

Summary

In this tasting we have seen the additional interest of colour in red wine and tried two very different noble red grape varieties – Nebbiolo and Pinot Noir. We also tried a strongly contrasted range of red wine styles, tasted tannin at very different levels, and experienced an excellent and a disastrous food and wine combination.

wine nonsense

Wine lore seems to be particularly rich in old wives' tales – these are a few of the most abiding bits of nonsense.

Old wine is better than young wine.
Occasionally, mostly not. (*See* p147.)

Where wine is concerned, anything goes – it's all just a matter of opinion anyway.
Plenty of opinions, and plenty of room for them. But we do have standards too! (*See* pp29–33.)

Don't use the freezer to chill wine.
Your freezer is less messy than the ice (and water) bucket and much, much quicker than the fridge. It is absolutely harmless, but absolutely essential to remember the bottle is there. So set your kitchen timer. (*See* p119.)

Salt and white wine remove freshly spilt red wine stains.
Not on the evidence of our tablecloths. They may cover them up and/or dilute them. They certainly create more mess, and possibly assuage the guilty hand. Remove stains they don't! If you are quick, and lucky, the washing machine might.

Great red wines don't taste good when they are young.
If they are likely to be good when they are old – no guarantee, mind you – they will taste impressive when young. This is especially clear when tasted from the barrel, when all their component parts will be in well-balanced proportions for their type. They may well go through an adolescent phase after bottling, when they seem unresolved, angular, maybe rough at the edges. But only the naïve or gullible believe that ugly youngsters make mature beauties. (*See* also p147).

Fine wines have a clear drinking peak.
Some fine wines are adolescent – and senescent, for that matter – longer than others. If they keep, try them and enjoy them for different reasons, at different ages, in different contexts. The perfect moment is about as easy to define as quicksilver. Specialist reference books and, above all, your own experience, will provide you with some answers. (*See* p147.)

Red burgundy should not be decanted.
Burgundian folklore. Burgundy is no different from other wines. If it has a deposit and you want pellucid wine, decant it. If you don't mind it murky to look at – and maybe to taste – then you needn't bother.

How many wines can you taste?
Presumably at one session. I am frequently asked this. It is about as intelligent a question as asking: how many pictures can you see in a gallery? All of them, if I canter round giving each a casual glance. But what would I get out of that? It depends on the quality of the wines, how much time I have, what I am trying to do and, maybe, how sore a head I want at the end. Quantity is rarely the issue. Except where you need to 'manage' impossible numbers.

A teaspoon suspended in a bottle of partly consumed Champagne will help it keep its fizz.
Oh yes? And water runs uphill! Silver or pewter spoon, Champagne or sparkling wine, this has to take the palm for the most tenacious piece of wine nonsense ever. Still, however, peddled as kosher by a few who know better in every other respect. To work it would have to defy the most elementary laws of gas pressure. Cold slows down the release of CO_2 gas, or a stopper. Nothing else.

ABOVE *Nonsense.*

BELOW *Common sense.*

tasting 6 terroir and quality in reds

Wines of real individuality and distinction come from grapes grown in particular locations. As its history proves, Bordeaux is a good point to start exploring this phenomenon, but time and experiments are revealing similarly promising site-soil-grape combinations all round the globe.

Serving temperature:
17–19°C (63–67°F).

Decanting:
check for deposit, decant if necessary, *see* p138.

General procedure:
remind yourself on pp117–19.

Aims: this tasting takes a look at two of the wine world's most famous red grape varieties, Cabernet Sauvignon* and Merlot*. You will get a glimpse of the infinite possibilities offered by blending wines from different grapes, taste again the difference that location can make to quality, and scent the underlying 'earthiness' that pervades claret – red Bordeaux that is – at almost any level. You will also discover two further measures of quality: the texture* of tannin, and the all-important middle-palate length*.

Buying advice: one aim of this tasting is to illustrate the difference between Merlot-based wines from Bordeaux's 'right bank'* and Cabernet Sauvignon-based wines from the 'left bank'*. A tall order, with only three wines. For this reason, careful choice will repay the effort. For wine 1, most Bordeaux Supérieur will guarantee you a largely Merlot-based wine, but a lesser St-Emilion would be a better example; and for wine 3 choose a St-Julien or a Pauillac if possible. Much of what we consider here would also apply to a New World trio, given similar price differentiations. A fine Coonawarra or Napa Valley Cabernet would work well as the third wine.

Serve wines 1 and 2, left (St-Emilion) to right (Médoc).

Appearance: wines 1 & 2

Examine them for depth and clarity from above.
Note that both wines are much darker than the Pinot Noir from the previous tasting, the Cabernet Sauvignon noticeably so. The right bank wine may be lighter in colour, both because it is a less expensive wine and because it is made largely from Merlot.

Examine the wines with the glasses tilted, next to each other. Note the core and rim colour.
Now you will be better able to see the more saturated colour of the Cabernet-based wine on the right. Given a similar age, the right bank, Merlot-based, wine is likely to look more brick hued, more mature at the rim. This is a function both of the grape variety, which 'matures' more rapidly, and of the lower quality level of this particular wine. Remind yourself about colour in red wine, and about the core and rim on pp10–11.

Ideal wines	Origin	Grape variety	Price	Style			Alternative wines	
				alcohol	acid	tannin		
1 1997/8 lesser St-Emilion or Bordeaux Supérieur	Bordeaux 'right bank', France	Merlot++*	£–££	med	mod	light	1 Merlot: Bulgarian or lesser New World	£
2 1995/6/7 Cru Bourgeois, Haut-Médoc or Médoc	Bordeaux 'left bank', France	Cabernet Sauvignon++*	££	med	fresh	mod	2 Premium New World Cabernet Sauvignon++	££
3 1995/6/7 Classed-growth 'second' or 'third wine'*	Bordeaux 'left bank', France	Cabernet Sauvignon++	£££	med	fresh	mod	3 Fine New World Cabernet Sauvignon++	£££

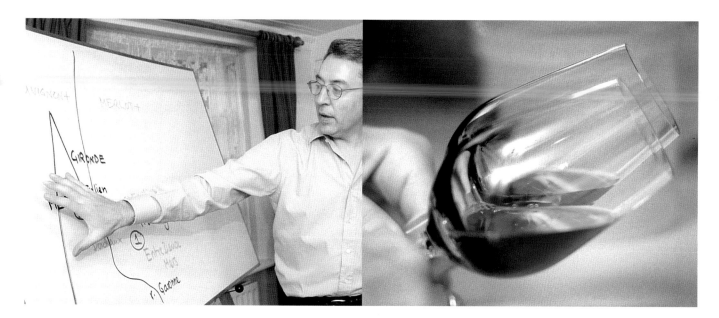

Nose: wines 1 & 2

Compare the noses of the two wines, still and swirled; concentrate, and note two or three adjectives for each.

The less expensive the right bank wine, the less you are likely to smell any oak. Unoaked Bordeaux Merlot usually has light, simple fruit aromas, reminiscent of stewed plums and fruit cake. It can be more or less sweet depending on the vintage, and possibly tinged with the vegetal characteristics of mown hay or grass. Any oak* will introduce butter and caramel. The Cabernet-based wine may well have a suggestion of cedary new oak, but it will certainly have a more blackcurranty core of fruit, and, especially after being swirled, a clear, light earthy aroma.

Taste: wines 1 & 2

Taste the wines left to right. First, what is the difference in the overall 'feel' and individual flavours of the wines?

Both of these will be only light- to medium-bodied wines, with a clear 'dryness' to them. 'Dry' because their fruit is not super-ripe and also because of their tannin. The Merlot-based right bank wine is likely to be straightforward, with a fluid, yet dry-edged feel to it; generally more supple in texture and more plummy in taste than the left bank wine. The Cabernet-based Médoc will be slightly sharper in its acidity, drier and more 'grippy' from more tannin, and with the distinctive raw blackcurrant/cassis Cabernet Sauvignon flavour at its centre.

Now taste and compare the difference in their 'aromatic' characters when you aerate the wines gently in the mouth.

The aromatic earthiness in the Médoc will be much more apparent and mouthfilling upon aeration.

NB: the two wine styles here of course represent an oversimplification of the difference between Bordeaux's right and left banks, but they make a useful start. (The essays on Merlot*, Cab Sauvignon* and the map on p168 help explain some of these differences.)

What is this 'earthiness'?

I was asked this question one summer evening when doing this very tasting. It had been still, close, sticky, and threatening a storm all day. Before I could answer, there was terrific clap of thunder and the heavens opened. As the flower beds outside slaked their thirst beneath the torrent, the breeze carried the aroma of their satisfaction around the net curtains into the room. I beamed, and everyone understood that there was my reply: the gentle scent of freshly moistened earth, as cleansing and refreshing to the evening air as claret to the palate. It was an extraordinary, illuminating coincidence. I have only once been indulged with such perfect timing!

Now serve wine 3 (classed-growth) to the right of wine 2 (Cru Bourgeois). Refresh wines 1 and 2.

ABOVE LEFT *For details of the 'left bank'/'right bank' distinction use the Bordeaux map p168, and refer to the Cabernet Sauvignon* and Merlot* essays.*

ABOVE RIGHT *As with white wines, colour is much easier to describe with two wines next to each other, as reference points for each other. But there is much more to observe in red wines, more to deduce too.*

*See also

cab sauvignon **83**
merlot **93**
middle-palate length **26-7**
oak **48**
right/left bank **83-4,93-4**
second/third wines **83, 84**
texture **28**

Appearance: wine 3

Check clarity, brightness and hue, as before.

Nose: wines 2 & 3

Compare the noses carefully, still and swirled, going to and fro, noting down the differences.

Wine 3 may well have more new oak apparent, the Cabernet cassis should be there; the earthiness, if present to smell, will seem more refined, less overt than in wine 2.

Taste: wines 2 & 3

For a brief general comparison. Remind yourself of the taste of wine 2 before trying wine 3.

In general wine 3 should taste richer, maybe riper, more mouthfilling in its aromas and longer on the finish. But let's look a bit more closely.

Have a rest, a biscuit and some water.

Taste for quality as revealed by tannin texture: this time taste wine 3 first. Pay attention just to the texture of the wine in your mouth. Taste wine 2 for the same thing immediately after. How does your impression of the tannin differ?

The tannins of wine 2 will seem coarser and rougher by comparison. The texture, or mouthfeel, of red wines is an important quality factor. One of the aspects we look for in expensive red wines is this 'fineness' of texture. (*See* p28.)

Taste for quality as revealed by middle-palate length: again, taste wine 3 first. As you gently alternate working and aerating the wine, see how long you want to savour it, how long its flavours continue to stimulate your palate as you keep it in your mouth, before it seems to fade. Do the same with wine 2 immediately after. What is the difference?

You will find that you cannot savour wine 2 for as long, you exhaust its possibilities sooner. It stimulates your taste-buds and imagination for a shorter time. It has a shorter middle-palate (*see* especially pp26–7).

Retasting, first wine 2 and then wine 3, will confirm this.

And this is as it should be. The last wine is more expensive, it should have more to offer – an important means to perceiving this is the middle-palate length. You will find a clear family resemblance between these two, but the last wine should not only be longer in the mouth and on the finish, but more aromatic and overall a more refined and clear-cut expression of similar characteristics.

Summary

Here we have had an all-too limited introductory glance at one of the world's most fascinating wine regions, Bordeaux; and at its wine, the light, dry, earth-backed, blackcurrant freshness that is claret. We have broached the flavours of Cabernet Sauvignon and Merlot, seen again what a difference location can make, and tried two more important measures of quality: texture and middle-palate length.

wines and age

Most wines don't age! The majority, by far, are designed to be enjoyed within a year or two of being made. Therefore, the rule for the vast proportion of what is on the shelves is: buy and drink the youngest available.

But as a beverage, wines are unique in that some not only keep for decades, but become more desirable with age, and thus repay keeping. These few undergo a magical transformation and develop a remarkable appeal to our senses of sight, smell, touch and taste. And although they represent a small proportion, once experienced, it is precisely these wines that turn the casual, if appreciative, drinker into the wine nut who delves deep into his or her pocket at the (often very unpredictable) prospect of future rapture.

What happens as wines age?

Sufficient acid and/or tannin will permit practically any wine to keep. But age by itself is not a virtue unless the wine improves with keeping. Wines which are likely to need ageing will often tell you so because, tasted young, their component parts, acid and tannin especially, seem individually obtrusive, sometimes harsh and raw. For those that improve over time, numerous minute chemical changes take place, rounding off the harsh edges, producing a smoother texture, a richer spectrum of flavours and aromas and a more harmonious effect overall. Reading and your own experience will reveal what you think is worth keeping. (*See* also p143.)

Which wines improve with age?

Price is an initial guide (more expensive wines are more likely to reward cellaring), specialist literature (*see* p159) is more useful. The principal international red grape varieties which age successfully are Cabernet Sauvignon, Merlot, Syrah/Shiraz, Nebbiolo, Sangiovese and, to a lesser extent, Pinot Noir. White varieties would be Riesling, Chardonnay and Loire Chenin Blanc. Add to these, botrytised dessert wines and Vintage port. Consult the White and Red Grapes and their Wines sections for suggestions as to individual wines and regions.

When are wines at their best?

You'd like a certainty, wouldn't you: 'tomorrow' …'November next year'… 'in 2007'? Because that's easy. But ask yourself when *you* are/were/will be at *your* best? Of course it varies with the wine, but it's more than that. Fine wines, like people, change with age: all vigour but not much subtlety when young, less muscle but a great deal more nuance when grey-haired… different ages, different virtues. There are also different moments of perfection, which vary according to taste, accompanying food, the occasion, different cultural traditions and so on.

There is plenty of guru guidance to be had, and the experience of others is a useful start. But experiment, and see which wines you prefer young or old. The saddest, all too frequent, negative approach is that which only regrets what the wine doesn't have, rather than enjoying what it does!

Tough, I agree, if you only have one bottle about which to make the decision. Even more reason then to relish rather than cavil, to see the glass as half full rather than half empty!

ABOVE *Two Rieslings: the 1988 Australian had poor bottling and absorbed too much oxygen; it looks, and tastes, old. In 2000, the 1985 Alsace was still a baby!* BELOW *Claret: a '94 Cabernet Sauvignon (left) and a '95 Merlot (right). The '95 looks older (more brick hued) as Merlot matures more rapidly than Cabernet.*

tasting 7

reds: old world v new world

Although grape variety is normally the single most important influence on style and character in wine, sometimes wines seem to smell and taste first of their geographical origin, and then of their grape – witness the Syrah and Shiraz here. *Terroir* on a grand scale? National style? See what you think.

Serving temperature:
17–19°C (63–67°F).

Decanting:
check for deposit, decant if necessary, *see* p138.

General procedure:
remind yourself on pp117–19.

Aims: this is last of the three red wine tastings. It first compares two classic, and very contrasting, expressions of Syrah: Old World Syrah from the northern Rhône, and New World Shiraz from South Australia. Then there are two examples of New World Cabernet Sauvignon at different price levels. Both pairs provide an opportunity to consider once again style differences, quality criteria, value for money, and to write notes* which make the differences clear.

Buying advice: as usual, consult the appropriate White and Red Grapes and their Wines sections for brands and producers. Try to buy the Syrah/Shiraz pair fairly close in price, and go for a mainstream Australian Shiraz from South Australia – Barossa or McLaren Vale. Chilean Cabernets abound, and the aim here is to get a good inexpensive Chilean to compare with California cream, primarily for a strong contrast of styles and quality. For wine 4, push the boat out for a really good Napa Valley or Australian Cabernet Sauvignon.

Serve wines 1 and 2, left (Syrah) to right (Shiraz).

Appearance: wines 1 & 2

Examine them as usual: for depth and clarity from above, for differences in hue with the glasses tilted. The principal difference, viewed either way, is likely to be that the Shiraz is a darker, more colour-saturated wine. Mainly an indication of riper grapes from a warmer climate.

Nose: wines 1 & 2

Compare the noses of the two wines, 'still' and 'swirled'; concentrate, and note two or three adjectives for each. How would you say they differ? The most immediate difference you will notice with the wines next to each other is the richer, oakier presence of the Shiraz. This is typically: blackberry, liquorice, jam, with the sweet vanilla and clove overlay of American oak*. By contrast the Rhône Syrah will seem more discreetly oaky, if there is new oak at all, and it will probably smell more peppery, possibly minerally, maybe with suggestions of singed meat. It will be 'drier' and less sweetly ripe overall.

If you are more familiar with French Syrah than with Australian Shiraz, the latter wine may well smell, initially

Ideal wines	Origin	Grape variety	Price	Style			Alternative wines		
				alcohol	acid	tannin			
1 1995/6/7 Crozes-Hermitage	Northern Rhône, France	Syrah*	£–££	med	mod–high	mod+	1 St-Joseph, France		££
							Valais, Switzerland		£££
2 1996/7/8 Shiraz	South Australia	Shiraz*	£–££	high	mod	mod	2 South Africa		££
3 1997/8/9 Cabernet Sauvignon	Chile	Cab Sauvignon*	£	med–high	mod	light	3 1999 Bulgaria, inexp.		£
							California, Argentina		£
4 1994/5/6 Cabernet Sauvignon	Napa Valley, California	Cab Sauvignon	£££	high	mod+	mod+	4 South or Western		
							Australia		£££

at least, more of Australian 'style' than of the Shiraz grape. The reverse is, of course, also true. In both cases this is a reflection of climate as well as of winemaking traditions.

Taste: wines 1 & 2

Taste them *individually* to begin with, making a 'taste' note for each. Look at actions 7 and 8, p133, and at the 'taste' notes on p135 for details of what to focus on. Taste the French wine first, and have a biscuit and some water before moving on to the Australian. When you come to taste the Shiraz, your impressions will be implicitly comparative but, as an exercise, make your initial description *without* reference to the Rhône wine.

NB: there are two reasons for doing this:
1 You can focus more objectively, and therefore accurately, on describing the wine in question in its own right, answering what is this like? rather than how is it different?
2 You avoid the tendency towards loaded words and an immediate rush to judgement: this is bigger, fuller, stronger (*ie* better?) or lighter, less concentrated (*ie* worse?).

As you know by now, I am all for comparisons because they can be so illuminating, but it is important to remember that comparing can be a distraction too, preventing you from seeing something for what it is, and instead seeing it mainly for what it isn't.

That done, however, you will want to make the comparisons. The Rhône wine will be higher in acidity, lower in alcohol, more earthily aromatic and peppery to taste; overall lighter, brighter and drier. The Shiraz will be fuller in alcohol, warmer, thicker and more mouthfilling, with more emphasis on ripe fruit and sweet oak. In terms of quality as measured by length they are likely to be very similar, but, as on the nose, their styles will be very different to taste. So much so, that it is difficult to credit they are the same grape variety! The wines seem to smell and taste at least as much of their origins, climate and winemaking traditions as they do of their grape. (*See* pp90–2 for more on these stylistic differences.)

Now serve wines 3 and 4, left (Chile) to right (California).

This is a demanding comparison of two wines because, apart from the fact that they are both New World Cabernet Sauvignons, in most respects you are not comparing like with like. The interest here is to taste two New World expressions of Cabernet to see how they differ in style, to see how you can perceive the quality differences there should be at this price differential, and then to consider each in terms of value for money.

Appearance: wines 3 & 4

Check for clarity and observe the differences in depth and hue.

ABOVE LEFT *Any container will do as a spittoon!*

ABOVE RIGHT *How do you prevent unfinished wine from spoiling? The cooler, and less contact with oxygen, the better. One method is to use a Vacuvin which sucks out air, and therefore oxygen; another, even more efficient, is to use food grade inert nitrogen gas from a canister (see p119); the nitrogen is heavier than air, and thus displaces it. Keeping the wine in the fridge will slow down its demise, as will filling, and corking, a half bottle.*

*See also

american oak **48**
cab sauvignon **83-5**
herbaceous/minty **38-9,** *86*
making notes **25-6, 134-5**
syrah/shiraz **90-2**

Taste: wines 3 & 4

The style differences you perceived on the nose will be reflected in the tastes of the wines too, and you will want to note these. But concentrate first on perceiving, and articulating in words, the differences in *quality* between these two wines. (*See* pp26–8 and action 8 p133.) Going to and fro will clarify the distinctions.

The differences should be most apparent in:

1 Texture, where the last wine should have 'finer' mouthfeel.

2 Middle-palate length, where its flavour should be more prolonged.

3 Balance of scent to fruit, where the expensive wine should have a greater aromatic presence.

4 Finish, which clearly should be much more persistent in the final wine.

But now ask yourself which, for you, represents better *value for money*? Wine 4 is probably three times the price of wine 3.

Finally, take a critical look at the descriptive information in your notes. See how clearly the words recall the wines, and see if you can rework them to make the note read more fluently.

Nose: wines 3 & 4

Follow the 'taste' instructions for wines 1 and 2, but here with 'smell', and make a brief, complete note of the nose of each wine *separately*. Look at actions 4 and 5 p133, and at the 'nose' notes p135 for the details of what to consider.

The expensive wine should have the more subtle and complex nose, and it should also be 'longer'. A longer nose? Yes. Longer in the sense that, rather like length of middle-palate and aftertaste, it will seem to persist in coming from the glass, and it will hold your attention for a greater length of time. The expensive wine is likely also to have more overt oak; ask yourself whether you think the level appropriate? And they should both smell of Cabernet Sauvignon of course, but the Chilean wine will probably be 'cooler', more in the 'raw' blackcurrant spectrum, a bit minty* and herbaceous*. Whereas the fine California should clearly be more intense, with riper, more cassis-like fruit under its oak. In quality terms it should also be more clear-cut and refined.

Summary

We have tasted Syrah and Shiraz next to each other, and seen once more how strong the influence of origin is on wine style. We have also seen that, for all the value of comparisons, it is sometimes important to taste without making immediate comparisons. And, finally, more detailed notes of yours have provided the basis for considering quality as opposed to value.

wine faults

Happily, faulty wines are rare today.

Innocent suspects (not faults)

Bubbles in a still wine: many light white wines and a few reds are deliberately left with a little CO_2 gas to add to and maintain their freshness. Nothing to worry about. (*See* p9.)

Cloudy wine: most likely to be mature, fine wine with its sediment stirred up. If you have poured, it's too late; if you haven't opened the bottle, allow it to settle, then decant (*see* p138).

Pieces of floating cork: not a corked wine but from a crumbly cork or blunt corkscrew. Pick them out with fingers or a teaspoon.

White or purple crystal deposit: *see* bottom illustration opposite, and illustration p50.

The real villains

The faults you are most likely to encounter are related to oxygen, sulphur and cork taint. 'Oxidised' is a generic description for wine faults resulting from absorbing excess oxygen, usually the result of poor (eg too warm) storage, or leaky corks. It is clearer to think of these as 'oxidised' *or* 'volatile' which may occur together or independently.

Oxidised appearance: *see* top and middle illustrations, opposite.

Oxidised nose: all wines lose freshness, smelling progressively flat or stale, with bruised-apple, and fino-sherry-like smells in white wines, bitter-sweet, caramely odours in reds.

Oxidised taste: mirrors the smell – tired, flat, hard in whites; sweet and sour in reds.

Volatile: the term refers to both the smell of acetic acid (vinegar), and its associated odour, that of ethyl acetate. The two 'volatile' faults may occur together, or independently:

Acetic acid gives wines the sour smell of vinegar, along with its thin, sharp taste.

Ethyl acetate smells of nail polish, chemical solvents, airplane glue. It is sometimes present in young wines, or wines that are in all other respects 'fresh'. It tends to make wine hard and hot to taste, especially on the finish. The degree to which you tolerate it is very personal; my own tolerance is low.

SO_2 (sulphur dioxide): SO_2 protects wine from oxygen. When there is too much present it can be both smelt, like the acrid whiff from a struck match, and sensed as a pricking sensation at the top of one's nose and back of the throat. It can be dissipated to some extent by 'splash' decanting or generous swirling. Individual sensitivity to it varies enormously.

H_2S (hydrogen sulphide): 'reduced' sulphur (combined with hydrogen) produces unpleasant smells of bad eggs or burning rubber. In a mild form (bottle stink), aeration will sometimes remove it. In extreme form it produces mercaptans, smelling of garlic, onion, sewage. There is nothing you can do about it then.

Corked/Corky: chlorine solutions used to sterilise corks and barrels can produce a substance called trichloranisole (TCA for short) when they come into contact with moulds in these items. TCA produces a chemical smell of mould, damp cellars, dustiness. It masks a wine's fruit, dries and shortens its taste, and becomes more marked the longer the bottle is open. Corkiness is the most prevalent fault today, and a compelling reason to change from cork to polypropylene, or screwcaps.

ABOVE *Bottles from the same case! The l/h bottle is badly ullaged from a poor fill. With more oxygen contact the colour difference is clear to see.*

ABOVE *Same red wine, different bottles. The right hand one had been open ten days longer. The oxydised 'bricking' is clear.*
BELOW LEFT *Tartrate crystals but on a red wine cork, see p50.*
BELOW RIGHT *So far Altec (see little symbol at the top?) has the most successful 'natural cork' solution to cork taint.*

tasting 8
medium-dry and sweet whites

The associations of sugar with bulging waistlines has made wines with any degree of sweetness unfashionable. But don't let prejudice put you off: sweet wines are some of the most delectable of all, often at very modest levels of alcohol. If you are sceptical, allow me to convince you – I love them!

Serving temperature:
6–8°C (43–47°F).

General procedure:
remind yourself on
pp117–119.

Aims: this tasting takes a glance at the Riesling* and Furmint* grapes, and at some of the consequences of 'noble rot'* in sweet wines. It covers a wide range of sweetness* and shows the crucial importance of acidity if wines are to remain appetising. Finally there is a brief consideration of these wines with food… or not!

Buying advice: this is the tasting where alternatives are likely to prove least satisfactory. Sauternes, New World Late Harvest Semillon or Riesling are all sufficiently sweet to stand in for the Tokaji. However, there is no real substitute for good Riesling Spätlese and Auslese from Germany, and there is little point in pretending otherwise. Read up the producers in the White Grapes and their Wines section, then buy the best you can afford – ideally a Spätlese* and Auslese* from the same year and producer.

NB: you will need some good Roquefort cheese for this tasting – nice and creamy in texture, please. Plus your favourite bread, freshly toasted, to put it on.

Serve wines 1 and 2, left (Liebfraumilch) to right (Riesling Spätlese).

Appearance: wines 1 & 2
Examine for clarity, brilliance and colour.
Both should be pale and bright, the Liebfraumilch probably with a more straw-coloured hue, the Spätlese almost colourless, with more lustre and maybe a greenish cast.

Nose: wines 1 & 2
Compare the noses of the two wines, still and after swirling; concentrate, and note down two or three adjectives for each.
Both will be light. The Müller-Thurgau will smell, if not very clearly, of elderflower, box hedge; and it may be a touch floral from the Morio-Muskat grape usually blended in with it. Don't expect much distinction. The Riesling should have a more clear-cut, floral and freshly grapey nose when still. It often smells faintly 'oily' as it settles after swirling, recalling petrol or kerosene – in the nicest way, you understand!

Taste: wines 1 and 2
Taste for sweetness: first just compare your impression of sweetness in these two wines.

Ideal wines	Origin	Grape variety	Price	Style		Alternative wines	
				alcohol	acid		
1 **Youngest available Liebfraumilch**	Rheinhessen, Germany	Müller-Thurgau++*	£	low	mod	1 Med-dry QBA, Germany	£
2 **1997/8/9 Riesling Spätlese**	Mosel, Germany	Riesling*	££	low	lively	2 Med-dry Riesling, New Zealand; Oregon, USA	£–££
3 **1997/8/9 Riesling Auslese**	Mosel, Germany	Riesling	££–£££	low	lively	3 Riesling Auslese, Pfalz, Nahe, Rheingau	££–£££
4 **1993/5 Tokaji Aszú 5 Puttonyos**	Tokaji, Hungary	Furmint++*	££–£££	med	high	Sauternes, Barsac, France	
						Late Harv Sem, Australia	££–£££

How would you describe each one? Choose a description from the following list of rising degrees of sweetness: *off-dry*, *medium-dry*, *medium-sweet*, *sweet*, *very sweet*, *intensely sweet*.

Of course this will vary with the wines you have in front of you, but there is often not much difference in their apparent sweetness. Even if the Spätlese has more measurable residual sugar, this is likely to be offset by a higher level of acidity. There is no objective measurement for describing sweetness; as you will see, it is a question of degree. Both these wines would normally be described as medium-dry or medium-sweet. Did you think they were 'sweet' or 'very sweet'?

Taste for quality as indicated by length:

Neither of these is likely to be very long on the finish, but the Riesling should have a clearer, fresher flavour, and greater persistence. If you are in any doubt, taste the Riesling first, then go back to the Liebfraumilch: not unpleasant, just mild and bland.

Now serve wine 3 (Auslese) to the right of wine 2 (Spätlese). Refresh wine 2 at the same time.

Appearance: wine 3

Check for clarity, brightness.

Nose: wines 2 & 3

Compare the noses, and note the differences.

Wine 3 should have similar characteristics to wine 2, but should be a bit more intense, richer. And, especially as it subsides after swirling, the Auslese is likely to have a more pronounced 'oily/petrolly' aroma, possibly with suggestions of raisins, musk, and spice. Auslese wines (see pp62–3) are made from late-picked, riper Riesling grapes from the best-exposed, warmest sites in the vineyard, and often with a degree of noble rot (see p42–3). The musk, raisin and spice characters are a couple of the aroma manifestations of noble rot (*Edelfäule* in German).

Taste: wines 2 & 3

This time taste wine 3 first and then taste wine 2, just to compare the sweetness. Again, choose a description from the list above to indicate the level of sweetness for each.

Tasted this way round, with an Auslese to begin with, you will probably want to adjust your earlier sweetness appraisal of the Spätlese. It tastes much drier when you have had the Auslese to put its sweetness in perspective first, doesn't it? Even so, the Auslese itself is a 'sweet' wine, not a 'very sweet' one.

Taste for quality: consider the overall breadth of flavour, middle-palate length and length of finish. Go to and fro to clarify differences.

The Auslese is not just sweeter from riper fruit and noble rot concentration, it has a subtle spice and raciness of flavour across the palate, one of the most desirable

ABOVE LEFT AND RIGHT
These three Muscats*, of very different styles, origins and alcohol levels, make a most interesting comparative trio. Find the youngest available if they are vintage wines.
1 Moscato d'Asti, Italy; 5%.
2 Elysium Black Muscat (Quady), California; 15%.
3 Australian Liqueur Muscat, Victoria, Australia; 18%. They differ in colour, scent and alcohol, but the family resemblance is clear. The Moscato, defies conventional wisdom by being drinkable with really quite strong desserts.

consequences of noble rot. The wine should be fuller and its aftertaste longer, with the everpresent acidity keeping its succulence fresh.

Notice the quality of the Riesling grape in both these wines.

There is nothing tiring about Mosel Rieslings. In spite of their sweetness they remain light, transparent in flavour, freshly delineated and deliciously grapey. (Return to the soft neutrality of the Müller-Thurgau for a comparison if you are in doubt.) And, at barely 8% alcohol, they can be delightful apéritifs; indeed, drunk on their own they are often at their refreshing best. In spite of their sweetness these are not, on the whole, food wines*; their delicacy and moderate sweetness are easily overwhelmed by desserts.

Now serve wine 4 (Tokaji), to the right of wine 3 (Auslese), which you might like to refresh at this point.

Appearance: wine 4

Compare its colour and viscosity with those of the previous wines.
Very different, isn't it? Almost amber in appearance, and much more viscous in the glass – *see* p77.

Nose: wine 4

Smell and note in the usual way.
Tokaji's Furmint grape has its stiff pepper and lemon personality intensified by noble rot. Here are penetrating aromas of raisins, Seville orange marmalade and caramelised sugar, all cut with a citrus piquancy. And made, as these are, with a high proportion of fully nobly rotten grapes, there is sometimes the merest telltale sign of mushroomy decay, too. Quite a personality, don't you think?

Taste: wine 4

Briefly taste the Auslese again, just to remind yourself of its sweetness, and then taste the Tokaji.
Now *that* (Tokaji) is sweet wine! Intensely so, and no mistake. But with that sweetness relieved throughout by a sharp thread of orange and lemon acidity. Sweet, viscous, yet surprisingly refreshing; and gently spiced and raisiny from noble rot. A sweet wine in a completely different style from the Riesling Auslese.

Sweet Tokaji makes a splendid digestif by itself, but it is also a particularly satisfying partner to Roquefort on toast. They match each other for intensity, and the sweet-salty opposition of flavours is a most complementary one, just as it is with Roquefort and Sauternes.

Summary

This quartet of contrasts, including Riesling and Furmint, provides a glimpse of the range of sweet wines there is to explore and enjoy. You will have seen that acidity to balance the sweetness is always the key, for this is a pleasure which becomes saccharine and palls rapidly without relief. If an intensely sweet, nobly rotten Tokaji can be a delight with food, many so-called 'dessert'* wines are not. The fresh, grapey purity of a Riesling Spätlese or Auslese is an apéritif joy on its own. Sweet wine sceptics, have I made you think again, momentarily at least? I hope so.

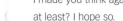

blind tasting

Blind tasting is tasting wines without seeing the shape of the bottle or the label, and thus knowing nothing – or in 'semi-blind', only a limited amount – about them. In an area fraught with prejudice, it aims to introduce a degree of objectivity. Its uses are several: a diverting game at home, the principal method by which much of the wine trade and wine press judge their product, and the best means, bar none, of training one's palate. It makes wines nervous because they have to perform without the benefits of hype or history. It makes people nervous because it tests their ability to taste.

A fine whetstone for the taster's palate

Where wine is concerned we are all enormously prone to suggestion. Tasting blind forces you to taste with real concentration, and to rely entirely on what your senses actually perceive rather than what various preconceptions suggest they ought to. Lack of knowledge encourages you to search more diligently, and this act of scrutiny reveals the wine to you in much greater detail. You will find it a challenging and rewarding discipline; one which rapidly helps you establish how you personally identify the individual characteristics of different grapes, regions, styles. Equally, uninfluenced by the knowledge of price, origin or reputation, you can assess quality objectively, once more relying solely on what your senses detect in terms of balance, complexity and length. But remember that in order to direct your attention efficiently you always need to be absolutely clear as to what you are blind tasting *for*.

Identification

Discovering style and distinguishing quality like this soon enables you to begin to identify wines blind. This commonly perceived main aim of blind tasting is a fascinating one, if by no means its most important, and beginners often hit the 'bullseye' more frequently than experienced tasters because they see fewer options.

A crude measure for deciding what's 'best'

Competition is essential in any field, if only to encourage excellence; and the theory behind tasting wines blind in competitions is that it creates a level playing field for judging. However, this objectivity is often illusory, for it is practically impossible to make line-ups fair in all respects: grape, origin, price, style and so on.

More to the point is that the implied notion of a single form of excellence is extremely limiting. Best for what? Not all wines are trying to do the same thing. We have different expectations of different examples even of the same generic type, we look for a variety of attributes in different contexts, and we drink wine with food. When judging large numbers of wines blind, at speed, there simply isn't time to consider all this. As a result, competitions tend to favour the fruity, the potent*, the obvious. Good wines, yes, but often bullies at the table. What they overlook are the (very real) pleasures of the delicate* or the individual. For these need time, food and company – precisely what palate-fatigued, time-pressed judges do not have.

ABOVE *When serving wines blind, they can either be decanted into anonymous bottles, or bagged like this to hide their identity – in which case you need to remove recognisable capsules too. We all grasp surreptitiously at any available clue, given the opportunity!*

tasting 9
sherry, port and madeira

The great fortified wines sherry, port and Madeira are neglected by wine-lovers. Outmoded image and insipid generic wines are two of the reasons. Ignore the image, pay a bit more, and you will not be disappointed. They are remarkable value and most, once opened, remain drinkable for some time.

Serving temperature:
manzanilla, 8–10°C (46–50°F); the others, 15–17°C (59–63°F).

Decanting:
the Vintage port, not the LBV, will need decanting, see p138.

General procedure:
remind yourself on pp117–19.

Aims: in addition to introducing you to three very different types of fortified wine, wines for 'sipping' rather than 'drinking', you will see that tasting and assessing wines at between 15% and 20% alcohol differs little from what you have done so far. However, their method of vinification (see pp110–15) so dominates grape character that, from a tasting point of view, varietal characteristics are unimportant. Style and quality are what matter. The two sherries* represent a contrast of style, the port* and Madeira* pairs are contrasts of quality*. And the two quality comparisons here are particularly telling: a summary, if you wish, of this most important aspect of tasting.

Buying advice: I have not given alternatives here. Madeira is unique and there is no other wine remotely like it. There are sherry-style and port-style wines made in Australia and South Africa, along with a number of good port look-alikes in California, but try to find the originals. For Madeira and port it is worth purchasing the 15 Year Old, and Single Quinta respectively if at all possible. The latter can be consumed over several days, if necessary; the former over several months, which I guarantee won't

be necessary! The manzanilla will not keep once opened.

NB: you will need a tin of manzanilla olives in brine (I like the Crespo brand best, especially those stuffed with anchovies) and shelled walnuts. A luxury would include home-made Madeira cake – a moist, lemon-zest flavoured sponge. Don't bother with 'commercial' Madeira cake, it is universally dry and tasteless.

Serve wine 1 (manzanilla) on its own.

Appearance: wine 1
This should be the palest of lemon yellow.

Nose: wine 1
Smelling carefully, how would you describe this?
The smell of a good manzanilla reminds me of the tang of green apples. *Manzana* means 'apple' in Spanish, *manzanilla* is its diminutive, also meaning 'camomile', whose leaves are apple scented. Is this smell just wishful thinking on my part? Some people can also detect a faintly yeasty character (see *flor* p110).

Ideal wines	Origin	Grape variety	Price	Style	
				alcohol	acid
1 Manzanilla sherry NV	Jerez*, Spain	Palomino	£–££	high	crisp
2 Sweet oloroso or cream sherry NV	Jerez, Spain	Palomino	££–£££	high	mod
3 3 or 5 Year Old Full/Rich Madeira	Madeira*, Portugal	Tinta Negra Mole	££	high	lively
4 10 or 15 Year Old Malmsey	Madeira, Portugal	Malvasia	££–£££	high	vivid
5 Ruby port NV	Douro, Portugal	Numerous	£	high	mod
6 1995/6 LBV or 1988/9 S Quinta Vintage port	Douro, Portugal	Numerous	£££	high	mod

Taste: wine 1

Have a good taste, on its own, and note your first impressions.

Do you screw up your face, from the sharpness of it? You are not alone. That's what 'bone-dry' is!

Now have a manzanilla olive first, and then try the sherry again.

That's better. The saltiness of the olives partly neutralises the acidity of the wine, and together they become distinctly 'moreish'. The salty partner could be cashew nuts, crisps, etc.

NB: good manzanilla is not a complex wine, that is not its point. But it should be whistle clean, tangily aromatic and mouthwatering, literally sharpening your appetite. I think this combination does just that. In fact I find it hard to resist making a meal just of the appetisers!

Serve sherry 2 (oloroso/cream sherry).

Appearance: wine 2

Check that it is clear and bright.

You can read about this wine's colour on p111.

Nose: wine 2

Smell still, and after swirling.

There is probably not a lot of difference between the two states, and don't expect to find any family resemblance with the manzanilla. You are not comparing these two; the oloroso is a completely contrasting style from the wide range of sherries. What you notice here is a gentle reminder of caramelised sugar, raisins and possibly a grapey Muscat-like perfume. (*See* again pp110–11.)

Taste: wine 2

Taste, and note down your impressions.

Full, rich, sweet and long. On the palate very much what you smelled on the nose. A smooth pleasure on its own; but if you want to flatter both its fruit and its sweetness, the slightly bitter gall of a walnut will do just that. When would you sip this wine? How about with walnuts as a winter's day snack, or with crisp apple slices and pecans as a simple dessert?

Serve wines 3 and 4 (the pair of Madeiras), the younger wine to the left.

Appearance: wines 3 & 4

Compare the two wines, from above and with the glasses tilted.

Both will have a golden to nut-brown colour, often with an olive tint at the rim, but the older wine will appear more brilliant.

Nose: wines 3 & 4

Compare the bouquets. How do they differ in character, clarity, complexity, persistence?

Much inexpensive (a euphemism here) Madeira tends to have a particularly undistinguished smell, grubby, cheesy.

ABOVE *Of course you can taste fortified wines without food, but I think the olives are essential to try with the Manzanilla (or you could have salted cashew nuts, even crisps).*

NB: and having concentrated and done the work tasting, sipping these quality wines with complementary nibbles is a reward worth making a little preparation for. If you have got this far, you do have something to celebrate after all.

You might be luckier. But the older wine will be a marked contrast: more intensely aromatic and clear-cut. A complex, heady and persistent combination of burnt caramel, lemon zest, crystallised violets, smoke….

Taste: wines 3 & 4

Compare these two, looking in particular at intensity of flavour, middle-palate length, aromatic character and length of finish. Aerate them well in the mouth, and make notes if it will help your concentration.

Chalk and cheese, isn't it? The lesser wine will be pleasant enough: a slightly tangy, burnt-caramel sweetness, but bland and brief, with little aroma or clarity. The finer Madeira will be richer and noticeably better defined; caramel and lemon sweet to start with, smooth yet sharp and penetrating across the palate, and then dry and lasting to finish from the Madeira soul, that constant cut of acidity. And a mouthfilling scent as you aerate and savour.

Then go back to the lesser Madeira.

Unfair? Maybe, but so revealing. An impressive demonstration of the lengths, clarity and aromatic complexities that characterise differences in quality! You find the older Malmsey a bit too incisive on its own? Temper its edge with a walnut or, best of all, a slice of that home-made Madeira cake.

Serve wines 5 and 6 (the ports), ruby to the left.

Appearance: wines 5 & 6

Compare the colours, in particular the hue at the rim of the two wines.

There is probably close to a ten-year age gap, but the Vintage port will not look ten years older at its rim. In wines of the same type, colour evolution reflects maturity and readiness to drink at least as much as age in years.

Nose: wines 5 & 6

Compare the noses, still and after swirling. How would you characterise the differences in quality apparent on the nose?

Both will have a combination of sweet fruit and pepperiness, but expressed in very different ways qualitatively. In the vintage wine you should notice a greater purity and concentration of fruit, more volume and subtlety of scent to smell, a superior clarity and separation of its characteristics. And a greater persistence or 'length' of bouquet.

Taste: wines 5 & 6

Compare in the same way as for the Madeiras.

Notice in this final pair that, as with all this group, well-balanced proportions mean you are not particularly aware of their high alcohol, apart, perhaps, from a pleasing fullness and warmth. Both ports will have their sweetness offset by a gentle peppery fire, and the *qualitative differences* will be similar to those between the two Madeiras: differences of richness, aromatic complexity, refinement and length.

Summary

Here we have looked at two very different styles of sherry, and at marked quality contrasts in port and Madeira. You will have seen that the process of tasting wines at between 15% and 20% alcohol is no different from that for other wines, and that the essential criteria for evaluating their qualities are those that we have used throughout these nine tastings: harmonious proportions for the style, the balance of aromatic and fruit interest, texture quality, length of middle-palate and length of finish.

Summary of the tasting course

1 Style and quality in dry whites
- The basic mechanical aspects of tasting
- Length of finish as a measure of quality
- Different grapes produce different styles
- Gewurztraminer, Muscadet

2 *Terroir* and quality in dry whites
- Aerating wines to taste more fully
- What is meant by an aromatic grape variety
- The influence of new oak on taste
- How vineyard location affects quality
- Sauvignon Blanc and Chardonnay 1

3 Dry whites: Old World v New World
- Smelling before and after swirling the wine
- The effect of warmer temperature
- The effect of climate on varietal character
- Sauvignon Blanc and Chardonnay 2

4 Sparkling wines: style and quality
- How to judge sparkling wines' bubbles
- How their styles also vary according to origin
- The good value of non-Champagne sparklers

5 Style and tannin in reds
- Colour in red wine
- Different levels of tannin
- Combining tannic red wines with food
- Pinot Noir, Nebbiolo, Tempranillo, Gamay

6 *Terroir* and quality in red wines
- Bordeaux and 'claret'
- Vineyard location affecting style and quality
- Texture and middle-palate length as a measure of quality
- Cabernet Sauvignon and Merlot

7 Reds: Old World v New World
- The influence of national origin on style
- Making detailed notes
- Quality as opposed to value
- Syrah and Shiraz

8 Medium dry and sweet whites
- The sweetness spectrum
- Acidity as the key to balancing sweetness
- Noble rot in sweet wines
- Sweet wines and food
- Riesling, Furmint, Müller-Thurgau

9 Sherry, port and Madeira
- Tasting wines between 15% and 20% alcohol
- Different styles of sherry
- Quality contrasts in port and Madeira

Further reading

There are many wine books and for a beginner it's difficult to know what to choose. Here are some proven volumes:

Major reference:
- *The Oxford Companion to Wine* editor Jancis Robinson (Oxford University Press)
- *The World Atlas of Wine* Hugh Johnson (Mitchell Beazley)
- *The New Sotheby's Wine Encyclopedia* Tom Stevenson (Dorling Kindersley)
- *Oz Clarke's Encyclopedia of Wine* (Little Brown) – more suitable as a first encyclopedia

Individual countries or regions:

The Faber & Faber series is excellent, only the Loire and South Africa volumes disappoint:
- *Bordeaux* David Peppercorn
- *Burgundy* Anthony Hanson
- *Alsace* Tom Stevenson
- *Rhône* John Livingstone-Learmonth
- *French Country Wines* Rosemary George
- *Wines of Northern Italy* Nicolas Belfrage
- *The Wines of California* Stephen Brook
- *Port and the Douro* Richard Mayson

And from other publishers:
- *World Encyclopedia of Champagne and Sparkling Wine* Tom Stevenson (Absolute Press)
- *The Wines of Chablis* Austen Biss and Owen Smith (Writers International)
- *A Wine and Food Guide to the Loire* Jacqueline Friedrich (Mitchell Beazley)
- *The New Spain* John Radford (Mitchell Beazley)
- *The Wine Atlas of Germany* Stuart Pigott (Mitchell Beazley)
- *South African Wines* John Platter (Platter)
- *The Wine Atlas of California* Bob Thompson (Mitchell Beazley)
- *Crush, the New Australian Wine Book* Max Allen (Mitchell Beazley)
- *Wines of Australia* James Halliday (Mitchell Beazley Pocket Guide)
- *Wines and Vineyards of New Zealand* Michael Cooper (Hodder Moa Beckett)

And two information-packed tailpieces:
- *Hugh Johnson's Pocket Wine Book* Hugh Johnson (Mitchell Beazley)
- *101 Things You Need to Know About Wine* Andrew Jefford (Simon & Schuster)

8. wine and food

a basic guide

Local cuisine, different cultures and personal preference make what seem perfectly acceptable wine and food combinations to some, appear unpleasant to others. Here are a few ideas for your own exploration.

My feelings about analysing wine and food combinations are schizophrenic. Personal experience tells me that it is, above all, an extremely flexible affair. Most of us know what we like to eat and what we like to drink. And common sense, more often than not, makes countless different, but satisfactory, combinations of the two. But you can, of course, be more rational about it. Here is one basic principle to bear in mind, and three specific questions to ask as you mull over your choices.

• Keep contrast and adaptation as a basic principle at the back of your mind.
1 Is either the wine or the food a priority?
2 What are the weight and flavour intensities that need to be matched?
3 Are there marked individual characteristics in the wine or food that will need 'managing'?

The basic principle: contrast and adaptation

We don't use wine to 'wash down' what we eat, nor do we make a soupy blend of wine and food before swallowing. We eat, and then we drink to lubricate and refresh our palates. This sets up a regular juxtaposition of tastes that

1 Medium-bodied, supple, uncomplicated wines

The three white wines here, a California Chardonnay, a northern Italian Soave and Pinot Bianco, are dry, smooth, supple, unoaked wines. The Californian is fairly full, but otherwise all three are moderate in alcohol, acid and flavour intensity. The red wines too are light, fresh, fruity and unoaked. As a group they typify the vast bulk of uncomplicated, 'slip-down' table wine whose lack of marked characteristics means they are very flexible with food. And the sort of food they partner easily has similar characteristics: simple, unembellished fare which is itself light in flavour, represented here by the cold meats mortadella, salami, mild ham and cold roast chicken. Countless comparable, undemanding wine and food combinations are probably what most of us enjoy on a regular basis.

either follow on from each other happily – or not. Thus the basic principles at work are those of 'contrast' and 'adaptation' (not surprisingly, the same ones that affect our experience of smell and taste in wines, *see* margin p20). Our palate having become accustomed to sweetness in the food, let's say, will be less sensitive to sweetness in a wine drunk subsequently because it has become 'adapted' to it. Equally, we will experience a different flavour from sweetness more keenly, precisely because of its 'contrast', its freshness to the palate.

Is either the wine or the food a priority?

In the vast majority of cases the answer will be no. But two prima donnas can be just as difficult at the same table as on the same stage; they tend to compete for attention at each other's expense. Therefore with the very finest wines, which often have so much to offer and to consider in their own right, it is often more satisfactory to serve relatively simple food. By the same token, the most exquisite food, especially if it needs to be eaten hot, is best partnered by good rather than 'great' wines.

2 Light- to medium-bodied wines, with a lively acidity that needs considering

Three of the white wines here, the Spanish Albariño, the Alsace Riesling and the Chablis are also light- to medium-bodied, unoaked and with moderately intense, pure, direct flavours. But all three also have a vivid acidity to consider. Such acidity can be both eased and complemented by salty food, hence the range of firm cheeses here: Beaufort, Gruyère, Austrian Bergkäse and Old Amsterdam (wonderful cheese, if you don't know it). These represent flavoursome rather than forceful fare, which comfortably 'matches' the sharpness of these wines. Similar salty fare might be oysters in their juices, olives in brine, a tasty ham, canapés and so on. An eager acidity can of course also be used to cut through, and provide a foil to, a rich mayonnaise, creamy sauces with all sorts of fish, and creamy cheese too – where a sharp white is much better than red wine.

In the background are a fine claret and a white burgundy, still representing middle-weight wines, and also with a fresh, but in this case less incisive, acidity. These wines have an extra richness, a light oak and an aromatic complexity of flavour which can certainly stand somewhat more elaborate, lightly sauced accompaniments. But if you wanted to relish the wine as a priority, they would be fine with the most simple, unadorned food, too.

Matching the weight and intensity of flavours

If you need rules, this is the simplest and most useful. It assumes, as is mostly the case, that you want to taste both the food *and* the wine, and that you don't want one to suppress the other. In plain terms this means that wine and food sharing broadly similar proportions and characteristics tend to go well together. Match delicate tastes with delicate wines; moderately flavoured food with unassertive, medium-bodied wines; strong wines with food that has

3 Forceful characters whose power and muscularity need matching and managing

The Barolo, California Zinfandel, and Australian Shiraz-Cabernet exemplify force and personality in every department: abundant tannin, intense flavours, no shortage of acidity, alcohol levels of 14% – and some higher! With considerable bottle-age, these wines mellow, but in practice many are drunk young and the danger then is that the wine simply smothers any dish put next to it. In the first place such wines call for food that will measure up to their weight and intensity: strongly flavoured stews and casseroles, wild game with rich gravy, full-flavoured roasts or pasta dishes, hard, granular cheeses. Indeed, without the cushion of food, they can rapidly exhaust rather than refresh the palate. The Parmesan here stands for that requisite combination of protein richness and pungency of flavour.

Traditional Barolo, like the one illustrated, is a rough diamond when young, with an astonishing natural astringency. Seeing how a fine Parmesan can absorb its tannin and allow the wine's fruit through is always a remarkable, if extreme, demonstration of 'managing' a very pronounced individual characteristic, and also of the mutually enhancing chemistry of some wine and food marriages (*see* pp140–2).

plenty of personality, and so on. Common sense (*see* pp140–2)! Bear in mind too, that for 'food' frequently read 'sauce', as this is usually a far more significant flavour component than the meat, fish or fowl it accompanies.

Managing marked individual characteristics

The main ones to consider here are pronounced saltiness, acidity or sweetness in the food, and a high level of acidity, sweetness or tannin in the wine. Such wines are a trifle more choosy about what they partner comfortably.

Saltiness: chemically, salt neutralises acidity; consequently salty food takes the 'edge' off and marries well with acid wines. Salt also brings out or complements sweetness in wine, and salty cheeses often partner sweet wines well, white or red (*see* pp154,157).

Acidity: noticeable acidity in wine or food will mellow and lessen the impression of acidity which follows (adaptation), and highlight subsequent sweetness (contrast). Food with plenty of acidity will make low-acid dry wines taste flat – and vice versa – but it may make a good foil for sweet wine. High-acid dry wines need salt (*see* p157) or acidity in the food to temper their sharpness. Rich food often requires wines with lively acidity to cut through its richness and refresh the palate.

Sweetness: sugar in wine or food will subdue the taste of sweetness in whichever follows. Its effect on acidity may be positive and complementary (a sweet wine with a sharp dessert), or negative and aggravating (sweet food with dry wine will make the wine taste unpleasantly acid). Both effects, of course, will depend very much on the relative degree(s) of sweetness.

Tannin: chemically, tannin binds with protein. Put oversimply, but usefully: in the absence of protein-rich food, tannin in wine will bind with the protein in your saliva, robbing it of its 'slipperiness', and so producing the dry, gripping astringency associated with tannin. But put plenty of food protein in its way, and it will gobble that up instead: meat that is not overcooked, rich sauces as a buffer, or hard, granular cheeses, for example. The Parmesan and Nebbiolo combination in Tasting 5 pp140–2, offers a dramatic demonstration of this.

Spice: very peppery, 'hot', spicy food tends to sensitise the lining of the mouth so much that all you wants is a balm such as milk, lager, or cold, mild, medium-dry white wine. Any noticeable alcohol, acid or tannin just inflame one's sensitivity. Or so I find.

Chocolate and wine: there seems to be an ongoing competition to find out which wines will stand up to the generously mouth-coating sweetness of many chocolate desserts. I love chocolate, and I love intensely sweet wines, but I mostly find the prospective surfeit of the two combined a positive turn-off. If we are talking surfeits, I prefer fresh cream with my chocolate, and good coffee to follow, please. There are better things which combine with sweet wines.

Summary: How's that? Helpful? Maybe. Imprecise? Certainly – this is not a precise business. And to judge by the depth to which others can explore wine and food combinations in writing, I simply don't have the appetite to think, or indeed read about them, in any great detail. The minutiae of either activity soon has my head spinning as I try to envisage all the variables, and I very soon give up. Back then to intuition, mostly, with just a modicum of reason. You see now what I mean about schizophrenic?

4 Medium-dry to intensely sweet wines offer plenty of opportunities other than dessert

The concept of 'dessert' or, worse, 'pudding' wines is not a helpful one, suggesting, as it does, that all such wines generally perform best with desserts. The four wines in this picture all contain residual sugar, and thus are sweet to some degree, but they vary enormously in their levels of alcohol, acidity and sweetness. The German Auslese in the background is light, unoaked and has only 7.5% alcohol, the Barsac, Château Nairac, is a rich barrel-fermented 14% alcohol; the Vouvray Demi-Sec is medium-dry, the Tokaji 6 Puttonyos intensely sweet… and so on.

Sweetness, however, is the key feature which needs managing. The most useful guideline with desserts is that the wine should be sweeter than the 'pudding' rather than the other way round, otherwise the wine seems inadequate. The Auslese is in the background because its delicate, fresh, grapey quality is easily overwhelmed, and these wines are often best on their own, possibly with the lightest of biscuits, or with a gently piquant fruit such as strawberries. The sharp-edged medium-dry to medium-sweet purity of Vouvray is just as good a foil to subtly cream-sauced river fish as it is to blander, not too sweet fruit tarts, such as those made with the apples or pears in the picture above. The two richer, and far sweeter wines here can cope with the richer dishes and more intense flavour, hence the citrus and passion-fruit, whose acidity complements sweetness so well. The attractive salt-sweet contrast is particularly successful with Roquefort, but numerous pairings of wines and salty, hard cheeses make for an appealing attractive alternative to 'pudding'.

Illustrations and captions

The illustrations in this section are not meant to be a comprehensive guide, but along with the captions they give you an idea as to how you might start to think about pairing four broadly different categories of wine with food.

reference

9. maps

maps and fact boxes

The purpose of the map section is to give a clear basic picture of where the main wine names are located, and to put the countries and regions in context with a few facts and figures.

Maps

Being able to see just where a wine comes from not only helps locate it in our memory, but often explains its style as well. Both are part of the pattern that we need to impose to make sense of this enormously diverse subject.

Inevitably limitations of space have meant it has been impossible to do justice to each country to the same extent, but there are numerous detailed wine atlases available to do this. France takes the lion's share because her regions, their wines and the grape varieties associated with them, are not only very well established, but also important reference points for so many major grapes and wine styles.

Clarity was the principal aim of these maps, I didn't want them to be too cluttered. With this in mind, and especially in order to avoid the duplication of names as far as possible, different typefaces have been used to distinguish between what is only a wine name, Côte-Rôtie for example, and what is a wine name as well as the name of a village, town, region etc, Sancerre for example. It is not a hierarchical distinction.

The key boxes are self-explanatory, and the system outlined above is consistent as far as possible, given the varying scales of the maps and the different methods of naming wines in different countries and regions. Latitude has been included because it is interesting to compare one region with another within countries as well as across the globe. Latitude is also important for distinguishing between regions and their styles. An occasional trig point is shown where it is of particular interest.

Fact boxes

These aim to provide a thumbnail statistical and grape variety sketch for each country or region. The idea behind the production figures was to put regions in context within a country (France, Italy, USA), to put individual countries into a global context, and to give an indication of the proportions of red and white wine.

Given limitations of space, the grape varieties shown feature for quality and local importance rather than quantity planted. The statistics are indicative rather than absolute and precise, and the mathematically pedantic will find few satisfying 100 per cent totals, but they do provide a useful comparative summary. The sources are a combination of the OIV (*Office Internationale de la Vigne et du Vin*) in Paris and national, generic bodies. The area under vine figure is for wine grapes, and, because individual years can vary so much, the annual production figure is an average of the three years 1996, '97 and '98.

Map key abbreviations

ha = hectares   hl = hectolitres
m = million   prod = production

vintages

Vintages in the New World wine regions do vary, but on the whole they are much more consistent in style and quality than those in northern Europe. This is a very brief guide to some vintages in a few crucial areas.

Bear in mind that good winemakers make attractive wines even in 'lesser' years.

Red Bordeaux (Claret)
1999 Ripe grapes rained on, early drinking.
1998 Excellent right bank, good left bank.
1997 Ripe, supple, early drinking wines.
1996 Very fine Cabernet; right bank lighter.
1995 Good, can be rather dry and sinewy.
1994 Good, savoury middleweights.
1993 Rain at harvest; pleasant, drink soon.
1992 Rain as in '93; diluted, if some charm.
1991 First of a trio of rain-marred vintages.
1990 Great beauty, if not great concentration.

Red burgundy
1999 Early reports full of ripe promise.
1998 Good, but mixed; best are juicy.
1997 Ripe, ample, fleshy; lowish acidity.
1996 Long-term reds, fine but austere.
1995 Good, firm, sinewy wines.
1994 Harvest rain, not bad; drink soon.
1993 Concentrated, tannic, long term.
1992 Light, but with sweet, ripe, easy charm.
1991 Varied, very good to very lean.
1990 Great; many still surprisingly firm.

White burgundy
1999 Good fresh to lively wines.
1998 Fresh, elegant; can be rather alcoholic.
1997 Good, but acidity tends be on low side.
1996 First rate; vivid, classy wines.

1995 The best are concentrated and vigorous.
1994 Tend to be hefty, low acid; drink soon.
1993 Best lovely and taut; many lean though.
1992 Very ripe fruit, fairly potent. Drink up.

Chablis
1999 Ripe fruit, but with some rain at harvest.
1998 Not bad, but a bit lacklustre after '96/7.
1997 Fresh, juicy, delightful Chablis.
1996 First-rate, classic, vivid long-term vintage.
1995 Good, solid wines; less stylish than '96/7.

Northern Rhône
1999 Looks outstanding.
1998 Excellent, concentrated wines.
1997 Rich and ripe; acidity on low side.
1996 Crisp, aromatic; not the flesh of '97.
1995 Firmly structured middleweights.
1994 Bit austere; rain at harvest time.

Piedmont (Nebbiolo)
Barolo, Barbaresco and Nebbiolo d'Alba had a run of five excellent vintages: 1999, 1998, 1997 (outstanding), 1996 and 1995; after a run of four difficult ones from 1991 to 1994.

Germany (Riesling)
From 1990 to 1999 Germany had a remarkably consistent run of good Riesling vintages. Only 1991 was weak in the decade, otherwise good from good producers.

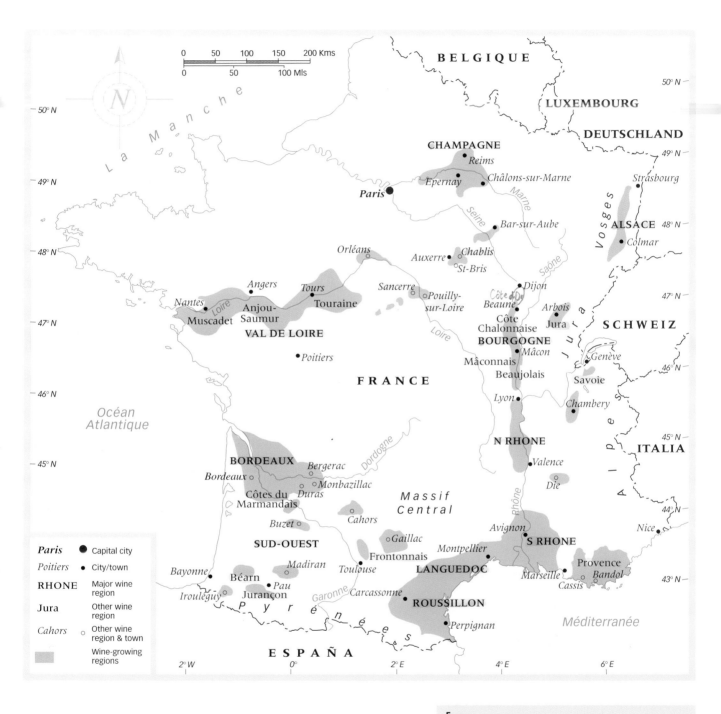

0   50   100   150   200 Kms

0   50   100 Mls

La Manche

BELGIQUE

LUXEMBOURG

DEUTSCHLAND

50° N

49° N

CHAMPAGNE
Reims
Epernay
Châlons-sur-Marne
Strasbourg

Paris

Bar-sur-Aube

Marne
Seine

Vosges

ALSACE
Colmar

48° N

Orléans
Auxerre
Chablis
St-Bris

Saône

47° N

Angers
Tours
Nantes
Loire
Anjou-
Saumur
Touraine
Sancerre
*Pouilly-
sur-Loire*

Côte d'Or
Dijon
Beaune
Côte
Chalonnaise
Arbois
Jura

SCHWEIZ

Muscadet

VAL DE LOIRE

BOURGOGNE
Mâcon

Loire

Mâconnais

Poitiers

Beaujolais

Genève

Savoie

46° N

FRANCE

Lyon

Chambery

Alpes

Océan
Atlantique

45° N

Dordogne

N RHONE

Valence

ITALIA

BORDEAUX
Bergerac
Bordeaux
Monbazillac
Côtes du
Marmandais
Duras

*Massif
Central*

Die

44° N

Buzet

Cahors

Rhône

Nice

Avignon

S RHONE

Gaillac

SUD-OUEST
Madiran
Bayonne
Béarn
Pau
Jurançon
Irouléguy

Frontonnais
Toulouse

LANGUEDOC
Montpellier

Marseille

Provence
Bandol
Cassis

43° N

Garonne
Carcassonne

ROUSSILLON

Méditerranée

Pyrénées

Perpignan

ESPAÑA

2° W   0°   2° E   4° E   6° E

Paris ● Capital city

Poitiers ● City/town

RHONE Major wine region

Jura Other wine region

Cahors ○ Other wine region & town

Wine-growing regions

50° N

49° N

48° N

47° N

46° N

45° N

44° N

43° N

France

Annual prod:	**% prod, red:** 61
54.4m hl	**% prod, white:** 39
Vine area:	**% world prod:** 20.6
873,000 ha	

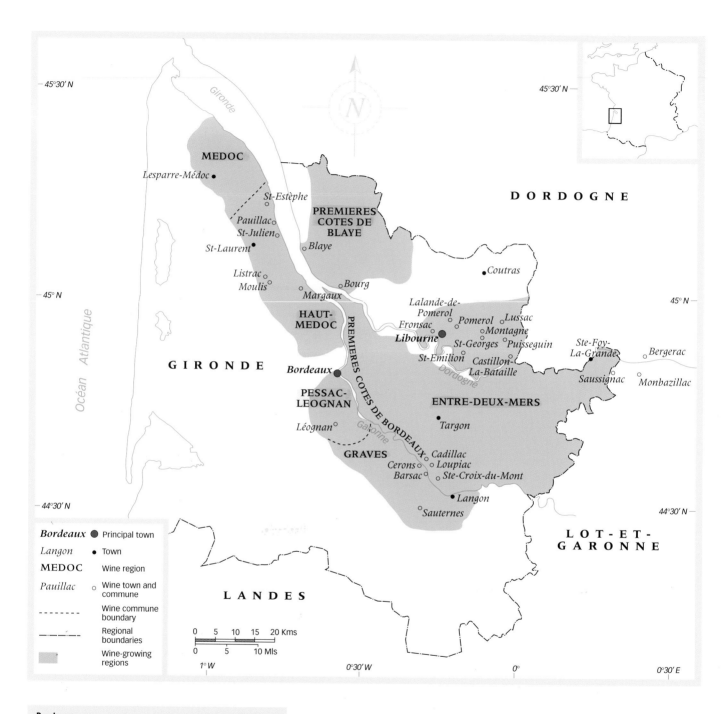

Bordeaux

Annual prod: 7m hl
Vine area: 116,000 ha
% prod, red: 86
% prod, white: 14
% French prod: 12.9

Key red grapes: Merlot, Cabernet Sauvignon, Cabernet Franc
Key white grapes: Semillon, Sauvignon Blanc

CHABLIS

48° N —   — 48° N

Serein
Ligny-le-Châtel
Pontigny
Tonnerre
Chablis
Auxerre
St-Bris
Irancy
Nitry

| 0 | 5 | 10 | 15 Kms |
| 0 | 5 | | 10 Mls |

5°E

Dijon

Marsannay

Fixin

Gevrey-Chambertin

Morey-St-Denis

Chambolle-Musigny

Vougeot

Vosne-Romanée

COTE DE NUITS

Nuits-St-Georges

N74

COTE D'OR

Pernand-Vergelesses

Aloxe-Corton

Savigny-lès-Beaune

Chorey-lès-Beaune

COTE DE BEAUNE

Pommard

St-Romain

Volnay

Beaune

N74

Monthélie

Auxey-Duresses

Meursault

St-Aubin

Puligny-Montrachet

Chassagne-Montrachet

Santenay

Chagny

47° N   — 47° N

| 0 | | 5 Kms |
| 0 | | 5 Mls |

Chablis

Dijon

Beaune

Mâcon

Lyon

| 0 | 25 | 50 Kms |
| 0 | 25 | 50 Mls |

TOP RIGHT BOX *Map of town placements shows the lie of Burgundy's wine regions.*

Chagny

COTE CHALONNAISE

Rully
Mercurey
Givry
Chalon-sur-Saône
Montagny
Buxy

Tournus

MACONNAIS

Chardonnay
Lugny
Viré
Clessé

Vergisson

Mâcon

Pouilly-Fuissé

Juliénas
St-Amour
Fleurie
Chénas
Chiroubles
Moulin-à-Vent
Beaujeu
Morgon
Régnié
Brouilly
Côte de Brouilly

BEAUJOLAIS

Villefranche-sur-Saône

46° N   — 46° N

Lyon *Rhône*

| 0 | 20 | 40 Kms |
| 0 | | 20 Mls |

Legend:

Dijon ● Principal town
Buxy • Town
CHABLIS   Wine region
Volnay ○ Wine town and commune
    Wine-growing regions

Burgundy

Annual prod: 1.6m hl
Vine area: 28,000 ha
% prod, red: 43
% prod, white: 57
% French prod: 3
Key red grape: Pinot Noir
Key white grapes: Chardonnay, Aligoté

Beaujolais

Annual prod: 1.4m hl
Vine area: 22,000 ha
% prod, red: 99
% prod, white: 1
% French prod: 2.6
Key red grape: Gamay

— Burgundy —
Chablis
Dijon
N Cote de Nuits
Cote de Beaune } Cote d'Or
— Chalonnaise (Cote)
Maconnais
Beaujolais
Lyon
Rhône (N)

Loire

Annual prod: 3.9m hl
Vine area: 71,000 ha
% prod, red: 48
% prod, white: 52
% French prod: 7.2
Key red grapes:
Cabernet Franc, Cabernet Sauvignon, Gamay
Key white grapes:
Chenin Blanc, Sauvignon Blanc, Muscadet

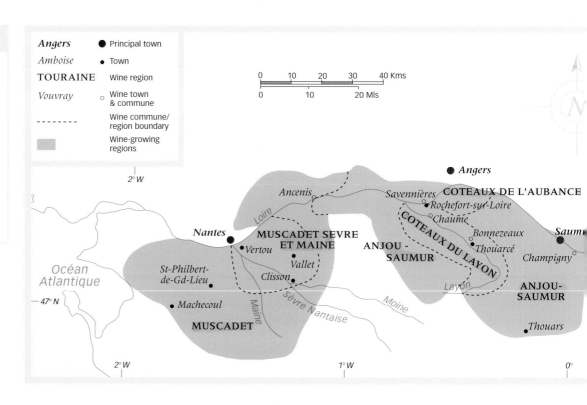

Angers ● Principal town
Amboise ● Town
TOURAINE Wine region
Vouvray ○ Wine town & commune
- - - - Wine commune/ region boundary
▨ Wine-growing regions

South West France

Annual prod: 3.7m hl
Vine area: 62,000 ha
% prod, red: 59
% prod, white: 41
% French prod: 6.8
Key red grapes:
Cabernet Sauvignon, Cabernet Franc, Merlot, Malbec, Tannat
Key white grapes:
Semillon, Sauvignon Blanc, Gros Manseng, Petit Manseng, Mauzac

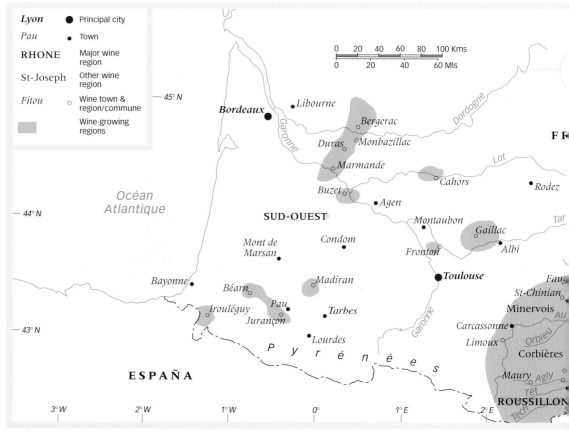

Lyon ● Principal city
Pau ● Town
RHONE Major wine region
St-Joseph Other wine region
Fitou ○ Wine town & region/commune
▨ Wine-growing regions

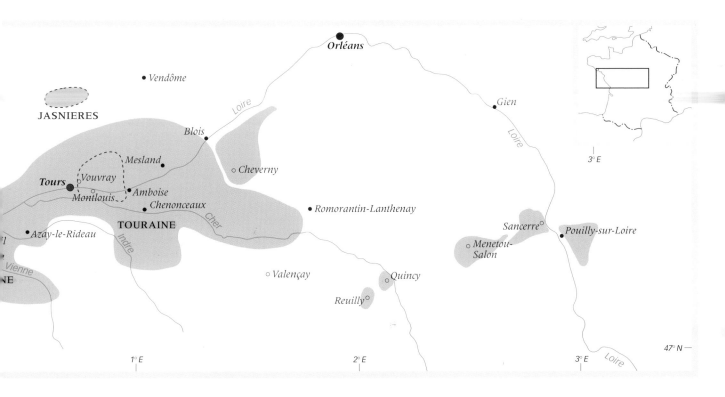

Languedoc-Roussillon

Annual prod: 11.2m hl
Vine area: 229,000 ha
% prod, red: 88
% prod, white: 12
% French prod: 20.7
Key red grapes:
Grenache, Carignan,
Mourvèdre, Syrah
Key white grapes:
Grenache Blanc,
Macabeo, Muscat

Rhône Valley

Annual prod: 8.7m hl
Vine area: 150,000 ha
% prod, red: 93
% prod, white: 7
% French prod: 16
Northern Rhône
Key red grape: Syrah
Key white grapes:
Marsanne, Rousanne,
Viognier
Southern Rhône
Key red grapes:
Grenache, Carignan, Syrah,
Cinsault
Key white grapes:
Marsanne, Rousanne,
Muscat
NB: Northern Rhône
(St-Péray to Côte-Rôtie)
represents less than
5 per cent of total Rhône
production – mainly red.

Provence

Annual prod: 2.1m hl
Vine area: 44,000 ha
% prod, red: 94
% prod, white: 6
% French prod: 4
Key red grapes:
Grenache, Cinsault, Syrah,
Mourvèdre, Cabernet
Sauvignon
Key white grapes:
Sauvignon Blanc, Ugni
Blanc, Clairette

Champagne

Annual prod: 2.7m hl
Vine area: 30,400 ha
% prod, red: 0.2
% prod, white: 99.8
% French prod: 5
Key red grapes:
Pinot Noir (28%),
Pinot Meunier (48%)
Key white grapes:
Chardonnay (24%)

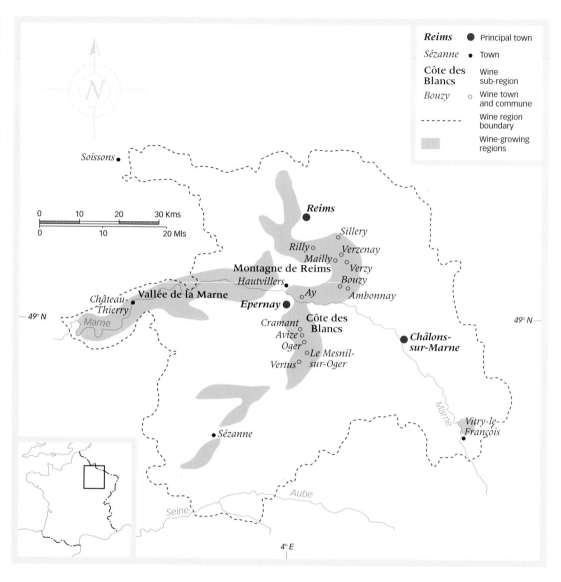

Reims ● Principal town
Sézanne ● Town
Côte des Blancs — Wine sub-region
Bouzy ○ Wine town and commune
– – – Wine region boundary
Wine-growing regions

Madeira*

Annual prod: 45,000 hl
Vine area: 750 ha
Key grapes: Sercial,
Verdelho, Bual, Malvasia,
Tinta Negra Mole

*fortified wine see p.114

Funchal ● Capital city
Seixal ● Town
Wine-growing regions

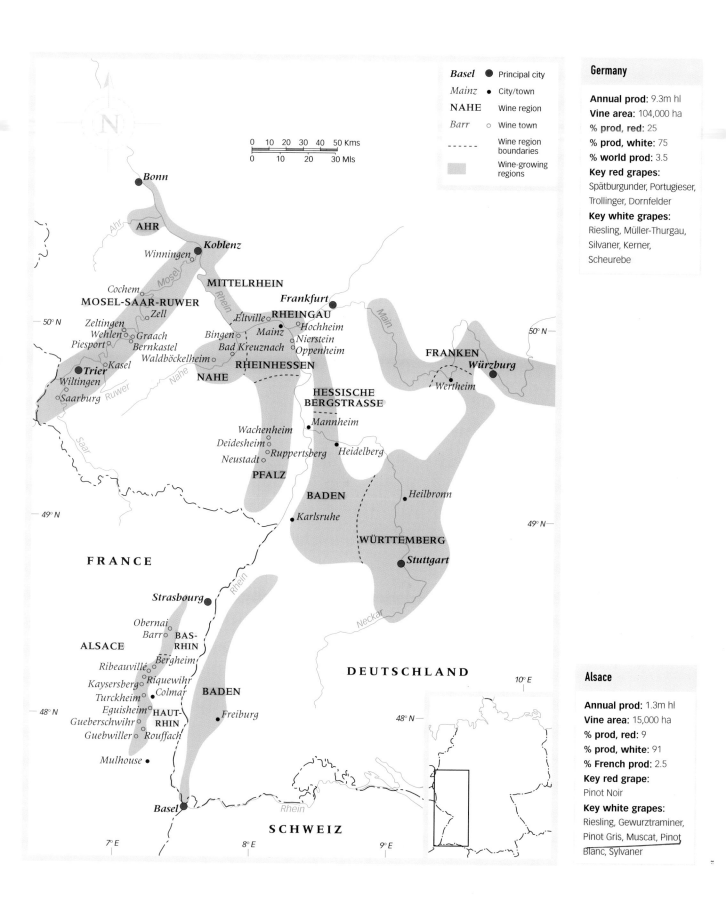

Legend

Basel ● Principal city
Mainz ● City/town
NAHE Wine region
Barr ○ Wine town
- - - - Wine region boundaries
░ Wine-growing regions

Germany

Annual prod: 9.3m hl
Vine area: 104,000 ha
% prod, red: 25
% prod, white: 75
% world prod: 3.5
Key red grapes:
Spätburgunder, Portugieser, Trollinger, Dornfelder
Key white grapes:
Riesling, Müller-Thurgau, Silvaner, Kerner, Scheurebe

Alsace

Annual prod: 1.3m hl
Vine area: 15,000 ha
% prod, red: 9
% prod, white: 91
% French prod: 2.5
Key red grape:
Pinot Noir
Key white grapes:
Riesling, Gewurztraminer, Pinot Gris, Muscat, Pinot Blanc, Sylvaner

Map labels:

Bonn
AHR
Ahr
Winningen
Koblenz
Cochem
MITTELRHEIN
Mosel
MOSEL-SAAR-RUWER
Zell
Zeltingen
Wehlen
Graach
Piesport
Bernkastel
Rhein
Eltville
RHEINGAU
Hochheim
Frankfurt
Mainz
Bingen
Nierstein
Bad Kreuznach
Oppenheim
Main
Trier
Kasel
Waldböckelheim
RHEINHESSEN
FRANKEN
Würzburg
Wiltingen
Ruwer
NAHE
Wertheim
Saarburg
Nahe
HESSISCHE BERGSTRASSE
Saar
Mannheim
Wachenheim
Deidesheim
Ruppertsberg
Heidelberg
Neustadt
PFALZ
BADEN
Heilbronn
Karlsruhe
WÜRTTEMBERG
49° N
Stuttgart
FRANCE
Rhein
Strasbourg
Obernai
Barr
BAS-RHIN
DEUTSCHLAND
Ribeauvillé
Bergheim
ALSACE
Kaysersberg
Riquewihr
Turckheim
Colmar
BADEN
Eguisheim
HAUT-RHIN
Gueberschwihr
Freiburg
Neckar
Guebwiller
Rouffach
Mulhouse
Basel
Rhein
SCHWEIZ

50° N
49° N
48° N
7° E
8° E
9° E
10° E
48° N

Scale: 0 10 20 30 40 50 Kms / 0 10 20 30 Mls

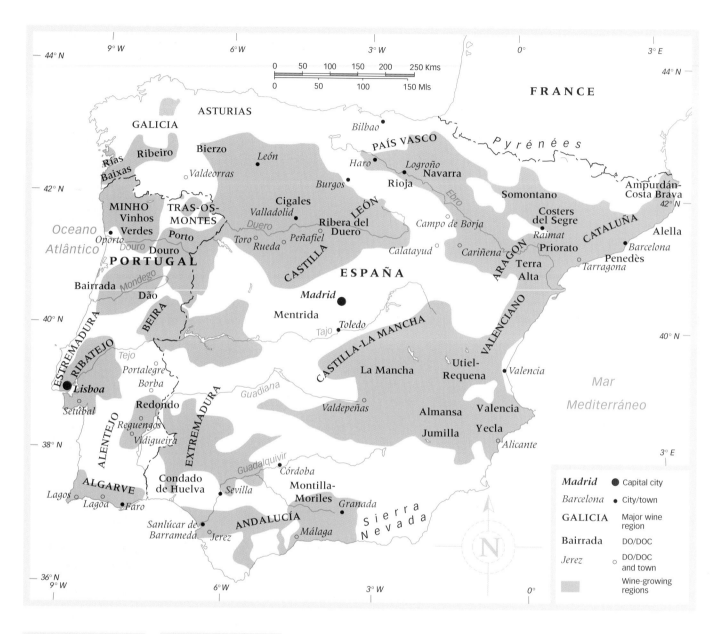

Portugal

Annual prod: 6.5m hl
Vine area: 116,000 ha
% prod, red: 60
% prod, white: 40
% world prod: 2.5
Key red grapes: Touriga Nacional, Tinta Roriz, Touriga Francesa, Baga
Key white grapes: Loureiro, Arinto, Bical, Alvarinho

Spain

Annual prod: 31.5m hl
Vine area: 650,000 ha
% prod, red: 60
% prod, white: 40
% world prod: 11.9
Key red grapes: Garnacha, Tempranillo, Graciano
Key white grapes: Albariño, Viura, Verdejo, Moscatel, Parellada, Palomino, Pedro Ximénez

Switzerland

Annual prod: 1.2m hl
Vine area: 15,000 ha
% prod, red: 53
% prod, white: 47
% world prod: 0.45
Key red grapes: Pinot Noir, Gamay, Merlot
Key white grapes: Chasselas, Müller-Thurgau, Sylvaner

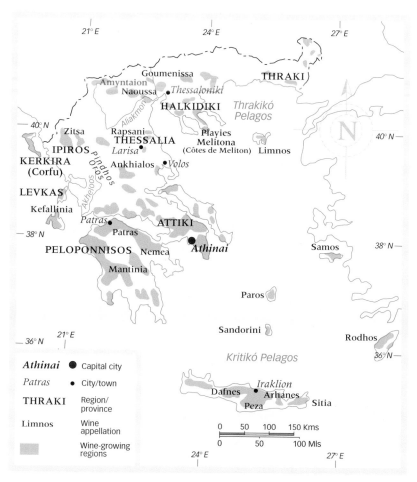

Athinai ● Capital city
Patras ● City/town
THRAKI Region/province
Limnos Wine appellation
Wine-growing regions

21° E 24° E 27° E

Goumenissa
Amyntaion THRAKI
Naoussa *Thessaloniki*
HALKIDIKI Thrakikó Pelagos
Zitsa Rapsani Playies Melitona
IPIROS THESSALIA (Côtes de Meliton)
KERKIRA *Larisa* Limnos
(Corfu) Ankhialos *Volos*
LEVKAS
Kefallinia ATTIKI
Patras Samos
Patras *Athinai*
PELOPONNISOS Nemea
Mantinia
Paros

Sandorini

Rodhos

Kritikó Pelagos

Dafnes *Iraklion*
Peza Arhanes Sitia

CESKA REPUBLIKA
Retz *Falkenstein*
Kamp *Mailberg*
KAMPTAL WEINVIERTEL
Krems *Langenlois*
Spitz DONAU-
WACHAU *Loiben* LAND *Klosterneuburg*
TRAISENTAL *Wien* WIEN
Melk *Donau*
CARNUNTUM
Baden NEUSIEDLER-
THERMEN- SEE
REGION *Eisenstadt*
ÖSTERREICH *Rust* *Illmitz*
NEUSIEDLERSEE- *Apetlon*
HÜGELLAND Neusiedler See
MITTEL-
BURGENLAND
Mur
SÜD-
BURGENLAND
Graz
STEIERMARK
(Styria)
Klöch
Gamlitz
SLOVENIJA

SLOVENSKA REPUBLIKA

● Capital city
● City/town
Major wine region
○ Wine town & commune
Wine-growing regions

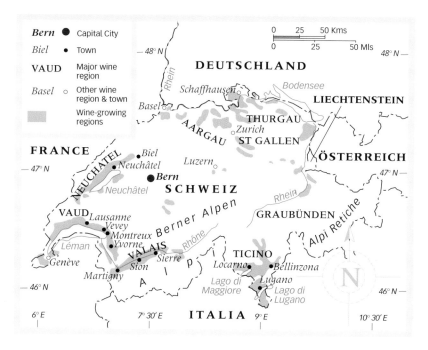

Bern ● Capital City
Biel ● Town
VAUD Major wine region
Basel ○ Other wine region & town
Wine-growing regions

DEUTSCHLAND
Schaffhausen Bodensee
LIECHTENSTEIN
Basel THURGAU
AARGAU *Zurich* ST GALLEN
FRANCE *Rhein* ÖSTERREICH
Biel *Luzern*
NEUCHÂTEL *Neuchâtel*
Bern SCHWEIZ
Neuchâtel *Rhein*
VAUD *Lausanne* GRAUBÜNDEN
Vevey Berner Alpen Alpi Retiche
Montreux VALAIS
Léman *Yvorne* TICINO
Genève *Sierre* p *Locarno* *Bellinzona*
Sion Lago di
Martigny A Maggiore *Lugano*
Lago di Lugano
ITALIA

Greece

Annual prod: 4m hl
Vine area: 70,000 ha
% prod, red: 26
% prod, white: 74
% world prod: 1.5
Key red grapes:
Agiorgitiko, Xynomavro, Limnio, Mavrodaphne
Key white grapes:
Savatiano, Assyrtiko, Roditis, Moscophilero

Austria

Annual prod: 2.2m hl
Vine area: 51,000 ha
% prod, red: 25
% prod, white: 75
% world prod: 0.8
Key red grapes:
Zweigelt, Blaufränkisch, Blauer Portugieser, St-Laurent
Key white grapes:
Grüner Veltliner, Welschriesling, Riesling, Müller-Thurgau, Neuburger, Weissburgunder

Italy

Annual prod: 54.6m hl
Vine area: 800,000 ha
% prod, red: 48.3
% prod, white: 51.7
% world prod: 20.7

North & Central Italy

Piemonte
Annual prod: 3.4 m hl
Key red grapes:
Nebbiolo, Barbera, Dolcetto
Key white grapes:
Moscato, Cortese, Arneis

Lombardia
Annual prod: 1.7m hl
Key red grapes:
Nebbiolo, Barbera
Key white grape:
Trebbiano di Lugana

Trentino-Alto Adige
Annual prod: 1m hl
Key red grapes:
Teroldego, Lagrein
Key white grapes:
Pinot Grigio, Pinot Bianco

Veneto
Annual prod: 6.8m hl
Key red grape: Corvina
Key white grapes:
Garganega, Prosecco

Friuli-Venezia Giulia
Annual prod: 1m hl
Key red grapes: Cabernet
Sauvignon, Merlot
Key white grapes: Tocai
Friulano, Pinot Grigio

Liguria
Annual prod: 164,000 hl
Key white grape:
Vermentino

Emilia-Romagna
Annual prod: 4.7m hl
Key red grapes:
Lambrusco
Key white grape: Albana

Toscana
Annual prod: 2.2m hl
Key red grape:
Sangiovese
Key white grapes:
Vermentino, Vernaccia

Marche
Annual prod: 1.8m hl

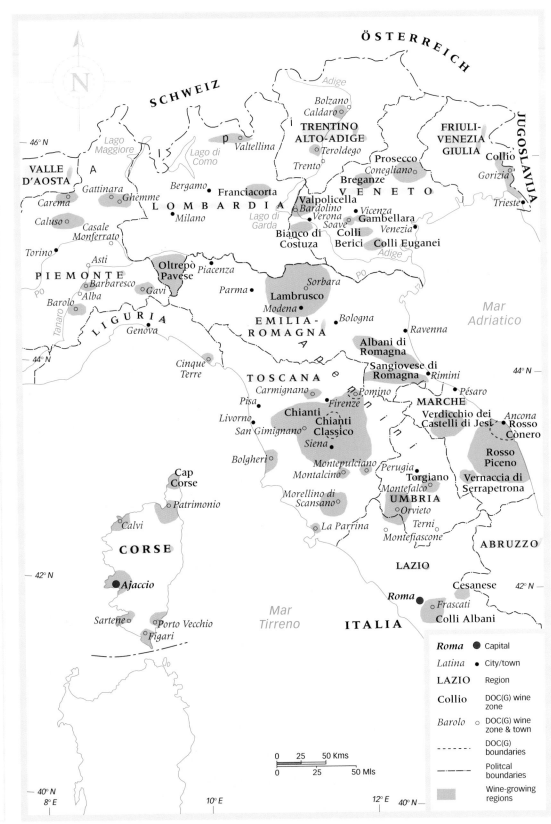

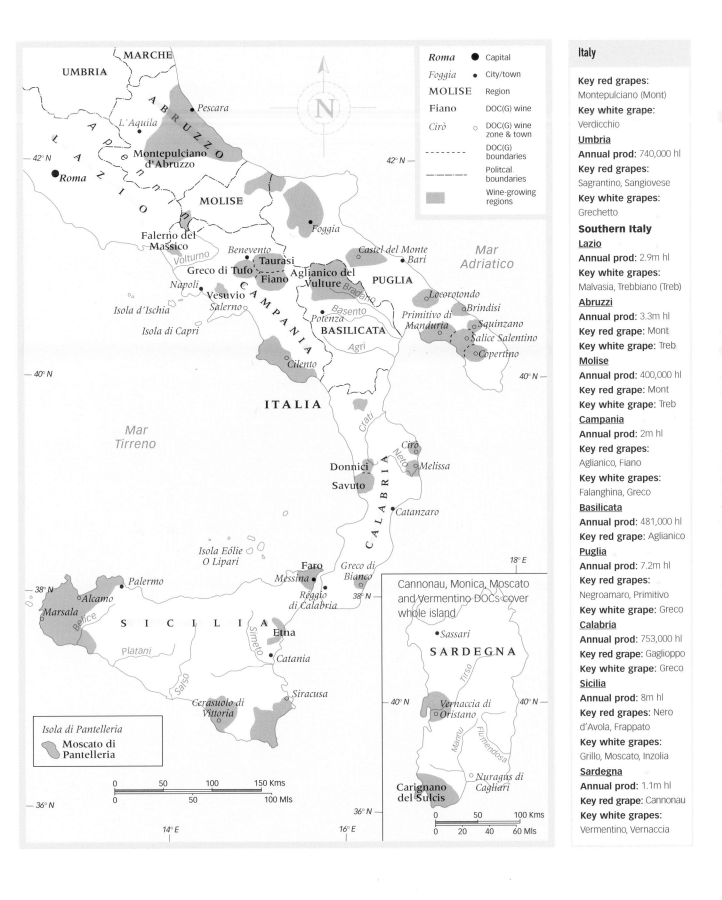

MARCHE

UMBRIA

A B R U Z Z O

• Pescara

L'Aquila

— 42° N
42° N —

Montepulciano d'Abruzzo

L A Z I O

• *Roma*

MOLISE

Falerno del Massico

Volturno

• *Foggia*

Benevento

Taurasi

Greco di Tufo

Aglianico del Vulture

Fiano

Castel del Monte

• Bari

Mar Adriatico

PUGLIA

Napoli

C A M P A N I A

Vesuvio

Salerno

Isola d'Ischia

Bradano

Locorotondo

Primitivo di Manduria

Brindisi

Basento

Potenza

BASILICATA

Squinzano

Salice Salentino

Isola di Capri

Agri

Copertino

— 40° N
40° N —

Cilento

I T A L I A

Mar Tirreno

Crati

Ciró

Neto

Donnici

Melissa

Savuto

C A L A B R I A

• Catanzaro

Isola Eólie O Lipari

Faro

Messina

Greco di Bianco

18° E

— 38° N
38° N —

Palermo

Alcamo

Réggio di Calabria

Marsala

Belice

S I C I L I A

Etna

Simeto

• Catania

Platani

Salso

• Siracusa

Cerasuolo di Vittoria

Isola di Pantelleria

Moscato di Pantelleria

0   50   100   150 Kms

0   50   100 Mls

— 36° N
36° N —

14° E

16° E

Legend:

Roma ● Capital

Foggia • City/town

MOLISE Region

Fiano DOC(G) wine

Ciró ○ DOC(G) wine zone & town

– – – DOC(G) boundaries

–·–·– Politcal boundaries

▨ Wine-growing regions

Cannonau, Monica, Moscato and Vermentino DOCs cover whole island

• *Sassari*

S A R D E G N A

— 40° N
40° N —

Vernaccia di Oristano

Tirso

Mannu

Flumendosa

Nuragus di Cagliari

Carignano del Sulcis

0   50   100 Kms

0   20   40   60 Mls

Italy

Key red grapes:
Montepulciano (Mont)

Key white grape:
Verdicchio

Umbria

Annual prod: 740,000 hl

Key red grapes:
Sagrantino, Sangiovese

Key white grapes:
Grechetto

Southern Italy

Lazio

Annual prod: 2.9m hl

Key white grapes:
Malvasia, Trebbiano (Treb)

Abruzzi

Annual prod: 3.3m hl

Key red grape: Mont

Key white grape: Treb

Molise

Annual prod: 400,000 hl

Key red grape: Mont

Key white grape: Treb

Campania

Annual prod: 2m hl

Key red grapes:
Aglianico, Fiano

Key white grapes:
Falanghina, Greco

Basilicata

Annual prod: 481,000 hl

Key red grape: Aglianico

Puglia

Annual prod: 7.2m hl

Key red grapes:
Negroamaro, Primitivo

Key white grape: Greco

Calabria

Annual prod: 753,000 hl

Key red grape: Gaglioppo

Key white grape: Greco

Sicilia

Annual prod: 8m hl

Key red grapes: Nero d'Avola, Frappato

Key white grapes:
Grillo, Moscato, Inzolia

Sardegna

Annual prod: 1.1m hl

Key red grape: Cannonau

Key white grapes:
Vermentino, Vernaccia

Hungary

Annual prod: 4.3m hl
Vine area: 130,000 ha
% prod, red: 25
% prod, white: 75
% world prod: 1.6
Key red grapes:
Kadarka, Kékfrankos
Key white grapes:
Furmint, Hárslevelü,
Leányka

Romania

Annual prod: 6.5m hl
Vine area: 250,000 ha
% prod, red: 60
% prod, white: 40
% world prod: 2.5
Key red grapes: Feteasca
Negra, Cab Sauv, Merlot,
Pinot Noir
Key white grapes:
Feteasca Alba, Welshriesling

Bulgaria

Annual prod: 6m hl
Vine area: 110,000 ha
% prod, red: 80
% prod, white: 20
% world prod: 2
Key red grapes: Merlot,
Cab Sauv, Mavrud, Melnik
Key white grapes:
Chardonnay, Sauvignon
Blanc, Dimiat

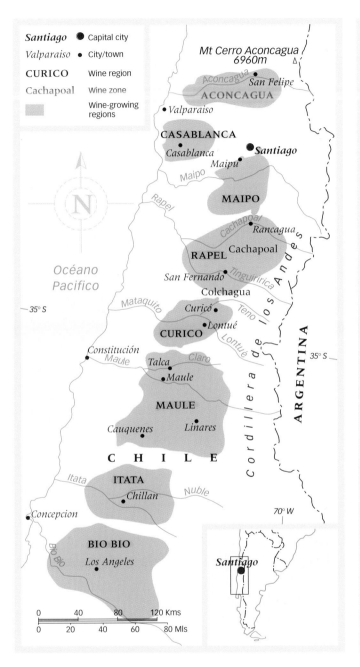

Chile

Annual prod: 4.6m hl
Vine area: 75,000 ha
% prod, red: 65
% prod, white: 35
% world prod: 1.7

Key red grapes: Cabernet Sauvignon, Merlot, Carmenère
Key white grapes: Chardonnay, Sauvignon Blanc

Argentina

Annual prod: 13m hl
Vine area: 210,500 ha
% prod, red: 60
% prod, white: 40
% world prod: 4.9

Key red grapes: Malbec, Cabernet Sauvignon, Merlot, Syrah
Key white grapes: Chardonnay, Torrontes

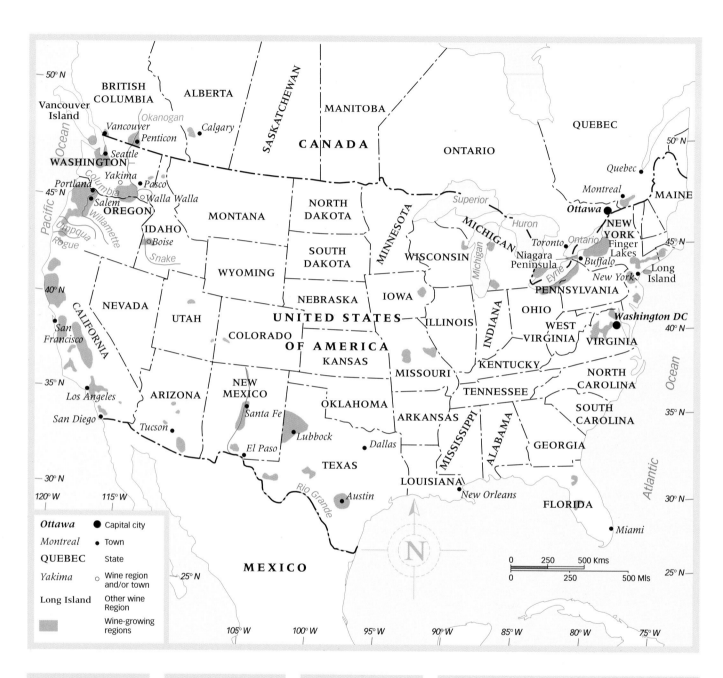

Legend:
- *Ottawa* ● Capital city
- *Montreal* • Town
- QUEBEC State
- *Yakima* ○ Wine region and/or town
- Long Island Other wine Region
- ▨ Wine-growing regions

Scale: 0 — 250 — 500 Kms / 0 — 250 — 500 Mls

United States

Annual prod: 20.4m hl
Vine area: 404,000 ha
% prod, red: 55
% prod, white: 45
% world prod: 7.7

Oregon

Annual prod: 76,000 hl
Vine area: 4,000 ha
% red: 52, **% white:** 48
% USA prod: 0.3
Key red grapes: Pinot Noir, Cab Sauvignon, Merlot
Key white grapes: Chardonnay, Pinot Gris, Riesling

Washington State

Annual prod: 380,000 hl
Vine area: 10,000 ha
% red: 56, **% white:** 44
% USA prod: 1.7
Key red grapes: Merlot, Cab Sauvignon, Syrah
Key white grapes: Chardonnay, Riesling, Sauvignon Blanc

Canada

Annual prod: 343,000 hl
Vine area: 10,000 ha
% prod, red: 27
% prod, white: 73
% world prod: 0.1

Key red grapes: Cabernet Franc, Cabernet Sauvignon, Merlot, Gamay, Pinot Noir
Key white grapes: Vidal, Chardonnay, Riesling, Pinot Gris, Gewurztraminer

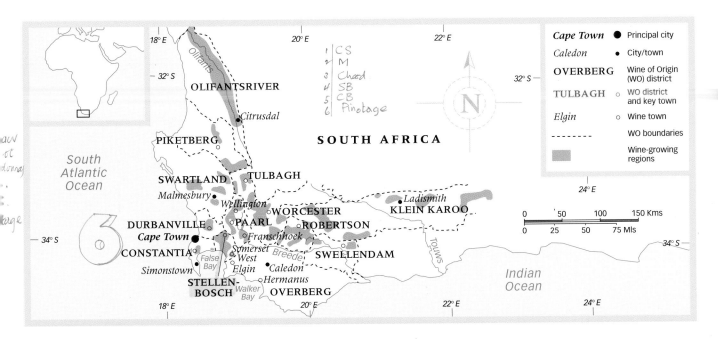

California

Annual prod: 19m hl
Vine area: 182,000 ha
% prod, red: 55
% prod, white: 45
% USA prod: 92
Key red grapes:
Cabernet Sauvignon,
Zinfandel, Merlot,
Pinot Noir, Syrah
Key white grapes:
Chardonnay, Sauvignon,
Blanc

South Africa

Annual prod: 8.5m hl
Vine area: 101,000 ha
% prod, red: 20
% prod, white: 80
% world prod: 3.2
Key red grapes:
Cabernet Sauvignon,
Pinotage, Pinot Noir,
Merlot, Shiraz
Key white grapes:
Chenin Blanc, Chardonnay,
Sauvignon Blanc

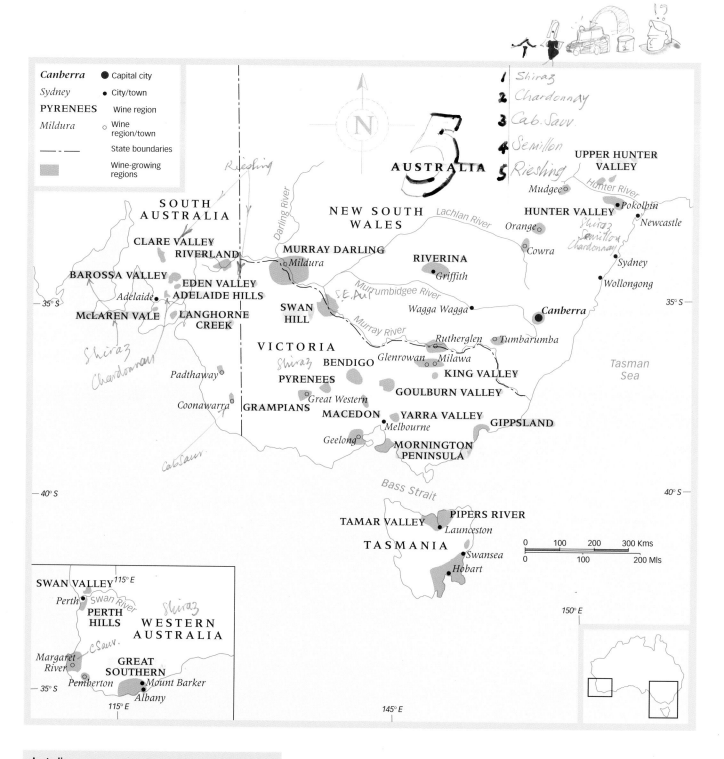

AUSTRALIA

1 Shiraz
2 Chardonnay
3 Cab. Sauv.
4 Semillon
5 Riesling

Australia

Annual prod: 6.8m hl
Vine area: 123,000 ha
% prod, red: 52
% prod, white: 48
% world prod: 2.6

Key red grapes: Shiraz, Cab Sauvignon, Pinot Noir
Key white grapes: Chardonnay, Semillon, Riesling, Muscat

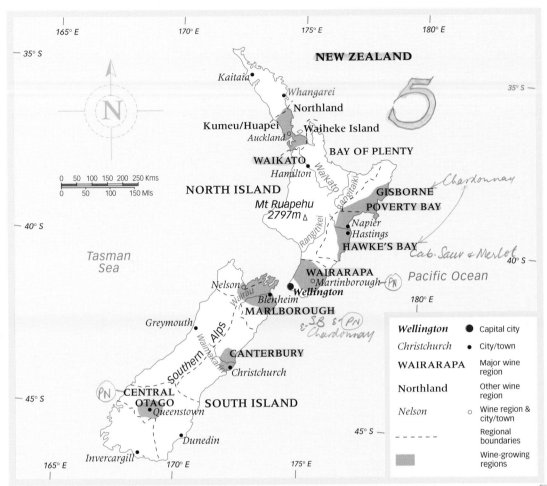

1 Cab Sauv.
2 Merlot
3 PN
4 Chardonnay
5 SB.

glossary of tasting terms

SMALL CAPS indicate words that are cross-referenced in the glossary.

Acescence/acescent The smell of ethyl acetate, a by-product of the formation of acetic acid (vinegar). The specific, HIGH-TONED, acetone smell is reminiscent of solvents such as airplane glue, nail-varnish remover, lacquers, and those boiled sweets called peardrops. An acescent wine is volatile. *See* p151.

Acetaldehyde A by-product of the oxidation of alcohol, as wine very gradually heads towards becoming vinegar. Usually imperceptible in light wines, but with a heavy, sweetish, sherry-like smell in fortified wines or faulty light white wines. *See* p151.

Acetic Smelling and tasting of acetic acid, *ie* vinegar. Also described as PRICKED.

Accessible Easy to drink early on; also used of wines normally requiring time.

Acid As a tasting term, indicates too much acidity.

Acrid A pungent, pricking, occasionally burning sensation sensed at the top of the nostrils and back of the throat; due to excess sulphur dioxide. *See* p151.

Aftertaste Synonymous with FINISH.

Aggressive Harshness of taste or texture usually due to excess tannin, acid, alcohol.

Alcoholic Wines with excess alcohol, and HEAVY or HOT to taste in consequence.

Aroma A nicer word for smell. Loosely interchangeable with BOUQUET, tends to be used to describe the fresh, fruit-based impressions of young wines.

Aromatic Applied to wines made from grapes with a particularly distinctive aroma, especially when young; eg Sauvignon Blanc, Gewurztraminer and Muscat. Also a useful term for distinguishing between fruit impressions in the mouth, as opposed to those gained by smell, especially on the MIDDLE-PALATE and FINISH of fine wines.

Astringent Dry, puckering effect on the gums produced by tannin. *See* p22.

Austere A hard, unyielding impression due to acid and/or tannin, usually said of young wines which need time to mellow. *See* p147.

Backward Less developed and mature than expected for its age or type. *See* p147.

Balance/balanced The relationship between alcohol, acid, fruit and tannin. This varies according to grape variety, geographical origin, winemaking practices and so on. A wine is well-balanced if no element appears to be lacking or unpleasantly obtrusive for its type. In young wines needing time to mature, the constituent parts often stand out individually, but when the proportions are perceived to be appropriate, they may be described as well balanced, even though they need time to harmonise.

Bite A marked, incisive level of acidity.

Bitter *See* pp21,121.

Blackcurrant The smell commonly associated with Cabernet Sauvignon. Needs qualifying: raw blackcurrant, blackcurrant jam, cassis, etc.

Blowsy Combination of high alcohol and low acidity making for heavy, overblown, shapeless wine.

Blunt Strong but dull.

Body Impression of weight and consistency in the mouth due to a combination of alcohol and EXTRACT. Alcohol is only part of the equation.

Bouquet Loosely interchangeable with AROMA, in practice used to describe the more mature, subtle smells that develop with bottle age.

Breed In the sense of thoroughbred, used of wines with particularly REFINED qualities.

Buttery As in the smell of melted butter; usually used, positively, of rich white wines.

Caramel Smell/taste of caramelised sugar.

Cassis *See* blackcurrant.

Casky Unpleasant, mouldy, smell of damp, rotting wood from old or unclean casks.

Cedary The smell of cedarwood, usually associated with wines aged in new oak, probably by association with the smell of the wood used in cigar boxes.

Chalky An impression of chalkiness from the soil; *see* EARTHY/*TERROIR*.

Charm/charming Plenty of immediate appeal, if not much COMPLEXITY; often used of wines that might be expected to have more of the latter.

Chewy So much matter, often tannin, one feels it could be chewed.

Cigar box CEDARY.

Citrussy Orange, lemon, lime, grapefruit scents and flavours.

Class/classy From the notion of classification, but top class is what is meant; very good quality,

Classic Both excellent and a model of its kind.

Clean Free of faults or impurities; sometimes suggests pure or FRESH as well.

Close-grained/close-knit/closely woven/closely wrought Descriptions of quality and feel by analogy with TEXTURE of fine fabrics, *see* p28.

Closed You feel there are qualities of AROMA and flavour which are presently hidden, but which will emerge with time.

Cloying Of sweet wines: sickly sweet because of inadequate acidity to balance.

Coarse (in texture) Usually due to the quality of tannin; lacking in refinement; also used of large, harsh bubbles in sparkling wine.

Common A more damning way of saying ordinary.

Compact Impressions of firmness and compression of constituent elements, the opposite of STRETCHED.

Complete For a given type, not lacking in any aspect of BOUQUET, taste and FINISH.

Complex/complexity Opposite of simple or one-dimensional; a multiplicity, intricacy, nuance of smells, tastes, textures. Quality of a high order. *See* pp32–3.

Concentrated Usually desirable, the opposite of dilute. Self-defeating at obsessive or extreme levels. *See* pp33, 36,39,50.

Constitution A wine's basic physical make-up – dimensions of alcohol, acid, fruit extract, tannin – as distinct from its actual tastes or quality. STRUCTURE is synonymous.

Cooked A critical description of tastes and smells that seem to have come from fruit subject to excess heat: JAMMY, burnt, baked, singed – all in a negative sense.

Corked A wine fault (*see* p151), indicated by mouldy, musty smells which mask the wine's fruit and both dry and shorten its PALATE.

Creamy Reminiscent of the rich, smooth consistency of cream. Mainly used of red wines, but also in reference to sparkling wines with a particularly fine MOUSSE.

Crisp A lively acidity; the kind you want in a juicy apple.

Crust The substantial deposit formed in bottles of mature Vintage port. *See* pp113,138–39.

Cut An incisive acidity; usually positive, as in 'a good cut of acidity'.

Definition A quality feature; well-defined wines give the impression of having a particularly clear-cut profile and distinctive flavours. *See* FOCUS.

Delicate Light but REFINED wine (unfashionable 'pianissimo' pleasure, but pleasure all the same). *See* p33.

Dense Used of AROMA/BOUQUET; an almost palpable abundance.

Depth Refers to a combination of intensity and COMPLEXITY of flavour.

Developed/undeveloped Of wines which need time to mature: ready to drink – or not.

Development (on/across the palate) A quality aspect relating to how, and for how long, a wine's flavours evolve as you keep and savour the wine in your mouth. *See* LENGTH, MIDDLE-PALATE; and pp26–7.

Dirty Having unpleasant, unclean flavours.

Distinctive Marked individuality of style.

Distinguished Exceptional character and quality.

Drive Wines so vital they seem to have an inner energy which you can feel as they cross your palate.

Drying out Losing fruit, sweetness, freshness to the extent that acid, alcohol and/or tannin dominate the taste. Drink up. The vinous equivalent of flesh withering on the bones!

Dumb Another word for CLOSED. Usually refers to smell: you sense there is something there, but you can't smell it much at present.

Earthy The impression on the nose, and as an AROMA on the palate, of damp earth (a dry garden after rain), usually used in a positive sense – by me anyway; *see* TERROIR, *and* p145.

Edgy An acidity which verges on being irritating, uncomfortable.

Elegant Refined flavours, harmonious balance, absence of coarseness.

Empty Absence of flavour and interest, similar to HOLLOW.

Ethyl acetate *See* ACESCENCE, HIGH-TONED, VOLATILE.

Eucalyptus Resinous aroma often, but not uniquely, associated with Australian red wines.

Extract In red wines especially: a high level of soluble solids, tannin above all, extracted during winemaking, producing dense, concentrated wines. In principle positive, but easily overdone, producing coarse, ASTRINGENT textures and flavours.

Farmyardy Animal and vegetable odours in mature wines which appeal to some, not to others!

Faulty *See* p151.

Fierce The aggressive, sometimes painful, sensations produced by high levels of alcohol and/or acid, and/or tannin.

Fine General term for a wine of high quality.

Finesse *See* REFINED.

Finish The sensations of taste, texture and smell you continue to perceive after swallowing. The longer the better (*see* LENGTH). The same as AFTERTASTE.

Firm A marked, but not excessive, acidity; a positive quality, especially in young wines which need time to mature. May refer to the texture of tannins as well.

Flabby Seriously deficient in acidity.

Flat Lacking in BOUQUET, fresh flavours and acidity; of a sparkling wine, one that has lost its bubbles.

Fleshy Mainly used of red wines: SOFT, plump, pulpy, smooth; with very little tannin.

Flinty A MINERALLY aroma usually associated with crisp, dry white wines such as Sancerre or Chablis.

Floral Aromas reminiscent of flowers.

Focus Usually 'well-focused', describing wines of great clarity of BOUQUET, flavour and TEXTURE. Similar to DEFINITION, but the usage is originally American. A useful analogy with photography.

Forward Mature and ready to drink earlier than expected for age and type; *see* BACKWARD.

Fragrant Delicate, scented, perfumed, particularly on the nose.

Fresh Youthful, lively, with an appealing acidity.

Fruity Overworked but difficult to avoid. Always implies abundant 'fruit', often

of a relatively simple character – but none the worse for that.

Full In BODY and/or flavour.

Generic Non-specific in origin, from a broad, general area. Usually simple, straightforward quality.

Generous Full, ample, mouthfilling, and usually easy to appreciate.

Glassy A personal usage, for a particularly smooth, pure, if slightly unyielding, texture; mainly in fine Riesling and Chenin Blanc.

Glossy The exceptionally smooth, polished feel of a fine, mature red wine, with all its youthful asperity gone.

Gooseberry For many the best description of the aroma of young, aromatic Sauvignon Blanc.

Graceful ELEGANT, HARMONIOUS and pleasing in a quiet way; *see* DELICATE.

Grapey A strong impression of the grape in its raw form, Muscats and German Rieslings especially.

Gravelly The specific earthiness associated with clarets from the Médoc and Graves; once suggested, difficult to ignore!

Green As in unripe fruit: high in acid, MEAN in flavour.

Grip An attractive firmness of texture, usually from tannin, which helps give DEFINITION to fine red wines.

Hard Pronounced firmness of texture due to tannin and/or acidity.

Harmonious Well-balanced proportions with no constituent lacking or obtrusive, and all the individual parts married and mellowed. Young wines can be well BALANCED but not yet harmonious.

Harsh In texture.

Heavy High in alcohol; usually critical, implying inadequate balancing acidity.

Herbaceous 'GREEN', vegetal characteristics: bruised leaf, bell/green pepper, olives and so on; associated with tannins that are not absolutely ripe in red wine grapes (*see* pp36–9), or with excessive extraction during winemaking (*see* pp45–6). Not necessarily critical when part of a cooler-climate style.

High-toned For me the sweet, chemical smells associated solvents, glues, lacquers etc, indicating ETHYL ACETATE, volatility. The degree to which you find them acceptable is very personal. My own tolerance is low, *ie* if I can smell them it's too much!

Hollow Evocative description for a wine that is SHORT and devoid of flavour.

Honeyed Self-explanatory.

Hot Excessive alcohol (for the wine in question) producing a warm-to-burning sensation, noticeable on the FINISH especially. *See* p21.

Inky A profound, opaque purple hue, or a metallic flavour associated with excessive extraction. See EXTRACT.

Jammy Hot-climate or hot-vintage character: super-ripe, fruity, commercial black-fruit jam characteristics, lacking DEFINITION.

Juicy Just that!

Lanolin A rich, oily impression recalling lanolin-derived wax polish, found on mature Sémillon-based wines, Sauternes especially.

Lean Not necessarily critical, but describing a rather austere style. In a critical sense: lacking ripe fruit.

Lees Sediment that settles at the bottom of a tank or barrel of wine after fermentation. Mainly dead yeast cells, also fragments of grape solids: pips, pulp, skin.

Lemony Self-explanatory, useful for dry white wine description.

Length Important measure of quality: 1) MIDDLE-PALATE length, length across the palate: the length of time for which a wine's flavours and aromas continue to stimulate one's palate whilst one keeps exploring it in the mouth; 2) length of FINISH/AFTERTASTE: in both cases the longer the better, assuming the sensations are agreeable. *See* pp26–7.

Light In body and/or flavour. Wines that are light-bodied may, however, be full of flavour.

Liquorous A liqueur-like unctuosity in sweet wines, complimentary.

Lively Acidity which gives an attractive zip and DEFINITION to a wine.

Loose/Loose-knit Not quite FLABBY, but implies a lack of acidity and poor DEFINITION. Opposite of TAUT.

Luscious Dessert wines: richly sweet, succulent yet fresh; a perfectly ripe peach is luscious.

Lustrous A particularly radiant beauty in the appearance of the very finest wines.

Maderised A critical term indicating excess oxidation in white wine that is darker in colour than appropriate for its type and age. The term derives from the madeira-like appearance. Generally used as a synonym for OXIDISED, with particular reference to white wines. For details, *see* p151.

Malic The sour taste of the 'green' apple acid.

Matt The fine, grainy texture of young red wine with good quality tannin which is still matt in feel rather than GLOSSY – think of photographic papers.

Mature Ready to drink. Opinions and cultures vary enormously as to when. *See* p147.

Mean High acid, unripe flavours; charmless.

Meaty Plenty of matter and a CHEWY quality.

Mellow SOFT and without harshness, but well balanced, not FLABBY.

Middle-palate A term for the phase of tasting before you swallow, during which you explore, savour, assess what the wine has to offer. The longer the wine is 'across the palate', ie the longer the middle-palate, the better the wine. *See* DEVELOPMENT and LENGTH, and pp26–7.

Minerally Suggestions to both nose and palate of stones: slate, granite, chalk, schist, and so on. Especially in wines from the Loire, N Rhône, Bordeaux, Burgundy, Douro, Mosel, Tokay etc. Fanciful? Maybe, but real enough to many winetasters; *see* TERROIR, p129.

Mint Not far from EUCALYPTUS as a smell; typically associated with Cabernet Sauvignon from California, Australia, and occasionally Bordeaux.

Mousse (Fr) The bubbles in a sparkling wine.

Mouthfeel Same as TEXTURE, *see* p28.

Musk The heady, heavy, wax and vegetal scent of mature Semillon, often on mature Sauternes, and sometimes Riesling, might be related to NOBLE ROT.

Neutral Bland, lacking any distinctive characteristics.

Noble rot See p43.

Nose General term for a wine's smell; *see* AROMA, BOUQUET.

Nutty Smell of various nuts (most often hazelnut, walnut, cashew), in various states (fresh, dried, roasted), but used as a generic description as well.

Oaky Numerous odours associated with wines that have been fermented or aged in new oak barrels, or that have been infused with oak chips: vanilla, cedar, toast, caramel, clove etc. *See* pp47–8.

Oily Can refer to TEXTURE (uncomplimentary), or to the BOUQUET of mature Riesling, Sémillon or Chenin Blanc, where it is a desirable quality.

Old age Objectively, of course, but perhaps more often pejoratively for a wine that is past its best and tiring or DRYING OUT.

Oxidised All wines contain oxygen, but oxidised refers generically to a series of faults resulting from excess contact with oxygen. *See* MADERISED and, for details, p151.

Phenols See POLYPHENOLS.

Phenolic A critical term used to describe ASTRINGENCY in white wines due to excess tannins leached from the grape skins or from wooden barrels during winemaking. *See* p40.

Palate In winespeak 'on the palate' means 'in the mouth'. *See* MIDDLE-PALATE.

Peak The period of time during which a wine tastes its best. Very subjective. *See* p147.

Penetrating Of BOUQUET: intense, CONCENTRATED; of taste: intensity of flavours which seem to search out and stimulate every niche of one's PALATE.

Peppery A distinct impression of pepperiness, white pepper in Grenache-based wines and Grüner Veltiner, ground black pepper in Northern Rhône Syrah, also clear in young port.

Perfumed FRAGRANT.

Persistent Used of a fine BOUQUET, and of length of FINISH. They are closely related.

Pétillant (Fr) Lightly sparkling.

Petrolly Smells reminiscent, in the most agreeable way, of petroleum-based products: oil, petrol, kerosene, paraffin. Found on mature Riesling in particular, to a lesser extent on mature Sémillon.

Piquant SHARP, possibly pleasantly so.

Plummy SOFT, round, supple, juicy – like ripe plums.

Polyphenols Pigmented compounds (anthocyanins and tannins) in the skin of red grapes. See pp10–11,21–2.

Pricked An evocative, old-fashioned term for a wine smelling of acetic acid (vinegar).

Prickle The delicate sensation of CO_2 on the tip of the tongue in a 'still' wine, as opposed to the MOUSSE of a sparkling one.

Racy A combination of energy and excitement in the mouth allied to finesse, a noticeably thoroughbred feel.

Rancio (Sp) Attractive buttery, nutty smells of acetals. These are formed by the slow combination of aldehydes (such as acetaldehyde) and alcohol. The term is associated mainly with fine old sherries and *vins doux naturels* such as Banyuls.

Raw Young wine whose elements of alcohol, acid and tannin, not yet mellowed and married, make for harsh, raw impressions.

Reduced Smells resulting from sulphur combined with hydrogen as opposed to oxygen; *see* p151.

Refined A total absence of coarseness in flavour and texture.

Residual sugar Sugar that remains in a finished wine because it has not been fermented out. *See* pp42–3.

Rich Abundance of flavour, opulence of texture. Does not, necessarily, mean sweet.

Ripe Natural sweetness of flavour resulting from fully ripe grapes.

Robust Full-bodied, VIGOROUS wine; finesse is not the point.

Rotten eggs The stink associated with hydrogen sulphide. *See* REDUCED, and p151.

Rubbery Another smell associated with hydrogen sulphide. *See* REDUCED, and p151.

Round Without hard edges, MELLOW.

Rustic COARSE, usually implying poor winemaking and its results.

Satin One of several materials whose 'feel' and appearance are used to help describe the TEXTURE of wine. Other commonly mentioned materials are silk, taffeta, lace, velvet. *See* p28.

Savoury Tasty, in a particularly appetising, maybe spicy, way.

Scope Multi-faceted, numerous impressions, a wide range of tastes and aromas and so on. I use this to indicate a wine with a considerable degree of COMPLEXITY and much to offer and explore.

Simple little SCOPE.

Searching *See* PENETRATING.

Sharp Acidity verging on the unpleasant.

Short Across the palate, and in AFTERTASTE. Quality wines have LENGTH.

Silky Along with VELVETY, the most frequently used material simile for TEXTURE. Particularly associated with fine, mature red burgundy – you should be so lucky! *See* SATIN.

Sinewy A combination of LEAN and muscular.

Slaty Mineral impression many tasters find in quality Rieslings from the Mosel.

Smoky An AROMATIC character in some Loire Sauvignon Blanc, Syrah from the Northern Rhône, and good-quality Bual Madeira.

Smooth Self-explanatory.

Soapy *See* UNCTUOUS.

Soft Refers in particular to the texture of tannin and/or level of acidity. Usually complimentary, not always so in the case of acidity, where 'soft' may indicate a deficiency.

Solid Firm, substantial, COMPACT, maybe CHEWY…

Spicy Usually non-specific impressions. Clear in Gewurztraminer, for example, and in good-quality Pomerols.

Spritzy Moderately sparkling, more so than PETILLANT.

Stalky/stemmy COARSE, often 'GREEN' astringency from unripe grapes, brutal crushing methods, excessive maceration or pressing. Mainly of red, very occasionally whites. *See* pp44–6.

Steely A severe acidity, appropriate and desirable in a limited number of quality white wines that benefit from long ageing: Premier Cru Chablis, Alsace Riesling, for example.

Stewed The analogy is with tea that has been infused for too long and with similar results in wine: dull to smell, lacking freshness, and ASTRINGENT.

Straightforward SIMPLE.

Stretched Dilute flavours from excess YIELD.

Stringy The comparison is with meat that is too sinewy. Lesser clarets in lean years.

Structure CONSTITUTION. 'Structured' means emphatic structure, on a grand scale; strong, solid, built to last.

Subtle COMPLEXITY and refinement which are not obvious.

Supple Of acidity or tannin: softness in a positive sense.

Tannic As a descriptive term indicates abundant tannin.

Tart Sharp, piquant acidity.

Taut In contrast to LOOSE, a positive, defining characteristic.

Tenacity Of flavour: the property of holding your attention and continuing to stimulate your palate and senses as you keep the wine in the mouth. The quality of great wines is an exceptional tenacity of flavour. *See* DEVELOPMENT, LENGTH, MIDDLE-PALATE.

Terroir EARTHY, MINERALLY impressions as part of the taste of a wine, but *see* also p129.

Texture Tactile qualities of a wine, often compared to the feel of fine materials. *See* p28.

Thin Dilute and lacking in flavour.

Tight-knit As opposed to LOOSE-KNIT. Firmly structured, usually CONCENTRATED wine with a multiplicity of well-defined flavours; generally used of a wine which needs to soften. By analogy with closely woven cloth. *See* p28.

Toasty Smell akin to fresh toast – particularly barrel-aged Chardonnay, mature Champagne.

Tough A coarse texture due to ASTRINGENT tannin.

Tired/limp, feeble, lacklustre.

Unbalanced One or more components noticeably lacking or dominant in the wine's make-up. *See* BALANCE.

Unctuous So rich and smooth as to be bordering on excess, at which point: soapy!

Varietal Relating to a specific grape variety.

Varietal wine A wine made from a single grape variety.

Vanilla One of the smells most commonly associated with ageing in new oak barrels. *See* OAKY, and pp47–8.

Vegetal Sometimes complimentary: FARMYARD and undergrowth smells in mature Pinot Noir; more often not: smells of bruised or rotting vegetation.

Velvety RICH flavour, sumptuous TEXTURE.

Vigorous A firm acidity, usually in the context of a full-bodied wine.

Volatile Smelling of excess acetic acid, *ie* vinegar, and possibly also of ETHYL ACETATE (*see* ACESCENT), both are faults; *see* p151.

Warm Not quite HOT!

Watery Low in alcohol, or dilute in flavour.

Waxy As in wax polish, candlewax; one of the smells associated with mature Sémillon and Chenin Blanc; partly an impression of TEXTURE as well.

Weak In structure, *ie* low in alcohol, acid, flavour, tannin.

Well-balanced *See* BALANCE, HARMONIOUS.

Wet wool A smell associated especially with unoaked Chablis, Loire Chenin and Bordeaux Semillon; probably intrinsic, but equally probably not unrelated to a somewhat heavy hand with the sulphur.

Yeasty The smell of active (*ie* fermenting) yeast, associated in a positive sense with young Champagne which has had prolonged contact with its yeast LEES.

Yield The relationship between a given area of vines or weight of fruit, and the volume of wine 'yielded'. *See* p36.

index

Grape varieties are in **bold**, as are page numbers of extended treatments of subjects. Page numbers in *italic* refer to boxed text and illustration captions. An 'm' following a page number indicates a map page for place names.

Acknowledgements

Key
CPL = Cephas Picture Library
MS = Michael Schuster
OPG = Octopus Publishing Group

b = bottom, t = top, l = left, r = right, c = centre

All pictures Octopus Publishing Group/Russell Sadur except the following:

6–7 OPG/Reuben Paris; 12b, 13tl, tr MS/Linden Artists Ltd; 15br MS; 16 MS; 19 MS/Linden Artists Ltd; 23 Science Photo Library/Frank Zullo; 24 MS; 25 MS; 27l, 27r MS/Linden Artists Ltd; 28l OPG/James Merrell; 28r OPG/Bill Batten; 29 Opera National de Paris; 29 Deutscher Fussball-Bund; 31 OPG; 31 Ch Le Pin; 32 Kettle's Yard/Henri Gaudier-Brzeska; 33 Bridgeman Art Library/Munch Museum/ Munch Estate/BONO, Oslo/DACs, London 2000; 34t MS; 34b CPL/Kevin Judd; 35 MS; 36 MS; 37t MS; 37b MS; 38t MS; 38b MS; 39l MS; 39r MS; 40t MS; 40b MS; 41 MS; 42 MS; 43t MS; 43b MS; 44 MS; 45t MS; 45b Pistolet Bleu/JJ Andreau; 46t MS; 46b MS; 47l Seguin Moreau; 47r Pascal

Chatonnet; 48t MS; 48b Seguin Moreau; 49 MS; 50bl MS; 50br CPL/Kevin Judd; 51l MS; 51r John Warne; 52-3 OPG/Reuben Paris; 57-58 Janet Price; 58 Janet Price; 59t MS; 59b MS; 60t Janet Price; 60c MS; 60b John Warne; 61 Janet Price; 62t MS; 62b MS; 63 Janet Price; 64b MS; 64t CPL/Walter Geiersperger; 65t Janet Price; 65b Root Stock/Montana Wines; 66 CPL/Alain Proust; 67 Steven Morris; 68 MS; 69 CPL/Mick Rock; 70 Janet Price; 71t Janet Price; 71b MS; 72 Janet Price; 73 CPL/Mick Rock; 74 MS; 75 MS; 76 Janet Price; 77l MS; 77r MS; 78 Janet Price; 79 CPL/Walter Geiersperger; 80 CPL/Mick Rock; 81 CPL/Mick Rock; 82 Janet Price; 83 MS; 84t MS; 84b John Warne; 85 Janet Price; 86 Steven Morris; 87t MS; 87b MS; 88 MS; 89 CPL/Bruce Fleming; 90 MS; 91 MS; 92 MS; 93 MS; 93r MS; 94 MS; 95t MS; 95b CPL/Mick Rock; 96 MS; 97t MS; 97b MS; 98 CPL/Mick Rock; 99t Janet Price; 99b Janet Price; 100 Janet Price; 101 Janet Price; 102r Janet Price; 102 Janet Price; 103 MS; 104t MS; 104b CPL/Mick Rock; 105 CPL/Ted Stefanski; 106 CPL/Mick Rock; 107 Janet Price; 108tl MS; 108tr CPL/Mick Rock; 108bl MS; 108br MS; 109t John Warne; 110 CPL/Mick Rock; 111 CPL/Mick Rock; 112t MS; 112b CPL/Mick Rock; 113 MS; 114 CPL/David Copeman; 115t MS; 115b MS; 116-117 OPG/Reuben Paris; 129 MS; 164-165 OPG/Reuben Paris.